D0307489

Stephen Smith is a Channel 4 News reporter, and a regular contributor to the *London Review of Books* and other newspapers.

Also by Stephen Smith

The Land of Miracles:
A Journey through Modern Cuba

Cocaine Train

*Tracing My Bloodline
Through Colombia*

Stephen Smith

An *Abacus* Book

First published in Great Britain by
Little, Brown and Company 1999
This edition published by Abacus 2000

Copyright © Stephen Smith 1999

The moral right of the author has been asserted.

All rights reserved.
No part of this publication may be reproduced, stored in
a retrieval system, or transmitted, in any form or by any
means, without the prior permission in writing of the
publisher, nor be otherwise circulated in any form of
binding or cover other than that in which it is published
and without a similar condition including this condition
being imposed on the subsequent purchaser.

A CIP catalogue record for this book
is available from the British Library.

ISBN 0 349 11114 6

Typeset in Melior by M Rules
Printed and bound in Great Britain
by Clays Ltd, St Ives plc

Abacus
A Division of
Little, Brown and Company (UK)
Brettenham House
Lancaster Place
London WC2E 7EN

In Memory of
Leslie Frost 1900–1966

Leslie Frost's map of Colombian railways

*The survey of the track was like
the tracing of the path of life.*

Joseph Conrad

Contents

1

Abandoned Railway

The train crept into the darkness as though it was dragging its feet, as though it was as reluctant as I was myself. We had been approaching the tunnel for hours, certainly a lot longer than the 'five, six minutes' promised so much earlier by the *chorizo* vendor with his tray of scandalizing sausage, but the blackness was still shocking after the brilliant morning. There were lampshades in the ceiling of the carriage but no light coming from them. Children squealed, half in terror, half in delight. Somewhere a deeper voice groaned. There was a sensation as though the benchseat beneath me was falling away, and then the train was gathering speed, the air sieving through the open windows. The bogies were slipping, there was a rasp of metal on metal. A spark threw a flaring, phosphorescent arc around the roof of the tunnel. The train was jumping the tracks. It was racing downhill. Or at least it felt as though it was racing: the shrieks of children, the rattle of wheels, the tumult of air. To look back over my shoulder, towards the open doorway at the rear of the carriage, was also to look up; it was an effort to turn my head. There was a smudge of light. I couldn't see it if I looked directly – I wasn't used to the dark – but it was there in

the corner of my eye. Where was the man who had been standing by the doorway? The man was as thickset as a bouncer. He
had a green shirt and a bull-neck and a crew cut. He had spent
most of the journey out on the footplate of the carriage, reading
a newspaper. He had shown an interest in me, I'd thought, or
perhaps it was an interest in my belongings. The man had held
a series of conversations with other people who had wandered
to the rear of the train. Sinister consultations, I had convinced
myself. Over my shoulder, the smudge that represented the end
of the tunnel dwindled until it was the size of a cameo brooch,
until it was like a memory of light. Where *was* the man? What
was he doing?

This was the train out of Medellin, the train I'd been warned
about, though frankly the same warning applied more or less
firmly to every train in Colombia. Every train and pretty well
everything else besides. Yes, the line out of Medellin was very
pretty, running alongside a river; no, the city was no longer the
fiefdom of the terrible Pablo Escobar, the late nabob of narcotics.
But the bad news was that people were robbed on the train. The
worse news was that it ran through territory controlled by guerrillas and the worst news of all was that from time to time they
boarded the train and kidnapped passengers. The guerrillas had
been very much on my mind as the train had wound up into the
mountains. At Porcecito, sixty-five kilometres out of Medellin,
where there had been a fire to clear sugar canes and ash hung in
the air, the initials of the ELN faction were painted on a shack.
The further we went, the thicker the graffiti on the breezeblock
walls beside the line. The reluctant train dragged itself past these
slogans and I found myself studying them with the concentration
you were supposed to bring to charcoals in a gallery. It wasn't
that they were good, or original, or had anything to say – anything to say that I wanted to hear right then, at any rate. But you
had to admit that a lot of work had gone into them. Someone
must have spent hours over them. This meant that the guerrillas
could do as they pleased with the peasants' shacks. Either that
or they lived in them themselves. I thought of a diplomat in the

capital, Bogota, who had told me that a foreigner – *any* foreigner – was irresistible bait to the guerrillas. 'If they think
anyone will pay for you – employer, family, whatever – they'll
take you,' he said. Colombia had the highest rate of kidnappings
in the world, an average of four a day. But the official rate was a
fraction of the true one, the diplomat claimed. 'There were two
thousand five hundred reported kidnaps last year but the real
total is – ten thousand? Who knows?' It was body-snatching as a
business proposition. 'Sit tight, pay up – you'll walk. The average
length of time of a kidnapping is five months. It might freak them
out if it happened any faster.' It might have been an estate agent
counselling patience to a first-time home buyer.

The diplomat told me a story about an embassy colleague, a
keen ornithologist, coming to the end of his posting with an
unfulfilled craving to see a Tolima dove. As well as having the
highest rate of kidnapping in the world, the Colombians also
had the greatest diversity of bird-life, with some species found
nowhere else on earth, the splendid *leptotila conoveri* among
them. 'Sides of neck and upper breast dark vinaceous buff, in
sharp contrast to buff lower breast and abdomen,' according to
Hilty and Brown's definitive *Guide to the Birds of Colombia*.
The Tolima dove was indigenous to a 'red zone', an area with
high guerrilla activity. The embassy man 'cracked', the diplomat
said, and took off to see the bird. He spent a long, fruitless day
in the red zone with his binoculars. As he was folding up his
stool and shaking out his flask, he was surprised by guerrillas.
'They took him off in his own vehicle, made him get behind the
wheel,' said the diplomat. 'As he was driving away, he saw a
flock of Tolima doves.'

As I say, the guerrillas had been uppermost in my thoughts as
we approached the tunnel, and might have been so still, if
anyone had told me about their spectacular record of derailing
the Medellin train, levering up the track in the darkness. But in
the whistling freefall of that mountain borehole, I was aware of
the man with the green shirt. I was aware of him and I was
aware of my neck, in the same way that a visit to the dentist's

concentrates your mind on your teeth. This was in anticipation of the forearm I expected around my throat at any moment.

In a nice example of comeuppance, I was a journalist with a cliché foisted upon him. Looking for light at the end of the tunnel was no longer a lazy image but an eye-straining vigil. And naturally it didn't help that I was crouching down in my seat the whole time. How long was this bloody tunnel, anyway? There was a jet of light, and a pool of light – snatches of light. But these were the flame of a cigarette lighter, the glow of a watch-face, the distress signals of my fellow passengers. We were all alone together in the headlong blackness. If you had seen us a few moments earlier, you would have been struck by the holiday atmosphere in our carriage. It was the weekend, after all, and the weather was fine. True, there had been an early start at the railway station in Medellin, people queuing since before seven o'clock in shorts and trainers. There had been a yapping dog, and a group who jumped the queue, a drunk among them – not a *harmless* drunk, you felt. Before long, though, we were diverted by *chulos*, vultures, making their toilet at the sulphur-smelling river, and by salesmen catwalking up and down the train: the man selling greasy meat rissoles from a bucket; the Hindu convert carrying a faggot of joss sticks like King Wenceslas's poor man with his winter fuel. The *medellinos* had adapted the old Spanish custom of *el paseo*, the promenade, taking the air. They had turned it into a day trip, an excuse to leave their city behind at the weekend in favour of a rustic spot in which to prepare a meal, a stew, for everyone to share. Understood in this way, *el paseo* caught the charabanc mood of my companions exactly. However, the expression has a second, ironic usage in Medellin. In recent times, it has come to mean being taken to the same out-of-town hollows in order to be killed: the roadsides of the holiday routes have been used for a number of years as a dumping ground for corpses.

In the darkness, something touched me, something brushed my shoulder. Someone was there! The man in the green shirt? I was terrified. I was exhilarated. I was more terrified than exhilarated. Hunching myself deeper into my seat, I knew a morbid vindication: I had been right all along, Colombia was as bad as I'd been told, as bad as I'd thought, and this was it. This was it. Without moving, I explored the rushing air – where was he? Where had he gone? There had been a man selling green mangoes in the carriage earlier. He had been sharpening a knife. I was bristling for a knife.

There were flashes of light on the carriage ceiling. They were bright, and getting brighter. Now they weren't flashes any more. This was incoming light. We careened into the sunshine and there was a man standing in the aisle beside me, a short man wearing a cap, with a leather bag, a *carriel*, slung around his neck. The *carriel* was level with my shoulder, close enough to rub against it . . . At the rear of the carriage, the man in the green shirt was leaning against the jamb of the door, opening up his newspaper again.

Hearts were lighter on the train. People were chatting busily, turning to look at their neighbours, happy to see faces and make eye contact. In the spirit of Medellin's authentic *paseo*, they were behaving as though they'd had a spree, as though they'd survived a scarcely licensable funfair ride and then found that their loose change had stayed in their pockets. I was smiling at the people across the aisle from me. I began to look forward to a late breakfast. The train was nearing the hamlet of Limon. From the map in my lap, I worked out that the tunnel had been more than two kilometres long. Alongside the carriage windows, the cane stood tall. In the middle distance were shacks, smoke, people. And then the train stopped and I saw the very last thing I wanted to see. Stepping towards us out of the cane were figures in camouflage fatigues. They were moving with the air of men who were breaking and entering. They were holding machine guns and they were boarding the train . . .

The train crept into the darkness. The following account is about darkness, a darkness which has overwhelmed an entire country, another which has fallen across a single life. It's also about reclaiming something from darkness, or attempting to – something that may be said clearly and verifiably about the country, details and truths about the life; something to remember them by. The country is Colombia, the life is my grandfather's.

Suffering Colombia is in danger of losing touch with the rest of the world. In his own rather less dramatic fashion, my grandfather is also shrinking over the horizon of recognisability. As I write these words, it strikes me that I have bracketed the pair of them together for as long as I can think: Fred Leslie Frost, my own flesh and blood, and a country separated from me by an entire hemisphere, to say nothing of other gulfs. For years, Colombia was a fuzzy outline, a blank space, Colombia was not known. As far as I was concerned, it went directly from being unknown to renowned – but that would happen much later. Leslie Frost, dead in his sixties, dead before I was six, belonged to a stripe of man I had no experience of: grandfathers. (The only other person to fit the bill, who was actually longer-lived than Leslie, had rejected his birthright, or perhaps I should say mine, on grounds of vanity, and insisted on the style of 'uncle' instead.) Like Colombia, Leslie Frost was a fuzzy outline. He was never known by a pet name, an intimate diminutive. He was never Grandpa, Pops, Gramps. I didn't know him well enough to remember him by anything less formal than Grandfather, than Leslie Frost. His life in Colombia was one of the few established biographical facts about him – established and dinned into us by rote, my grandmother returning to the subject at Sunday lunchtimes, so much so that the word 'Manizales', the name of a city where my grandparents and my mother had lived, became a private joke among younger members of the family, Gran's innocent mentions of it enough to provoke cretinous giggling. Colombia was the place where Leslie had been; Leslie was the handsome man in the black-and-white photograph who had been to Colombia. Thinking about the one put me in mind of the other. Not that I did think about either of them much.

Λ Colombian railway of the 1950s

The train crept into the darkness. Another black-and-white photograph, secured by cardboard corners to a page in an album belonging to my mother. A locomotive and tender are disappearing out of the left-hand side of the picture. There's a tree on the right of the shot and a mountain or peak in the background. The engine appears to be running through a valley, or perhaps across a plateau. The photograph was taken in the 1950s, before my mother left Colombia to come home to Great Britain, before the private railway company which employed my grandfather was nationalised and sights like the one in the photograph became a good deal rarer. Leslie Frost had been manager of the La Dorada line – the Railway of Gold – and of a stupendous aerial ropeway which spanned the Andes. In the course of half a lifetime spent in Colombia, he'd travelled across the country by railroad, mapping the tracks, carrying out surveys in areas where it was proposed to extend them. It must have been idyllic – why else would he have stayed so long? Colombia was renowned, now, but it had an unsung beauty. The story went that when God was creating the Earth, he decided to give Colombia the best coffee, the most breathtaking mountains, fertile lowlands, its own oil supply, the Tolima dove . . . finally, the angels could contain their curiosity no longer. 'Are you trying to turn Colombia into Paradise?' asked one. 'You haven't seen the Colombians yet,' replied God.

After the government got hold of the railway lines, they failed to put any money into them. The guerrillas blew them up or stuck them up and the rain washed them away. I bought an updated map. The index included a symbol for *ferrocarril*, railway. It was a neat and tidy stitch, of the kind that a cosmetic surgeon might leave behind, with an assurance that it would drop out by itself within a few days. Next to this character was another, representing *ferrocarril abandonado*, abandoned railway: also a stitch, but one suggesting a mortician's sinewy hand. This coarse needlework was more common on the map itself. It seemed that little remained of the railways my grandfather mapped and ran.

The train crept into the darkness . . . This story is bound up in death, the death of the Colombian railway, for one. According to one of the few generally available guidebooks to the country, 'There have been several short-term campaigns launched to bring the train back to life but nothing much has come of it. Actually, it would mean rebuilding the railway from scratch, as the abandoned railtrack has been largely dismantled by locals and enterprising trade operators.'

The demise of the Colombian railway is not surprising when you bear in mind the death of the host country. This has been so gore-spattered and melodramatic that good taste practically insists that you look away – except that it happened, except that it's all true. In the United States, which has a well-merited reputation for violent crime, nine people in every 100,000 are murdered. You might expect the Colombian picture to be rather grimmer, you might brace yourself for a murder rate double that of America, or quadruple, or even quintuple. For the true multiplying factor, however, there is no -*uple* available in everyday speech. Colombia kills more of her own than the United States by nine times. Visualising football grounds is a favourite way of grasping population statistics: I'm afraid it's as though, for every

Colombian stadium, there is a Hillsborough disaster, with more than eighty people in every 100,000 meeting untimely ends. Violence has officially been the primary cause of death for the past twenty years. Police records for 1997 show that 31,808 people were killed. In 1998, it was 36,000 – that's ninety-nine a day. Many of these fatalities were as a result of mass killings, of which there were more than a hundred: 'massacre' has entered the language of demographics in Colombia, the only place where it has done so, a term as coolly neutral as 'road traffic accident' or 'natural causes'. During an average twenty-four hour spell there were also 204 assaults or muggings, eight highway robberies and two bank raids. If average is the word

Colombia is shocking. This is a place where paramilitaries behead their victims with chainsaws – and then eat their brains, or so trembling villagers have claimed. It's a place where insurers quote politicians against assassination and insist on bulletproof vests and bodyguards the way the man from the Pru is pernickety about window locks and smoke alarms. Blue-chip companies allow for extortion payments in their annual budgets. Criminals have been caught attempting to move drugs by way of everything from a 1977 Ford hearse to a cashiered atomic submarine and a Colombian air force Hercules transporter (the Hercules was seized in the United States in November 1998 with a ton of cocaine in the cargo bay: the Colombian president had just been on a state visit to Washington). The authorities in Bogota have considered banning alcohol on 20 September, Love and Friendship Day, the Colombian equivalent of St Valentine's Day, because of the staggering body count. 'It's traditionally been the day when the number of *bogotanos* who are willing to kill their neighbours soars,' said the mayor. 'The Day of Love and Friendship is the day when we love the most and kill the most.' Some families were so violently divided against each other – father in the army; son with the guerrillas – that they could only be left together safely at Christmas. 'If they come across each other at any other time, they kill each other,' said a director who made pro-peace commercials. Even a dispute over

local government jobs could be shocking: after the mayor of a
town called Cartago announced plans to lay off 150 workers,
three of them crucified themselves. 'As they bit down on cloth,
supporters drove six-inch nails into the men's hands,' according
to an eyewitness.

Colombia is shocking. On the other hand, as you can't help
noticing, no one is behaving as though they're shocked.
Colombia is shocking, but has become virtually unshockable.
Think of the worst, the most outrageous thing that can happen:
in Colombia, it's already happened. Many of the hair-whiten-
ing facts above have been carried to the outside world by
means of international news agency wires, but few of them
have been given airtime or page-space by subscribing outlets.
I've read the wires – I've read the wires on Colombia obses-
sively – and I've thought about why editors haven't made
anything of them. I can imagine their arguments: that Colombia
is a faraway place, with few obvious links to a country like
Great Britain; that it's an expensive, and dangerous, story to
cover; that it's become bogged down: it's drugs and guns, drugs
and guns, over and over again. I can see their point. But at the
same time I find myself thinking of another explanation. It's
ridiculous, so ridiculous that I hesitate to mention it. On the
other hand, I'm sure that it's true; that it contains an element of
truth, at any rate. What keeps Colombia out of the newspapers
and off the television screens is embarrassment. Colombia is
unshockable – it can't be embarrassed – but to everyone else
it's embarrassing: *Dear God, what have they done this time?*
This embarrassment perhaps conceals a measure of guilt, on
the reasoning that drugs are at the root of Colombia's affliction
and most of them are consumed outside the country. Or, as
the Colombian Gabriel Garcia Marquez has described it, 'a
human tragedy for which the consuming nations bore primary
responsibility.' Partly it's a question of getting started: how do
you fill in the back-story on news items, items about the death
of a country, without inadvertently letting on that this has
been going on for years without your having made much of a

fuss about it? (And I'm just the same, I'm just as bad, I looked away for years.) Really it's about the way Colombia confounds us, the way it confounds our principles – even our elastic principles – of how people behave towards one another. As a government spokesman admitted in 1997, 'In Colombia, the notion of the value of human life has been largely lost.' The country is as abandoned as its railways. It took the catastrophe of an earthquake in January 1999, in which as many as 1,200 people were killed – a natural calamity, I note, an act of God – to focus the world's attention.

As it happens, the media's assumptions about Colombia are wrong. The drugs didn't produce the guns; the guns were there first. Comfortably first. The drugs didn't produce the guns; if anything, it was the other way round. There was a ready-made labour force for narcotics-trafficking among young men hitherto talented only in violence. When *coca* was still just a pleasantly anaesthetic leaf that the *campesinos*, peasants, liked to chew, my grandparents and my mother postponed a journey to Britain for three months because they dared not move for gunfire. 'There was a lot of shooting, and bombs on the railway line,' my mother said. This was at a turning point for Colombian society and, in its own unremarked way, for my family too. In the late 1940s and 1950s, Colombians lived through *La Violencia*; or some of them did. *La Violencia* was a period of internecine bloodletting so savage as to render even the respected academics of the Latin American Bureau speechless ('beyond the powers of human beings to comprehend or control'). It was the beginning of Colombia's travails, the antecedents of what is by some margin the longest-running civil conflict in Latin America; it was the beginning of the end.

Luckily for them, my relatives came home, my grandmother accompanying my mother, who was about to go to college. My grandfather followed some years later, having overseen the transfer of La Dorada Railway Company into government hands. Thousands died in Colombia during *La Violencia*, but he wasn't

Rosemary Smith, née Frost, and Leslie Frost

one of them. Colombia didn't kill him; it was leaving Colombia that killed him – that would become the invariable postscript to his life. (I think of one of my mother's sayings, something she probably picked up from Leslie, something you never hear now: 'It wasn't the cough that carried him off, it was the coffin they carried him off in.' I used to think, *Well, yes, but what about it? What about this coffin?*)

Family history catches up with Leslie again in the guise of a village postmaster in the West Country. He's there in my mum and dad's wedding photographs, and some years after they were taken he came to stay with us, though I remember this interlude only for the house calls of Leslie's barber, Mr Robinson, who was also put upon to give my brother and me a trim, seeing as he was there anyway, and had the scissors out. I don't remember my grandfather as a physical presence, I can't close my eyes and hear his voice. But I do know the smell of him, his scent. There was always a bottle of bay rum in a bathroom cabinet while Leslie was alive, and, I think, for some time after he died, too, its masculine tang perhaps a source of comfort to my grandmother.

This peppery solution was like a distillation of Leslie's old-fashioned qualities, I imagined. Rub the bottle of bay rum and you would release a genie of Englishness. Rub the bottle and it might rub off. I didn't appreciate that it was part of an invalid's medicine chest, a preparation used by a man too ill to go to the barber's, or even to wash his hair for himself.

And then there was a cemetery next to a dual carriageway which we visited for a while, and pieces of exotic armour hanging in the hall – a breastplate and a pudding-bowl helmet – which I convinced myself were trophies that Leslie had won in battle, childishly mindless of the anachronism. And always the black-and-white photograph: a pullover; a book and a pair of tortoiseshell glasses in my grandfather's hand; an unreadable expression. No, not unreadable; full of *conflicting* meanings. A smile, which became a level return of the camera's gaze, which turned into a minatory expression, one which seemed to say, 'You won't get anything out of me.'

I learnt more about Leslie as I got older: he was born in the first year of the century, on 10 June 1900; he had been a smoker, he died of emphysema (I'm sorry to say it *was* the cough that carried him off); he had spent some time as Her Majesty's Consular Agent in a town called Mariquita – *His* Majesty's, rather: this was in 1950, at the time of *La Violencia*. This seemed right. He bore a striking resemblance to Clark Gable and, by my mother's account, possessed something of the actor's screen charm and self-assurance. I imagined that he had been approached because he was the only British householder for miles around. In him, however, the King's representatives lit upon the very model of the cool, resourceful Englishman you would expect to find serving his country in some flyblown spot. Frost by name, Frost by nature, as it were. My mother said that Leslie had been strict with her, but she idolised him all the same, perhaps because of this very sternness. And he loved her; although he had really wanted a boy, a son, she told me.

I liked hearing about him, of course. He *was* my grandfather, after all, and with the film-star good looks and inscrutable

expression disclosed by the photograph, he had the makings of
an enigma. He had been, or should I say he would have been, an
indulgent grandparent. There had been a telegram for my
mother when I was born (CONGRATULATIONS FONDEST
LOVE TO YOU AND OUR GRANDSON = MUMMIE AND
POP + +) and a postcard a few days later, a cartoon showing
storks flying over a village, one of them carrying a baby in a
sling which was tied around its bill, and the caption 'Now then
girls – watch your step!'. Leslie wrote to his daughter, 'Glad to
hear all is going well with you and junior and am looking forward to seeing you all. Hope you will be able to pay us a visit
before the end of summer. In the meantime, I shall have to be
satisfied with second-hand accounts – lots of love to you all . . .'
On the front of the card, next to the tot in the sling, he had
printed 'JUNIOR'.

But I didn't remember him, and I wasn't prepared to invest
the curiosity which was required to make Leslie enigmatic. As
far as I was concerned, he couldn't really compete with relatives
on my dad's side of the family, colourful, eccentric people who
ran boarding houses and sailed tugboats on the Mersey, and
who knew how to lay their hands on Cup Final tickets. At a
time when children increasingly counted themselves lucky if
they knew their fathers, it didn't occur to me to feel hard-done-
by on the grounds of an unknown grandfather.

That would have been the long and the short of it if it hadn't
been for another death; another death, and a life. I was having
dinner with my parents at a hotel in Yorkshire. My mother's
train of conversation returned to her girlhood in Colombia, as
it does with minutely greater frequency year by year. In
Mariquita, where the Frosts had lived for some years at a house
known as 'Number Two', she had been a favourite with the
servants: she was the teenager who was always riding a horse.
My mother told me again how she'd kept in touch with friends
in Mariquita after she came home to England. I was only half-
listening. I was thinking back to the afternoon, to a walk in the
Dales. It was October but the sun had been warm, the paths by

the Wharfe dry. I was surprised how far Dad had walked. One day, a letter had arrived, my mother said. It was news of Leslie. There was something in my mother's voice. The news was shattering, she said. I was looking directly at her by now. Her father had had an affair. And it wasn't an act of loneliness with an American or European, the wife of a coffee planter, a bored ex-pat. My mother's friends said that Leslie's lover had been a Colombian, a woman of Mariquita. Well, not so much a woman; more of a girl, a teenager. ('They mature earlier there.') And it had been less of an affair than a common-law marriage. They had lived together, not at the old place, not at Number Two, but just down the road, at Number Five. There had been a baby, a boy.

I said, 'I've got an uncle!' I didn't have an uncle. I'd *never* had an uncle. Oh, I'd had *uncles*: 'Uncle' Stephen, my namesake, was my other grandfather, the one who had declined the role because he thought it would age him; and there was good old Uncle George, an explorer and climber, who had married my Aunty June. I had had any number of great-uncles and honorary uncles and godfathers. But I'd never had real, blood uncles, for what they might be worth. Well, now I did; a half-uncle, anyway. My mother had a half-brother. Leslie had had his longed-for son. I was waking up in a hurry to the puzzle of the man in the photograph.

It was a story my mother had forgotten about for forty years, she said — had *deliberately* forgotten about. She had kept it a secret from my grandmother, who only learnt the truth after Leslie had finally returned to Britain. And then it had come out in the most banal way, Gran discovering some letters when she was patting down a suit that was going off to the cleaners, a cornered Leslie passing off his involvement as a fling, a one-night stand. Except that it hadn't come out, not really. My brother and sister and I had never had an inkling of it. I'd never have imagined my grandfather as the sort of man who'd have a mistress on his arm. I could tell by my father's face that this was news he had heard before; *not* news, in fact. But also that it wasn't a story which had been brought out and turned over and considered very often, even when my parents had been alone together.

Now my mother was saying that Leslie had been quite open about the relationship in Colombia. According to her correspondents, who were servants working for another of the ex-pats in Mariquita, my grandfather and his girl would join the promenade on Saturday evenings, the local version of the *paseo*, he in his mid-fifties, she still a teenager. They used to push the pram together. The idea of the very proper, very English Leslie taking a turn about the town with his fancy woman and their son was almost as staggering as the affair itself. It transcended class and age; it transgressed the taboo of race. What on earth had made him do it? Apart from sex, I mean. Had he loved her?

My mother guessed how I would react to her secret: Leslie's life in Colombia was a good story. It was all so long ago and so far away that it didn't hurt her any more, she said, and it couldn't touch me, the grandson who had never known Leslie Frost; or that's how it seemed at the time. It was not something that could be looked into immediately, however. Nothing more needed to be said – did my dad, at the table with us, know it too, I wonder now. It was inconceivable that I would go to Colombia while he was so ill – while he was dying – that was the truth of it, though I didn't put it in those terms at the time, not even to myself.

And then something changed, and going to Colombia was no longer just about gathering a story but also about that taken-for-granted thing, family. My family was the club with the large membership roll and open-house entry policy which I had belonged to for as long as I could remember, and which had dwindled without my noticing it into a fringe movement, a minority interest. I thought, my uncle would be in his forties now, not all that much older than me, perhaps with a family of his own, my cousins; a thriving branch of the old club. My mother didn't know his name. She couldn't remember the

name of Leslie's mistress. 'That female,' as she called her, with
as much resentment as you were likely to hear from her, had
been related to Elvia Quintero, the Frosts' cook. But the mistress's name, the name written on the long-ago letter from
Mariquita, was one detail of her vividly remembered Colombia
which eluded her. What did my uncle do, I wondered. Was he
a peasant, a football star? Was he a presidential hopeful, a
narco-baron? Was he alive?

It was my grandfather's map I had in front of me on the train
outside Medellin when the sugar canes parted like a safety curtain and the camouflaged gunmen climbed aboard. It was the
army, someone said. They weren't the guerrillas, they were
looking for the guerrillas. I suppose that this was intended to
ensure the peace of mind of passengers, though I can vouch
that it didn't have that effect in every case. The soldiers passed
down the train. They didn't give a very convincing impression
that they expected to encounter their quarry. I felt a stirring of
sympathy for them. What was I doing but chasing shadows, following marks along the way just as they were tracking graffiti on
breezeblock walls? I was retracing my grandfather's travels on
the railways. His annotated map, dated 1941, with its blue
rivers, red roads and thick black *ferrocarrils*, was like a set of
instructions he had left behind: the fluke of it having endured
among his foxed and incomplete papers made me think of it, or
allowed me to think of it, as instructions for me to follow. From
the map, I knew that we had travelled through Villa and Bosque
and Acevado and Bello . . .

Reports of the death of the Colombian train had been exaggerated – though not greatly, not greatly at all. It was on its last
legs, all right. Of the lines Leslie had known, the surviving
routes could be reckoned on the fingers of one hand. In a year
or two, they might all be gone. Little boys famously like train
sets – older boys, too – and I had at last tumbled to my grandfather's full-scale train set in Colombia. I wanted to have a go on

it. Coming round to the mystery of my grandfather, I was prepared to invest the curiosity to get to know him, and the train
was a rusty, fatigued – but still tangible – connection. Colombia
was at the heart of it; this story of sex and drugs and rolling-
stock.

So I was looking for Colombia and for Leslie himself, for a
lost country and a missing person. Two missing people, in fact –
there was Leslie's son to find, my Colombian uncle, the man
who had been excluded from the family club: this seemed a
dauntingly tall order. I didn't have a name. I didn't have a photograph or a telephone number. I didn't have a clue in the
world, really. If I did but know it, though, this task was as nothing compared to the one of finding Colombia, of discovering
Leslie Frost.

2

The Saint
in the Suit

It was a very English life. He was the son of a shopkeeper and he became an engineer. In the dog days of empire, he went to far-off places where his skills were employed in making things work, and where his foreignness still conferred social distinction, the best seats at *fiestas* on saints' days. He was dry, independent, practical; qualities that look from a distance like stoicism. Being duly rewarded was important to him – a number of his surviving letters concerned remuneration – but I didn't think that money explained the lonely exiles of his career. He enlisted as a teenager to fight in the First World War and offered his services in the Second. He was partial to a drink and to cigarettes, and maintained a necessarily distant interest in the fortunes of Swindon Town Football Club. He had a wife and daughter whom he loved, though he was as 'proper', or undemonstrative, as his own parents had been, and a frowning paterfamilias. It was a very English life with a late-flowering Latin affair which was impossible to reconcile with the rest of my grandfather's biography.

He had been dead for thirty years. Gran was dead, too. My mother went to a hypnotist in an attempt to recall the name of

'Isabel', niece of the Frosts' cook (second from left)

Leslie's mistress. She came up with 'Isabel': Isabel had been a relation of the Frosts' cook – her niece, mother remembered, or dredged up. But she didn't feel she had 'gone under' at the hypnotist's; she wasn't sure of what had been *recovered*, in the jargon. The shock of the initial discovery, in her teens, had been like a flash of light on the tender membrane of a film: the memory had been over-exposed. Enough of it survived for my mother to connect the name Isabel to the picture of a girl in one of her albums: pretty, brown-eyed, smiling, her chin cupped in her hand. I was doing *my* best to recover Leslie. I thought of the black-and-white photograph, the bottle of bay rum, a soda syphon which had seen a lot of service. They were like objects on a tray in the old parlour game to test memory.

There was no word of my grandfather's secret history among his papers: I looked in vain among memoranda, accounts,

receipts. As for his railway map, with its smudged notes and
ghostly blottings, its somehow *knowing* question marks – here
and there, *?*s had been pencilled in, as daunting in their way as
skulls and crossbones – if this really was a set of instructions
that Leslie had left behind, then he must have calculated that
there was no danger of it leading anyone to *him*. His past resisted breaking and entering; it was a foolproof life.

He grew up in the shadow of his father, Major Frederick
Frost, who, even in peacetime, made a point of his rank and,
whenever possible, his uniform, an ensemble of knee-length
boots, underwired jodhpurs and a tunic of bright and valorous
plumage. Major Frost, who was a greengrocer in Civvy Street,
took the revolutionary step of stocking only the choicest produce at his chain of shops in Swindon, and selling it at a fair
price – with the result that housewives and rival traders flocked
to him, albeit for different reasons. His wife, Leslie's mother, ran
a sideline in cut blooms, the zenith of her floristry being the
wreath sent on behalf of the people of Swindon on the death of
George V. The proceeds of the business allowed the Major to
become a traveller and man of affairs. In a trunk of Leslie's
memorabilia, I discovered his father's jaunty press cuttings and
letters-to-the-editor. One of the first Britons to hold a driving
licence, he was still getting plenty of use out of it as a game
octogenarian. 'When his car stopped, undaunted Mr F. J. Frost
lit a little fire of petrol and twigs on the side of the road and
started it again,' read one sere clipping from the early 1960s. 'It
wasn't during this century, but at the end of the last, when he
was driving a Butler one and three-quarter horsepower single-
cylinder horseless carriage with a top speed of 16 miles an hour.
At 87, Mr Frost is the oldest driver in the British Isles except for
Lord Brabazon . . .' Leslie's *sang froid* seemed all the more *froid*
when he was viewed alongside the Major. My mother told me,
'He hardly ever saw his father and they were terribly formal
with each other. He adored his mother but had very little to say
about his father. He admired him but I think he felt he had
abandoned the family.'

The volubility of the Major's archive was equalled by the taciturnity of his son's. Secured by a corroded paperclip to his letter of application for the village postmaster's job was what would now be considered Leslie's CV or résumé: in fact, an unheaded, typewritten summary on a single sheet of paper, with no mention of hobbies or societies or interests. It explained concisely that he had attended Swindon High School and been apprenticed at sixteen to the Great Western Railway, one of the most famous names in the history of the train. Leslie had attended GWR's yards at Swindon between July 1916 and July 1921, gaining 'experience in workshop, testing house, drawing office and footplate', for all but ten months of those five years. His passing-out certificate was no more revealing, composed of school-report blandishments: 'During the time Frost was with us he bore a good character, conducted himself to our entire satisfaction, and displayed good ability both as a craftsman and a draughtsman.'

His absence from the company was explained: it had been the Great War and he had joined up, serving in the Royal Flying Corps. He was demobilised in the rank of second lieutenant; not that I would have known this if I hadn't stumbled across a distressed parchment from 'our court at Saint James' dated 1920. From Leslie's surviving sister, Babs, twelve years his junior, I discovered that he had lied about his age. 'He was a pilot and he was shot down, over France, I think. His plane caught on fire. His foot was slightly crushed but he survived. It was a miracle, really.' My grandfather had been a fighter ace – I'd had no idea. Not even my mother had known. She said, 'That must have been how he hurt his hands – both of his little fingers had breaks in them.' Leslie hadn't been one to make anything of a war record. His father, who was, without fail gave Leslie an RAF tie at Christmases and birthdays.

I half-believed that Leslie's documents had been tampered with to thwart investigation. Mould had been cultivated on them like cress on a blotter, I decided; they had been aerosoled with fun-dust. An exhaustive correspondence over the purchase of the post office had been preserved, but not so much as a leaf of a diary or a paragraph of a billet-doux. The only emotion on view was the very English one that masquerades as a lack of emotion, proverbially given away by a stiff upper lip. But I kept looking.

My grandfather first went to Colombia as a single man. He had just turned twenty one when he joined the Barranquilla Railway & Pier Company. He found a flat in Barranquilla, on the Caribbean coast, my mother said, and a Chinese to do for him, to look after his clothes and keep the flat clean. Leslie's records showed that he returned to Britain six years later. He went to stay with his cousin, Elsie Short, who lived in a beautiful mansion on a vast estate in Reading – Bulmershe Court. Elsie was a leading light of the town, famous for her summer pageants. It was while he was staying at Bulmershe Court that Leslie met Peggie Langston. 'She had a trail of boyfriends,' my mother said. 'But she fell for my father hook, line and sinker. He was very good-looking.' They married in 1927 and almost immediately left for the Sudan, as it was then called. Leslie had found work with a Greek business magnate who owned a cotton plantation. He looked after the estate office and the engineering department, and Gran continued to enjoy the social life she had known in Reading. The Frosts belonged to a tennis club, they went to garden parties and to the races. They had servants.

When Peggie fell pregnant, she returned to England to have the baby. 'Pop didn't see me until I was nine months old, when he came home on leave,' my mother recalled. 'When I was very small I didn't see very much of him because he was at work all day and then out in the evenings.' Leslie made her toys – he was very practical. They were wooden toys, mechanical toys, toys for a boy. The Frosts came home from Sudan when Rosemary, my mother, was five years old. She said, 'I don't know why. I don't know whether the Greek got fed up and left . . .' Leslie was unemployed for a year before he got the job with the La Dorada company which took him back to Colombia.

He had disappeared from his papers but he couldn't absent

himself from his daughter. 'My father was typically Victorian, but we got on very well,' she said. 'I really adored him. We had a similar sense of humour: he teased me and I teased him back. Mother teased people but she used to get uppity and put out if *she* was teased. My father used to call me "Stinka" from when I was very young because I used to go rolling around in the garden.'

Finally I found documents which suggested a different side to my grandfather, a side my mother had known. Documents which hadn't been hidden with sufficient care. There was a letter to my mother when she was six ('My dearest Baba') in which Leslie had sketched the animals of the Frost household, demonstrating that his eye had fully merited GWR's praise. The drawings were accompanied by ditties, such as the following elegy for Sapito the pig:

> *'Poor Sapito! Sad your fate!*
> *You'll be the bacon on my plate.*
> *And if the hens their duty do*
> *They'll give the eggs to fry with you.'*

On what looked like a corner of best stationery, there was a more sober poem, or homily, perhaps attributed to 'J.K. Ullman' (it was difficult to read the handwriting).

> *'Whatever the journey*
> *Whatever the cost,*
> *I must find out*
> *What is behind*
> *the hills.'*

And there was a typewritten, uncredited passage, unfamiliar to me, repeated twice on a piece of blue writing paper:

> *'Yet it may be that as we draw to the*
> *end of our travels, these may become a*

weariness and that the last of our
travels may well prove our last
adventure in life. But whether our
last adventure will be full of darkness
or full of light we cannot know.'

The first of these verses might have been copied out by Leslie's father. It looked a little like his hand; in a self-dramatising fashion, it caught the wanderlust of the travelling Major. But it was difficult to read the second, typed extract without thinking of Leslie, to read 'the last adventure in life' without thinking of his affair, his son, in what had proved to be the final decade of his life, before darkness had enveloped everything.

In all the years I'd spent not thinking about Leslie and Colombia, I'd never thought of going to Colombia, either. Not once had I considered boarding a plane to Bogota. But after what my mother told me, I did; I thought about going to Colombia. Almost immediately, I thought about *not* going to Colombia instead. Dare I confess that I'm not a fearless, an *intrepid* traveller? On the contrary, I'm a fearful traveller; it's something I've taught myself to be. If I don't worry, I'll come to a sticky end. Fear is a stimulant, a well-recognised defence mechanism; but it's also a penance to be served in return for coming back in one piece, or so I've superstitiously persuaded myself. No departure into the unknown has been complete without me staring back at myself from the toilet mirror of the aircraft, demanding to know how I let myself get into this mess. To this extent, I'm a bad flier. I get last-minute nerves. In the case of Colombia, though, I got first-minute nerves too.

My career had taken me dry-mouthed into one or two risky places, but Colombia exerted a particular tug of dread. I recognised the source of this as the prospect of my being kidnapped. I discovered I had a phobia about becoming a hostage. Before I

La Camelia.

Sez you!

Marcel - The horse which couldn't slip
Over a boulder he did trip
And when he came down
with a bump.
He fetched a bruise up
on his hump.

(and no more!)

LADY JANE

MARCEL.

Sept. 9th. 1936.

BILLY.

My dearest Baba,

I tried to draw some
of our animals for you, but although
Marcel, looks quite as sad and
pathetic as this when he has to
start out on a long trip over
the mountains, I am afraid that
poor old Billy has got mixed up with a camel.
Never mind, we have so many animals here that they
are bound to get mixed up sometimes. Shall I
tell you their names? There are three mules,
La Reina, Gabriella and Nacho Diamante; one horse,
Marcel; three dogs, Alfonso, Lady Jane and Puppy Dan;
a baby pig, Lupito; two goats, Billy and Sarah Jane;
two ducks, Jim & Jenny; twelve cows, six calves,
twenty five chickens and twenty pigeons.

The mules, cows and calves belong
to the Company but all the rest are ours. Mr.
Blackett gave me the two dogs, Alfonso & Lady Jane,
but Dan was born here and so were nearly all
the other animals. Lupito, the piggie, is so fat
that he can hardly move but is ever such a clean
animal and sleeps with the dogs, and the puppie
plays with him and pretends to bite his ears and
tail. Poor Marcel, the horse, has had
a bad leg, where he fell down on some
hard stones with me, but we have been

A letter of Leslie's to his daughter, 9 September 1936

Sapito is a funny pig.
(Not the one who danced the jig)
He eats and sleeps the whole daylong,
and says a piggie can't go wrong.

He does not like a sty or run,
But likes to be out in the sun.
But when tis dark & cold at night
He stows himself way out of sight.

Poor Sapito! Sad your fate!
You'll be the bacon on my plate.
And if the hens their duty do,
They'll give the eggs to fry with you.

SAMMY.

SAPITO.

BILLY HEDGEHOG.

been fixing him up and he is getting better. Poor Lady
Jane and Puppie Tini have been ever so ill with
distemper, and we had to give them lots of medicine,
but they are now better and Tini is as frisky as ever.

I have picked out a nice chestnut pony for
you when you come out — This will be instead of an
ordinary birthday & christmas present and we shall
have to save up our pennies to buy a nice saddle
and bridle for it. You are getting such a big girl
now that you will be able to ride a horse instead
of a donkey. Do write and tell me what you want
your pony to be called.

With lots of love & many happy returns
of the day.
Dada

Dear me! I missed Billy Hedgehog from
our animals — Billy is a naughty boy and
damages the garden & he really doesn't deserve
to be put in your birthday letter.

A poor old hedgehog, called Bill,
Eat turnips and got very ill.
To get over his pain
He went out in the rain,
Instead of taking a pill.

went – during the period when I was *not* going, in fact – I vacillated between a fear of Colombia and a sense of the essential foolishness of this fear (the odds were I *wouldn't* be kidnapped, weren't they?), and back to a fear of Colombia again. Actually, these feelings accompanied me during the period when I *was* going to Colombia, too, and never left me as long as I was there. My confidence waxed and waned according to the last press agency wire I read – whimsical feature or teeth-chattering despatch – and the last person I spoke to – doubtful colleague or nostalgia-filled parent. In a London bookshop, I hesitated over a morbid volume entitled *The World's Most Dangerous Places* before reading, in a gazpacho of perspiration, that 'more than 800 people are being held captive in Colombia as this ink dries.' (The book went on to rate Colombia the chanciest spot on the globe, among nations where it wasn't straightforwardly suicidal just to show your infidel face.)

Whether or not you have any idea what I'm talking about probably depends on whether you grew up believing in the bogeyman. As far as I was concerned, the kidnappers of Colombia were the bogeymen, the bogeymen in the jungle. The thought of them struck me with the force of a childhood terror. There was no cast-iron reason to think that they would snatch me – that the bogeyman would get me – and, as far as I could make out, there was no cast-iron reason to think that they wouldn't. Fear of being kidnapped scarcely equates to *being* kidnapped, needless to say. But when I read a line of Garcia Marquez's, about letters written home by a hostage – 'thunderous truths that seem ridiculous to anyone who has not lived through them' – I presumed to see in it my own much less justifiable sense-of-humour failure, my now-you-see-it, now-you-don't flip-flops of panic and fleeting, shamefaced calm.

Fortunately for me, I had a friend who had been to Colombia and who wanted to go back. You could say that Dom was an intrepid traveller – especially if you knew why she wanted to go back. Her boyfriend, who was as intrepid as Dom was herself, had been in Colombia, although not with Dom, on the day he was murdered. It was a mugging which had turned into a stabbing.

Dom was tall and slim, much travelled in Latin America: she had just finished a guidebook to Honduras and El Salvador. I first met her when we found ourselves covering a Lambeth conference vote on gay priests. She kept nipping out for a smoke: a strikingly redundant nubile vision, in those surroundings. Dom had a fund of hard-won stories – 'I was up this volcano in Nicaragua,' one began – which were distinguished not only by being true, but also because Dom was present in them only to lend quiet authenticity to her impressive knowledge. She knew that 'Chilean' didn't rhyme with 'Gillian' but with 'Himalayan', though it was only when you happened to hear her say it that you realised you mispronounced it. She wanted to go back to Colombia because it was South America, because it was *away*, and because she wanted to know more about Laurent's death, she said; to go to the scene herself, to say goodbye.

There was another twist. Dom and I talked about a trip, my first trip to Colombia. As we began finalising what was by now *the trip*, I realised I knew very little of the circumstances surrounding Laurent's death – I had wanted to know but I hadn't wanted to ask. When I finally got around to finding out where she intended going, where it had happened – we were in a pub called The World's End, I remember – Dom named the place and I recognised it at once as a point on Leslie's map, a location in his history; a stop on the journey. It was Manizales, the four syllables which my grandmother had only to utter at Sunday lunchtimes, which she used to do unfailingly, to provoke laughter – suppressed, unheard laughter. My grandparents had lived in Manizales because Leslie was for many years the general manager of *El Cable*, the aerial ropeway moving cargo across the Andes, and one end of the line was in that city. It was a supreme feat of engineering: the longest conveyor belt in the world. Like the off-centre photograph of a train which had survived among

Leslie's effects, there were innocently careless snaps of *El Cable* – in one, the wheels of a pulley appear over Gran's shoulder like primitive UFOs – pictures taken when it was assumed that the cable to Mariquita, like the railway, would be an unvarying feature of the Colombian landscape.

Dom and I had Manizales in common, thanks to serendipity, or whatever the opposite of serendipity is: this was the sort of thing a worried man seizes on as a sign. The blackest of black clouds had a silver lining, at least for me. It was an unhappy coincidence.

'*Cuanda pretendian atracarto asesinan ciudadano frances*,' said the newspaper. During an attempted hold-up, a French citizen was murdered. It happened here in Manizales, the paper continued: a foreigner aged thirty, stabbed in the chest. Laurent had been in a *barrio* on a Saturday night when he was accosted. A magistrate by the name of Dr Castro Castro was in charge of the case. Dom and I were in the high-ceilinged reading room of the National Library. Beyond the window were the mountains of Bogota, a sight which was to become very familiar to me. In the same January 1995 edition of *La Patria* of Manizales which carried the report of Laurent's death, there were pieces about Colombia's Ruiz earthquake and the United Nations pulling out of Somalia. Tom Cruise's *Interview with the Vampire* was showing at the Manizales fleapit. Turning through a sheaf of back numbers, Dom said, 'There's a death being reported every day, a murder.'

'I thought it was a nice quiet town,' I said, remembering the contented look which used to settle upon my grandmother's face at the dinner table. I could hear the sound of a bell tolling somewhere – or was it altitude sickness, a ringing in my ears? – and I wondered, 'Why do they kill each other such a lot?' From the window of the library, I watched a man in the park across the road. He was walking on stilts. A middle-aged businessman was sitting to a packed lunch at a tree stump as though he were

a newsreader behind his desk. Colombians were unfathomable,
I thought.

At a café opposite Manizales cathedral, a cripple selling lottery
tickets went between the tables on all fours, like a dog. An old
boy was looking like James Brown does now: business suit,
immaculate white blouse, tie and pin. But the old boy no longer
attended a place of business, dragging out pitch-black elevenses
with his cronies instead. Bootblacks circulated. Dom and I had
arrived in the city where Laurent had been killed. She lit a cigarette. She said, 'I feel I could cry.' And then she did, bowing
her head, letting the tears come. I wanted to say something, but
I sat uselessly by, saying nothing, hoping that this was by
chance the right thing to do.

She had met Laurent on her travels in South America. He
was French, a geologist with a social conscience who was
making a good if uneasy living out of the oil business. He was
impossibly promising. 'Very handsome,' Dom had told me with
a frown, as though this had been immaterial, a man's looks
something she could take or leave, or thought she could. They
ran into each other in Honduras, and then again by chance in
Peru ('That's where everything started'), the way you do meet
people by chance when you're travelling, Dom explained.
Abandoning their separate itineraries, they had pitched a tent
on a vast, empty beach and simply taken to it, one or the other
reluctantly emerging every few days to hitch a lift to the nearest
available supplies. In due course, Dom had met Laurent's
family. I had the impression that a long-term arrangement had
been on the cards and that there had been no one else for Dom
since his death.

In the café, I thought: Laurent should never have died here.
The lawless stews of Bogota or Cali or Medellin – I could understand such a thing happening there; I could certainly imagine
it – but in this temperate, pleasant-seeming spot? Manizales
was the heart of *la zona cafeteria*, the coffee belt: this region

more than any other was responsible for producing eleven million bags of coffee every year, accounting for up to 20 per cent of Colombia's exports. The city was watered with 3,500 mm of rain a year. The average temperature was 17°C; the average temperature was *room* temperature. There were buxom bowers of bougainvillaea – I don't believe I have ever seen so much bougainvillaea in a major conurbation. The city was more than 2,000 metres above sea-level. In fact, it was falling off a mountain: the apartment buildings which appeared at intervals along this rarefied precipice were like sentry posts on the ramparts of a Nepalese city. The image of a redoubt wasn't wholly fanciful. Manizales had been founded, as recently as 1848, by refugees from the Antioquia department, to the north, who were fleeing civil disturbances. There was a connection with violence, after all. In Colombia, there usually was.

As I've already indicated, Dom was the gutsy type, but she broke down for a second time when we were at Manizales police headquarters. It was as she was telling the officers on the front desk why she was there, what had happened to Laurent. She was hoping that they could give her more information. Stern in their photographs – the police station guard of honour; employee-of-the-month – and forbidding in their dress insignia – a rifle crossed with a sword appeared on one shoulder; pistols rampant on another – the officers were sympathetic in person, moved by Dom's courage. They directed us to the police station in the *barrio* where Laurent had been killed. There, houses tottered on spindly wooden legs – I thought of the man I had seen on stilts in the Bogota park. In the middle of these pick-up-sticks homes was the wooden police station itself. It was like a lifeguard booth in *Baywatch*. The policemen dug out their old ledgers and leafed through them, kneeling on the tiled floor. They had very shiny boots, like the old boys in the café opposite the cathedral. Up a hill from the police station, small children were playing in a yard. On a wall of the yard was a fabulous mural made of shells and stones, a mural which depicted small children at play.

The police officers had a portable television set and a kitch-enette. There was a woman in a Pisces T-shirt who apparently did for them. They had a pump-action shotgun and a grotty-looking puppy, and they were more interested in the puppy, which crapped tinily, than in Dom's enquiry. We were getting nowhere. 'What the fuck was he doing in a place like this?' Dom asked, or asked herself. But the *barrio*, all the better for bright sunshine, no doubt, was congenial, full of the sounds of children playing and of policemen indulging a puppy. It was as unlikely a place for a killing as Manizales was as a whole. Suddenly, all eyes faced the street – was it a road smash? A mugging? Following the narrowed gaze of the constabulary, I saw that an elderly dog had flopped onto its side. The officers watched anxiously – did one reach for binoculars? – until the pet had righted itself and shuffled on.

The man at the *Fiscalia*, the records office, wasn't much help either, a spare character with his shirt open to the navel, belatedly advising us that the *barrio* where Laurent's murder had happened was a bad place, we shouldn't go there. He folded the blade of a penknife back into its stock without looking at it, pressing the blunt face against his wooden desk. He was sitting at a type-writer. Everywhere there were bundles of typewritten documents, sealed with yellow string. In the next room, a man who had metal hooks for hands joined us at the counter while a cool brunette in a trouser suit logged on at her computer terminal, made calls, apparently on Dom's behalf. This room, also full of documents bound in yellow string, had a view over roof tiles to the deep valley below Manizales and the mist-hidden Villa Maria, 'the vil-lage of flowers'. The documents concerned matters such as extortion, corruption and – a large pile – homicide. A poster on the door showed a policeman cuddling a baby. Puppies and babies – the Manizales force didn't wholly fill you with confi-dence as to the remorselessness of its manhunts. At this office in the *Fiscalia*, they had nothing on Laurent's death, the staff told us.

The last place to try was the courthouse, where the dread-noughts in blue serge posted on the door were engrossed in assembling a clock. In the office of Juzgados Penal de Circuito, an official produced a file of paper the thickness of a telephone directory. Something had been scrawled freehand in blue felt-tip on the covering page. I couldn't make it out, it was upside down. Perhaps it said the case was closed. It was Laurent's file.

The official flicked through it. Laurent had gone out to dinner by himself on a Saturday night. After he had eaten and settled his bill, he was approached on the street by an *atracador*, a mugger, Freddy Holguin Arango, who had nervously demanded money. He had been carrying a knife. Laurent had refused to pay and there had been a struggle. He was stabbed. An ambulance was called to the *barrio*. It was unclear how long it had taken to arrive. Laurent was taken to hospital: twenty minutes later, he was pronounced dead. On 7 October 1996, Holguin had been sentenced to twenty-five years in prison. He was serving his time in Manizales.

The official looked at Dom, his thumb keeping his place in the file. He was willing to let her see more information but she hesitated. Having come so far to learn the truth, she shrank from it. Or perhaps she knew enough now. I prompted her to ask for the name of the restaurant – she had said she wanted to go to the scene – but I felt as though I was pushing her. It was plain that visiting Manizales was affecting her: the way she had wept a little at the café by the cathedral; her voice breaking when she heard herself going over the details with the police.

Inevitably, it was different for me: Laurent was a name, an idea; he was like the half-uncle I might or might not finally meet. I had been wondering how I felt about *him*; assuming there *was* a him, still. I hoped that there was, hoped that I would be able to find him. I reluctantly conceded that it would be neat and tidy (though, granted, not for my uncle) if he turned out to be a dead narcotrafficker, say. Dead, at any rate. If he was still alive, what if anything would I recognise if I had the opportunity of looking into his face? Would he be horrified by me, by what I'd tell him, accustomed to a version of his parentage at odds with the one I knew?

The official flicked through the pages again, as though inviting Dom to change her mind. When he had done this earlier, I had glimpsed what looked like photographs, and guessed what they must be. This time – perhaps his thumb moved less rapidly – I saw distinctly enough the pale image of a good-looking man, his eyes slightly open.

In the lobby of our hotel, a radiant beauty looked down from a picture frame. Beneath her, in *administracion*, a woman of middle years was wearing a pink cocktail dress with matching mules at one o'clock in the afternoon, studying a compact and applying lipstick. There was gold at each of her wrists and an amulet on her bosom. She was in conversation with a man wearing a ponytail and a bumbag. His ears pricked up at our accents.

'How you all doing?' he asked us.

'Doing fine, I think. How *you* doing?' I said.

'Just fine. I just come to this hotel to relax. They know me here. I'm Steven.'

'*I'm* Stephen.'

He had an American accent and a fruit-pulping handshake. 'You passing through or what?'

'Yes,' I said, 'just for a day or two.'

An eyeball-roll of heartfelt recognition. 'Same here,' said Steven. 'I pass through for a day, I go away for a month, I pass through for a day. I have a business in the mountains.'

What kind of business could *that* be? Not drugs, surely: he would hardly be so upfront about it. Perhaps he dabbled in emeralds – the indigenous stones were among the best in the world – a *gringo* prospecting in Colombia like my grandfather in his youth: what was Leslie's surveying, after all, but prospecting for rail? Steven went on, 'That there is Antonio –' a reference to a bespectacled young man using a payphone. And then he said, 'Look, if there's anything you need   '

'Sure. Thanks.' *If there's anything you need?*

'They know me here,' Steven repeated. He was the kind of person for whom helping others was a way of showing off.

'OK, well, be seeing you.'

'Do you want any money?' said Steven.

Money? We shook our heads at this curious offer.

I had been thinking – *hoping* – that the beauty in the painting in the hotel lobby was a younger version of the woman who titivated herself directly beneath the picture frame; either that, or an idealised presentation of her. In fact, the pretty sitter was someone else altogether, a former Colombian Miss World, a girl from Manizales – the only *colombiana* to have lifted the diamanté mace, as it happened. This was in 1958, just after my family's association with Colombia ceased, or had appeared to.

My grandfather had arrived in town in October 1935. He was taking up the job with the La Dorada company and going out ahead of his family to set up home, Gran and Mum, who was then aged six, following by cargo boat to Buenaventura on the Pacific, and by train up into the mountains. I had photographs of the Frosts' place in Manizales. It was the sort of single-storey property you could imagine plantation owners inhabiting, or the Kenyan 'quality' who used to get up to white mischief. A property for which the term 'bungalow' was entirely inadequate. The black-and-white compositions disclosed abundant gardens and servants. Leslie allowed a local farmer the run of the grounds and in return there was milk from the farmer's cow. My mother was surrounded by the menagerie she had first encountered in Leslie's sketches and doggerel, but anthropomorphic whimsy was discouraged. There was no such thing as the spaying of bitches, so male dogs were taken up the garden when necessary by the mule boy and the gardener: the animals were held down and had their balls cut off.

My mother learnt to ride. She did her lessons in Spanish in the mornings with Sylvia, a Colombian girl, and in English in the afternoons with Gran. My grandparents enjoyed a busy

social life, mixing with Americans who were in coffee and
banking, Germans who were training the Colombian army. My
mother had written to me in an effort to recall Manizales: 'The
ropeway headquarters and terminal were on the outskirts of the
city and opposite (nearly) the largish hospital,' her letter said.
'Our house was down in the valley not far from the ropeway station.' I was hoping to find the station and the house while Dom
and I were in the city.

Trees grew dreadlocks of catkins on the streets of luxuriant
Manizales, and a butcher's window was hung with plaits of
intestines: commerce mimicking nature. Dom said she thought
the city was very European. 'Very soothing for nervous
Europeans frightened by Colombia,' was how she put it. From
either end of Calle 22, you could see that this road went through
the middle of Manizales like a wave. And it seemed as though a
church breasted every swell: there was a dazzling white church
with black frogging; and the concrete cathedral, the successor to
two fire-crisped wooden structures (and itself damaged by an
earthquake in 1979), in which the crucified Christ was ascend-
ing to heaven in a winding cloth which might have been
knotted bedsheets, the essential mystery of Christianity revealed
as an Indian rope trick.

I was attracted to a shop selling religious artefacts: figurines
of the Madonna, rosaries, candles. A cabinet was lined with
holy household names: the Virgin, St Lazarus – and a pink-
faced, middle-aged businessman in a three-piece suit and
homburg. In place of a sacred heart, there was a triangle of white
handkerchief over his left breast. His image appeared on a
prayer-card and on a lamp (which came with an electrical cable
and a two-pin plug). On these items, the businessman was holding the same pose as the statuette – hands clasped loosely
behind his back – while a figure in surgical scrubs attended a
man on a palliasse.

I made enquiries. Sure enough, the accountant-type boasted
a saintly prefix: according to the prayer-card, he was St José
Gregorio, though I understood that the 'José' was largely

dropped, which seemed right. Like the public school old boy he somewhat resembled, he didn't look as though he would be comfortable on first-name terms. I was pleased to part with 3,000 *pesos* for the statuette. I didn't think it was daft to have a loss-adjuster, or whatever he was, as a saint; I thought it was rather a good idea. The shop assistant couldn't tell me much more about him but in due course I discovered that St Gregorio was not an accountant but a doctor (a professional gentleman, all the same, then). He wasn't strictly speaking a saint, come to that, though a great many Colombians hoped to see him canonised. St Gregorio was originally from Venezuela and came to Bogota in the 1920s or 1930s. He had met with success, and even after he was dead, people believed that he could heal the sick, through the offices of mediums.

Dom and I showed the statuette to a man named Umberto Gallego, a bald-headed, donnish figure attached to the cultural institute in Manizales. He told me, 'Gentlemen dressed this way at the time your grandfather lived here.' A three-piece suit had been appropriate both for the city's chilly climes and for its polite society. My reason for calling on Sr Gallego was the hope that he could help me to find the old Frost property and the cable station, to enlighten me about *El Cable* in general. I didn't know very much about this heroic contraption, apart from its unrivalled length and the indisputable fact that it didn't work any more. The gloom I felt about the dilapidated railways didn't seem to attach itself to the lost ropeway, perhaps because it had seemed such a precarious mode of transport in the first place: the wonder of it was that it had worked at all. In my grandfather's old photographs, it looked like an early ski-lift on which bursting horsehair sofas did service as gondolas: actually, these were the tarpaulined consignments of freight for which the cable was intended. It wasn't a passenger service, though Leslie and other members of staff used to ride on it, suspended hundreds of feet over Andean abysses. They were taking huge risks. In a high wind, the rope would 'float', slip off the trestles, and everything on it would tumble into a ravine. It was gruelling

El Cable, the longest aerial ropeway in the world

work to retrieve the rope and lash up the cable once more. On one occasion, my grandfather had been inspecting some machinery when he fell down a shaft and cracked several ribs. 'They managed to get him back to Manizales by road,' my mother had told me. 'He must have been in agony. I remember the doctor coming to do something called cupping. Alcohol was involved. Pop was strapped up in a tight bandage and the doctor set fire to these cups and put them on his skin, to prevent clotting on his lungs.' I wondered whether Leslie's accident had had anything to do with his emphysema. His accident, or his treatment, for that matter.

With Sr Gallego's help, we established that the ropeway station, *La Oficina del Cable*, still stood, a wooden building which, I now realised, had been in the background of a couple

Leslie Frost (right) at the ropeway offices in Manizales

of my grandfather's photographs – photographs which showed off a spanking new car: not Leslie's, I think, but belonging to the somehow American-looking gentleman who had a proprietorial arm on a rear door (in leather blouson and britches, what he actually looked like was the director of a silent movie). Leslie was my age or younger as he stood shyly in front of a whitewall tyre; he wasn't as good-looking as he later became, the toothbrush moustache suggesting Chaplin rather than Gable; he was wearing a check jacket and a tie, the off-the-peg vestments favoured by St Gregorio, my grandfather's hallowed contemporary.

Like the cable office, a wooden tower was still standing, a tower which used to moor one extremity of the ropeway to the

city. In fact, it had been preserved as a national monument. Its
legs stood in protective concrete. The tower had been made in
Germany and transported to South America by boat. It looked
like an early electricity pylon: foursquare; every bolt spannered
fast. The winding gear had gone, but apparently a memory of a
slight cable spanning the mountains had inspired the
Colombian authorities with a vision of *per ardua ad astra*:
spelled out around the base of the tower was the universal dec-
laration of human rights, a project as foolish-seeming in that
land as a slender wire sustaining trade across the Andes.

My mother's 'largish hospital' was perhaps the maternity unit
not far from the tower, but in the valley where the Frost place
once stood were only grey slate roofs, apartments, shanties; the
white steeple of a church, satellite dishes, and gardeners toiling.
I invited Sr Gallego to look at my photographs of Leslie's house.
'This style – it is called Republican – most of it has disappeared,'
he said.

He had a book, *Manizales de Ayer y de Hoy*, Manizales
Yesterday and Today, which went into raptures over *El Cable*:
'watchtower of the future,' it called it, 'symbol of progress; irra-
diating focus of everlasting energy; leading light of creative will;
crackling forge where triumphs of steel are made.' Inaugurated
in May 1922, this wonder looped over the mountains for fully
seventy-two kilometres. It was suspended between 400 towers,
some of them more than 3,000 metres above sea-level. The
longest gap between them was greater than 800 metres. Cargoes
of coffee and fruit rumbled between the towers at a rate of
between four and seven kilometres an hour, propelled by nine
steam engines which produced forty horsepower each. *El Cable*
moved 100 tons a day in each direction and the journey could
take as little as ten hours, or as long as fifteen. Feasibility studies had been carried out as early as 1912, and work began in
1913, but the ropeway was ten years in the making, partly
because materials from Europe were unobtainable during the
Great War. Sr Gallego said, 'They needed to ship coffee from *la
zona cafeteria* to the Magdalena river, but the roads through

the *Cordillera* were impassable for most of the year. That's why they built *El Cable*.'

According to Sr Gallego's sources, it was in service for fifty years, from 1923 to 1973. It had come through *La Violencia*; it had seen off my grandfather; it was still running when I was in my teens. When I'd thought of it as precarious, never likely to last, I'd been doing an injustice to Leslie and his colleagues. But then it wasn't only the physical environment I'd been taking into account, it was also the political surroundings – except that I'd been going by the times and conditions that I was experiencing. Sr Gallego said there were plans to resurrect the ropeway, this time as a passenger service, a tourist attraction – 'This is a very conservative city and it would be a way of asserting our history,' he said – but *El Cable* was unthinkable in the Colombia of today, I felt, no feasibility study likely to find a way of accommodating the country's topography of instability.

The ropeway had stopped running at about the same time as the train had last called in Manizales. The railway line, *El Ferrocarril de Caldas*, had linked the coffee belt with the Pacific. According to another of Sr Gallego's books, it had been envisaged as part of a mighty railroad, *la gran linea ferrea*, stretching from the frontier of Ecuador to the Atlantic. A special tunnel had been smashed through the mountainside, and a station built in Manizales. The tunnel was now filled in, memorialised by a *trompe l'oeil* mural on the city's ring road: a locomotive appeared to be bursting out of the concrete, making straight for the lines of traffic. The station had been taken over by Manizales University as a lecture theatre, though it looked like a cathedral with its high, pea-green cupola: the handmade wooden booth in its vaulted ticket hall might have been the Pope's private confessional. Outside the station were a couple of static railway carriages – they had been converted into a student refectory – and, elsewhere in the city, at the centre of a busy roundabout, a cashiered engine puffed noiselessly up a plinth. '*En 1970 se levantaron los rieles en una decision que hoy todavia duele y no tiene explication,*' said Sr Gallego's book. In 1970, they took up the track in a decision without explanation, a sorrow to everyone. 'But the government approved it,' said Sr Gallego, with the look of a man who has seen through something.

Dom and I said our goodbyes to him at the doorway of the Cultural Institute. We were buffeted by a man with wild hair who claimed to be the secretary of the establishment. He was wearing a shapeless cotton jacket and a shirt with no collar. He and I exchanged a greeting of '*buenas tardes*'.

He said, 'Speak English?'

I said, 'Yes. Do *you* speak English?'

'Ha, ha!' said the secretary. The laughter wasn't out of amusement; it was for emphasis. 'Speak English.' He wasn't asking me, I realised, he was telling me. All of Manizales enjoyed a two-hour lunch break. The secretary seemed to have enjoyed it more than most. His voice dropped to a mumble. This was what I heard: '*Mumble, mumble, mumble.* French?!'

'A little,' I said.

'Ah. I live *Francia*, France. Paris.'

'Very nice.'

'Yes, yes.' The secretary faltered. He swayed. 'Shakespeare!' he ejaculated.

'Oh, yes.'

He appeared to be trying to remember something – a quotation from the Swan of Avon, possibly. 'Speak English!' he repeated.

'Yes. I do.'

'Ha! Ha, ha. Speak English.' This time he *was* laughing. 'Speak English, *mumble, mumble, mumble.*' He was attempting to pass off the mumbling as a few words in my language. 'Balzac!' he said suddenly.

It had been drizzling. I tried to place the smell; it was the old, newly unfamiliar smell of a city after it's been raining. Dom said, 'Maybe the sun will be out in the morning.' She hoped to lay flowers on the spot where Laurent had been attacked. She said, 'The reason I didn't want to see more of that file at the courthouse was because I knew there would be pictures of Laurent.'

The next morning, we took a taxi to the *barrio* where Laurent had been having dinner on the night he died. The driver pulled up at the address which appeared in Laurent's file: it wasn't a restaurant but a *tienda*, a family grocery store. Dom stood by herself to one side of the *tienda*, where there was a good view of the valley below. The sun was out. Above us were the pick-up-sticks *casas* of the *barrio*. A fat, uncomprehending boy was watching Dom, watching her crying.

Afterwards I held her and said – it was all I could think of – 'Well done.' In the taxi, I said, 'That was a lovely thing.' She nodded: she didn't want to talk. We got out of the cab in the middle of town. 'I'm sure Laurent would have greatly appreciated what you've done,' I heard myself say. If I couldn't think of an intelligent remark, at least I could buy the poor girl a drink: I steered her to a café, *La Cigarra*. There were men at the tables around us in their twos and threes, smoking, sipping coffee from tiny china cups, having their shoes shined in breach of a faded notice – '*No se admiten lustrabotas ni vendedores ambulantes*' – and gossiping. On a wall was an election poster on behalf of an unusual-looking senatorial candidate, with an unusual-sounding pitch: 'Vote Jesus Pinacue, vote serenity,' said the motto beneath an image of a *mestizo* in a tracksuit top, who was sporting dreadlocks and beatific smile. (Jesus Pinacue went on to win his seat, and be courted by French fashion houses on account of his cheekbones. He belonged to a tribe of Indians, the Paez. After he disregarded their instructions over a crucial vote, the Paez tossed him naked into an icy mountain lake in the expectation that its holy waters would purify him.)

La Cigarra, the regulars arriving at their usual time to take coffee together at their accustomed tables: this cycle of comfort

was unchanging, a quiet defiance of the random, endemic violence taking place on the streets, even the streets of
European-seeming Manizales, where there was one unlawful
killing every day. In this sanctuary, Dom's mood lifted. She
had done what she had set out to do. She said, 'To me, what's
important is the coincidence of it all: Laurent and I happened
to check into the same hotel in Peru on the same day – another
day earlier or later and we wouldn't have met again. He happened to finish dinner in Manizales at a certain time – another
fifteen minutes later and he'd be alive. Think of the fluke of
you meeting me and our deciding to go to Colombia. The arbi-
trariness of fate.' Dom knew more about Laurent's death now.
She had been to the scene herself. She had said goodbye.
There would always be insoluble questions: even when you
knew why, you still didn't know *why*. But something had been
settled.

I thought about the violence of Colombia. History told you
that the killing which had made it notorious in the past twenty
years or so, far from being a grisly aberration, was as character-
istic as the mingling of Spanish and Indian blood. 'The republic
of Colombia was born in violence,' wrote the Latin American
specialist Colin Harding, referring to the acute labour pains of
the country's emergence from Spanish rule in the early nineteenth century. Barely a decade after the republic of Gran
Colombia was inaugurated, it fell apart   or fell in on itself,
rather, the regions asserting themselves against each other and
against the centre. Local leaders and their followers marched on
Bogota from cities like Cali. The parallels with the activities of
the cartels 150 years later were inescapable.

There was a coup and a brief military dictatorship in 1853,
followed in 1876 by civil war. In 1899, Colombia embarked on
the War of the Thousand Days, at the end of which 100,000
people were dead – and this out of a population which was
then only four million-strong, a rate of attrition which put even
the homicidal excesses of the *narcos* and the guerrillas into the
shade. The most calamitous of many civil conflicts erupted in

1948. This was the unambiguously, *despairingly*, named *La Violencia*, and it consumed 300,000 lives, securing it a place as one of the three most savage episodes in the history of the Americas (the others being the Mexican Revolution and the American Civil War). And now there was a struggle involving security forces, paramilitaries, rebels and drug-runners, and one in ten of the murders committed anywhere on the globe was taking place on Colombian soil.

What made the Colombians like this? For decades, it had had a lot to do with politics, most commentators said. There were, and *are*, two major political parties in Colombia: the Liberals, the party of modernisation, of secularism and federalism; and the Conservatives, representing the landed interest, the Catholic Church, the unified nation state. Reflecting on the period of *La Violencia*, a Polish traveller, Krzysztof Dydynski, wrote, 'To comprehend the brutality of this period, one must understand that Colombians were traditionally born either a Liberal or a Conservative and reared with a mistrust of the members of the other party. In the 1940s and 1950s, these "hereditary hatreds" prevailed over any rational difference of ideology or politics, and were the cause of countless atrocities, rapes and murders, particularly in rural areas. Hundreds of thousands of people took to the hills and shot each other for nothing more than the name of their party.'

There was a black comedy in all of this: despite their differences, the two parties had a lot in common. Both recruited politicians from the middle classes and drew support from workers in cities, *campesinos* on farms and ranches. Moreover, in the twentieth century, leading figures from each party appeared to go out of their way to follow policies associated with their supposed opponents. As Dydynski said, rationality had very little to do with Colombia's political killings. It was difficult to say exactly how significant they were in terms of *all* murders. Of the 30,000 and more unlawful killings recorded in 1997, for example, only 6,000 were as a result of the civil conflict, according to the security police – though critics would say that they had a vested interest in downplaying political killing, in which the forces of the state were often implicated.

Nor did it get you very far to imagine that the murders going on now could be explained away by cocaine – the assumptions that westerners brought with them didn't travel well. Drugs accounted for a surprisingly small share of gross domestic product, only about 5 per cent in the mid-1990s: in other words, *very few people were involved*. Of course, you could argue that the economics statistics didn't reflect the true picture. But the calculation of 5 per cent of GDP was the *highest* estimate offered by reputable analysts, and even if it erred on the modest side, the real scale of the drugs economy was clearly nothing like the one you would have guessed.

So, politics was a factor in Colombian violence, and geography, and, yes, drugs. But how to explain the nightly harvest of corpses? Poverty was surely at, or near, the root of a lot of violence. Urban unemployment stood at almost 15 per cent in March 1998, and there were glaring inequalities of wealth. The police offered apparently banal conclusions. They put the killing down to common crime, to personal vendettas, the booming trade in firearms, high levels of drinking . . . Even when you knew why, you still didn't know *why*.

There was a dull, brownish watercolour in *La Cigarra*. Had my grandfather smoked and ruminated beneath it? Pedro Gomez, eighty years old, told me that it used to take three days to move anything over the *Cordillera* until the ropeway had started running. '*El Cable era estupendo*,' said his companion, who was sixty-six. In the old days, the only way of reaching Mariquita had been on horseback, resumed Sr Gomez. Leslie had ridden out along the route of the ropeway himself when he was checking on the towers. My mother would sometimes accompany him. Photographs survived of father and daughter hitting the trail together: I had them with me. Sr Gomez examined my pictures: pictures of the *camino de herradura*, the mountain bridleway; *la oficina del cable*; the old Frost place in Manizales – no longer standing; and also of Number Two,

The mountain trail from Manizales

Mariquita. Sr Gomez spooned sugar into his strong, black *tinto* and said, 'We used to call Mariquita "The Home of the English".'

The waitresses sat down beside their customers. Although the women were highly personable, there was no hint of the escort bar or the lap-dance venue about *La Cigarra*. They merely kept the men company while they waited for their regular partners in the rituals of black coffee, shoeshine and gossip; the antique freemasonry of the *tinto*.

3

Kidnappability

Naked and covered in oil at a private members' club in Bogota, I had Esperanza's expert hands all over me, and I was wondering about my new friend, Ivan. Through a thin screen, I could hear him talking about me with the other men as they were getting undressed. 'I was just telling them that you might get up to what your grandfather did,' he called out with his high, empty laugh. I looked up at Esperanza: under normal circumstances, this would have been impossible, because although Esperanza undeniably had her charms, height wasn't one of them. She was extremely short, and had no neck. As it was, however, I was lying on her slippery couch. She was smiling at me. She was turning on a vibrator: it looked a little like a travelling iron.

The club was the one place where Ivan could truly unwind, he said. It wasn't just being at the club that did the trick for him, but being *of* the club too. It was very satisfactory to him that his membership application had been accepted. 'This is a very exclusive place. They only have businessmen, dentists, people like that,' he said. Ivan's father was a dentist. It was very satisfactory that Ivan's Renault Twingo was recognised by the doorman, whose wine livery would not have looked out of place in St James's. It was a country club, a health lido – Ivan visiting a brothel ('a house of appointments', Colombians called them) was somehow unimaginable, and Esperanza's toy of relief, with a noise like an oven-timer winding down, was an innocent massaging device. Health clubs were all the rage among successful Colombians: one of the first things Pablo Escobar had done with his money was to go out and buy one. Ivan liked to swim and take a Turkish bath. There were three chambers in the sauna, like descending circles of hell; I sat in the outer room – the temperature toasty, stalactites of condensation dropping into my drink – and watched Ivan in the cauldron next door, fast asleep in his bikini briefs. What Ivan *chiefly* liked to do at his club was to know people, and be known. There was an offer of a ride home in the Twingo to Carlos, who swept the locker-room floor; in a corridor, there was a chuck of the cheek for the daughter of a regular. In the middle of towelling himself down after his lengths, it occurred fo Ivan to flip-flop back to the poolside and offer his best wishes to the swimming team, who were in training for an important match.

Ivan's club was a revelation to me: I hadn't thought he cared for anything apart from money. He was forty-five years old and he sometimes worked for a western embassy, only now he was working for me, too, running me about the city in the Twingo, calling people on his cellular phone. Dom had returned to England; she was writing to France, to Laurent's family. Despite the loss of my guardian, Dom, I was in Bogota. I wanted to see what I could find out about my grandfather at the British Embassy and the railway offices, and to ride on one of Colombia's last remaining trains. The afternoon before the invitation to Ivan's club, he and I had been sitting in the lobby of the Hotel Tequendama, the oldest hotel in the downtown district: I was groggy with altitude sickness, scarcely curious about whether Leslie might have known the hotel's emerald shop, the marble urinals – when Ivan had started in about

money again. 'If it were possible that you could advance
me . . .'

We had already agreed a fabulous sum as his daily rate. It was
the price he could command in his regular occupation as a
simultaneous translator. 'I *love* simultaneous translation,' he
said: here was a source of professional fulfilment – but love? I
knew by now that Ivan's exultations were often uttered in a
spirit of total cynicism. I had tried to beat him down to a figure
which was merely ruinous – half his regular fee. 'Well, it would
be very interesting to work with you,' he'd said with a profound
lack of conviction. 'I'd *love* to do it, of course; but if we could
agree that in the event of a simultaneous translation coming
along . . .' Somehow simultaneous translations would be
coming along *ad infinitem*, I suspected, and Ivan would be
declaring himself unavailable. And, I had to admit, he was
extremely good: in offices, on the street, he gave a running commentary on conversations as they were going on in front of us,
as though we were invisible to the speakers. He knew where to
find the best cup of coffee in Bogota, and pointed out the city's
oldest blue movie cinema – I could imagine Ivan the simultaneous translator dubbing whimpers and moans onto a soft-porn
soundtrack, sipping take-out coffee between recordings, thinking of nothing except his fee and his club.

He would prefer it if I could pay half the money into a bank
account in Philadelphia, he said as we sat in the Tequendama.
As to the other half, well, he had bills coming in, and corporate
clients could be very slow settling their accounts, and it was
going to be a holiday weekend . . . So we went to a bank near
the hotel and I withdrew a staggering amount of money on a
credit card and Ivan sighed, 'I like you *so* much more now.'
The bank had recently been bought by a bigger concern in
Bilbao. 'The workers are exploited by the Spanish.' Ivan was
decoding the words on a poster in the window, which were
back-to-front from where we were standing. Like people who
always have to be reading – the print on a sauce bottle, if nothing else is to hand – he had a compulsion for simultaneous

translation. Perhaps he did love it, after all. Over the shoulders
of the bank tellers, a man peered from a hole in the wall. He
was watching the notes flicking through the hands of the
cashiers. He had the look of a casino boss checking up on the
croupiers. Perhaps he was one of the Spanish innovations that
had upset the staff.

'Should I count it?' Even though the inch-thick wad of large-
denomination *pesos* was in Ivan's hands – or rather, in an inside
pocket of his small holdall by now – he was not at ease. Before
the money was safe, he had to leave the bank, cross a street, and
go into a branch of his own bank where it could be deposited. It
was a journey of perhaps 500 yards, but it loomed in Ivan's
mind like a trek through no man's land under withering fire.
'No, I won't count it,' he said at last, and I could only guess how
much the words had cost him. 'We'll have to watch each other
very carefully.'

'I'll watch *you* very carefully,' I said, meaning he could look
after the bloody money all by himself if it meant so much to
him. But then I felt a pang of shame, and the pair of us went
across the street together under a light rain, Ivan with his curious, precise walk and a small holdall stuffed with cash.

Bogota was the only place where Ivan felt at home, he said. At
times I allowed myself the uncharitable reflection that it was the
only place that would have him. Refugees, runaways – misfits
of every sort – they came to the capital all the time. Colombia
was in a state of constant turnover. More than a million people
had been displaced from their homes in a decade, chased away
by guerrillas or paramilitaries, and most of them were fetching
up in the larger cities. The population of Bogota was being propelled towards a total of 10 million – though that was just a
guess, the demographers admitted. The constituency of the
unknown was vast: the last national census, undertaken in
1994, had still not appeared four years later. Many of Colombia's
internal exiles settled in the slums of southern Bogota, only to

find that the influence of the left-wing guerrillas extended even
there, to within a few blocks of the nominal seat of government.
Administration in many parts of the city, such as it was, came
from the rebels. Formally, the duty was shouldered by a mathe-
matician called Antanas Mockus, whose time in office was
distinguished by a flash of the mayoral buttocks in public, and
by the occasion of his marriage, reverently conducted in a tiger's
cage in the municipal zoo.

Like all big cities, Bogota was really a number of small cities,
operating in a more or less loose confederation. There was
Centro, downtown, where Ivan and I had bootlegged money
from one side of the street to the other. Confusingly, Centro
wasn't the area *bogotanos* thought of as the centre of their
hometown. That distinction was reserved for the quarter next to
the Plaza de Bolivar, which had been the nucleus in Spanish
times. This was a precinct of commerce and bustle, of dereliction and loss, home to high-rise businesses and stores, home to
the homeless. This was where you would find the head offices
of the manufacturing companies which contributed about 20
per cent of GDP: textiles, clothing, food processing, chemicals,
metal-working, paper, and so on. You had a sense of citizens
getting on with their affairs. There was order in the chaos. But
the order wasn't wholly plausible: there was an armed guard on
the Wimpy Bar. It wouldn't have surprised you to find the
plazas filling with security forces, the vendors of fresh fruit and
luridly battered snacks wheeling their barrows out of harm's
way: perhaps it was only the altitude, working on you like a
mild hallucinogen, or Bogota's brownish smog tainting your
view.

Quarters of town identified themselves according to the
trades which were plied on their streets. Entering the city
limits from the countryside, with Bogota looming out of the
haze – advertisements as big as apartment buildings for beer,
cigarettes – you passed electrical wholesalers for block after
block; then there were car parts, then vets, then pets. As if they
were a typing pool on a plantation, elderly black men sat before

similarly venerable Remingtons on one Bogota corner – 'Take a letter, Sr Gomez!' – bashing out while-you-wait job applications and wills and insurance claims. Gents in bow ties stood by for their fair copies, mingling with a little beggar girl who had a burned and withered leg, and a matron in a respectable suit, notable only for her dwarfish size. If customers knew exactly where to go for what they wanted, criminals did too: a gang which was reportedly helping itself to 'household items' at a warehouse in April 1997 was interrupted by the police. The raiders opened fire with assault rifles, shotguns and automatic pistols. 'The shooting started inside the warehouse but spilled into the street, but there was no risk to bystanders,' assured a police spokesman. Nonetheless, at the end of a two-hour shoot-out, nine men lay dead. The previous October, there had been a heist in the jewellery quarter – six people dead – and, in the same month, a break-in at one of several lorry pounds (seven dead). There was chaos in the order.

Amid all this zoning of goods and services, which allowed the law-abiding and the law-breaking alike to orientate themselves, it would have been strange if vice didn't enjoy regular premises. Sure enough, the red light area practically had its own postcode, so well established was it on a couple of blocks of Caracas Avenue. As Ivan and I were driving on that street one night, I noticed at the kerb not the customary hot pants and stilettos but a pair of spangled trousers, bulging at the thigh; a little further on, a figure was gesturing towards us in a tight bolero jacket; loitering at the following junction were three street professionals who were wearing – was I seeing things? – who were wearing *sombreros*. The pavement was busy with night owls in *gaucho* boots. It hadn't escaped my attention that all of them were men. That didn't tell me much in itself – what was this weakness *bogotanos* had for cartoon Mexicans? Judging by the numbers of hooped moustaches under the streetlights, it was an urge that a great many surrendered to on their way home. Was it sex, I wondered – I mean, *just* sex – or was it that old tear-jerker, men whose wives didn't understand them?

Did they yearn to crawl under a *poncho* with a strong, silent *caballero*, to talk about the endless *pampas* and perhaps share a numbing shot of tequila or two?

Ivan said, 'They are musicians in the Mexican style, *mariachi* men,' and I saw that several of them were leaning on guitar cases, and that the illuminated shop fronts in which many waited were displaying trumpets and maracas. It was all as innocent as Ivan's club. The form was as follows. The motorist wound down his window, just as he might further along Caracas Avenue, and in response to the question, 'Psst – looking for a good tune?', he would reply, 'Yes, it's my parents' golden wedding on Saturday and I need a trio from eight thirty.'

'Are you kidnappable?' Ivan asked me one day. 'You're a journalist, okay. But are you more, let's say, *The Guardian* than *Jane's Defence Weekly*?' Perhaps his point was that my political affiliations might have a bearing on whether or not I was snatched – my kidnappability; was that what he called it? – though I doubted it and I think he did too.

'You tell me, am I kidnappable?'

'Well, you look right,' said Ivan. 'You're a *gringo*.'

'Is it something *you* worry about, being kidnapped?'

'Not really. It's in the air we breathe. You get used to it.' A man who had a house across the street from Ivan's parents, a house in a nice part of town, had been taken, Ivan said. 'He had two Mercedes. They're so expensive in Colombia.' The cars were an advertisement of the man's kidnappability. Ivan made a phone call; I thought about the idea he had introduced me to: if there was such a thing as an ability to be kidnapped, perhaps there was a corresponding *dis*ability – what would that be? To pauperise yourself, to affect cast-offs? It sounded like an ability but really it was a predisposition, it was something like clubbability. You couldn't turn it off, or choose not to use it, as you could with an ability. That left you with the question: are kidnap victims predisposed?

I had read enough about kidnapping in Colombia – read enough and *sweated* enough – to know how it would happen. You would be on the street, making a familiar journey – to or from your place of employment, for example, or perhaps taking the air outside your habitual hotel. The kidnappers would probably be disguised, and certainly armed, though they could expect to strike with impunity except in cases of extreme bad luck on their part. Colombia's security forces were as colourful and varied as the banknotes, and, like the banknotes, the most exotic were of lowest value: compared to the in-country *narco*-busters in their grungy fatigues, a Bogota squad affecting white accessories – they looked like mime artists, or troupers in a Michael Jackson revue – were unconvincing, particularly as they never put in an appearance before lunch. Your kidnappers would force you into the back of a car, or perhaps the boot, so that you were unable to see where you were going. You would be taken to a house in an outlying part of the city, kept in a room admitting no natural light. Perhaps your location would be rotated – your guards would be. Who were they, who were they working for? One of the left-wing guerrilla factions, probably, or common-or-garden criminals. You might never find out. I don't mean that to sound unduly sinister: the chances are you would be treated quite well – fed and watered, permitted escorted visits to the bathroom, even allowed television and papers. And you would very likely be freed, your captors having named a surprisingly, almost hurtfully, reasonable price. (In my case – a *gringo*, but not one working for a household-name multinational – it might be no more than five figures.) It would all take time, however: the leisurely preparation and issuing of a ransom demand, and then the unhurried negotiations, as pungently folkloric as haggling in a souk. Of the 1,439 kidnappings in 1996 for which the police had paperwork, 7 per cent of the hostages involved had escaped a year later, 15 per cent had been freed in raids, 30 per cent had been released upon payment of a ransom and 39 per cent were still in the custody of their abductors. Nine per cent, a hundred or so, were dead.

With a view to minimising my kidnappability, I had been in touch with the British Embassy. There had been a series of harrowing telephone conversations with a security officer, in the most recent of which he had advised that if I was determined to travel the railways of Colombia, I should seriously entertain the idea of going with a unit. 'I'll have to see if we can put you in touch with a unit,' he went on, perplexingly. A unit? A travel agency, did he mean? 'An *armed* unit,' said the security officer. 'Two or three guys with guns.'

The embassy encouraged nationals to register themselves at its fortified apartments, which occupied one floor of a high-rise in northern Bogota. Officials suggested that visitors left a note of their itineraries. The security officer to whom I'd spoken over the telephone stood in front of a relief map of Colombia. Two local advisers, *mestizos* in lounge suits, were called into his office to adjudicate on the safety or otherwise of my proposed destinations. The security officer wasn't familiar with Mariquita, where my grandfather's son had been born. The two Indian security men let us know – they blinked; briefly, they turned down their mouths – that Mariquita was okay by them. The officer was doubtful about La Dorada but one of the Indians approved of it. It was the town at one end of the railway which Leslie had run during his last years in Colombia, and it had lent its name to the route: the La Dorada line.

The railway ran through Barrancabermeja, a town north-east of Bogota. When I pointed to 'Barranca' on the map, the security officer actually spluttered – it was something between maniacal laughter and fright. 'That's about the hottest place there is! That's just about as hot as you can get!' he said. Barrancabermeja was a major oil-producing centre. The state oil company, Ecopetrol, had a refinery there which filled 185,000 barrels a day and employed 5,000 people. The papers that morning had reported that rebels had set fire to three buses in the town. A fortnight earlier, a bomb had gone off as Ecopetrol executives were meeting.

Oil was the real wealth of Colombia, the leading export earner, generating much more revenue than illegal narcotics: BP, one of the largest investors in Colombia, exploited oilfields estimated to be worth £25 billion. The company has been criticised over its links with the Colombian armed forces, who provide protection for oil pipelines but have also been accused of human rights abuses. The guerrillas condemned Colombia's foreign partners like BP for exploiting the country's natural resources; the pipelines were their most important targets. The Cano–Limon pipeline, through which 170,000 barrels of crude oil flowed every day, was repeatedly bombed: when it was blown up on 20 April 1998, it was for the sixteenth time that year. It was also the most catastrophic rupture to date: the spill threatened to reach Venezuela.

Barrancabermeja was a powerbase of the communist-led oil-workers' union, and a stronghold of the leftist ELN guerrillas. It was frequently subjected to attacks by right-wing vigilantes. In May 1998, at least eleven people were killed and forty-two went missing – forced onto lorries, feared dead – after vigilantes attacked the impoverished *barrio* of Nino Divino before dawn one Sunday. 'Keep quiet, sons of bitches. Nobody move, we're here to fumigate this place,' said the leader of the masked, heavily armed mob of fifty or so, all of whom were wearing military fatigues. They checked names against a list – a familiar m.o. of the death squads – targeting those they suspected of sympathising with the guerrillas. Some were killed on a football pitch, where they had been dancing the night away to the accordion rhythms of *vallenato* music; others were executed in a billiard hall. All the time the killers shouted, 'We're the fumigators!' Some of the hostages were later freed but others had not returned from the mountains. It was said that they had been trussed up in the branches of trees.

What had happened in Barranca followed the established seesaw routine of unlawful killing in Colombia. In the north-west, on the border with Panama, guerrillas were in the habit of lining up busloads of peasants and shooting them, the security officer said. It was to dissuade the locals from working for foreign fruit-growers. The next day, another bus party would be shot by a right-leaning death squad, to ensure that the *campesinos* loyally picked fruit. Hundreds of plantation workers had been murdered according to this pitiful sequence, which seemed to pick up where Garcia Marquez had left off in *One Hundred Years of Solitude*, itself written in the knowledge of a massacre of banana workers at Cienaga on the Caribbean coast in 1928, when the workers had gone on strike and the army had opened fire on them. Here was another corrective to the established verity that Colombia's violence was exclusively linked to drugs. Growing fruit might be a prosaic occupation, but it was a valuable one – Colombia producing some 86 million boxes a year – and 'an even more dangerous game than *coca*,' according to the Latin America Bureau.

The security officer discussed kidnappability. 'The kidnappers work on routine. They're after wealthy *gringos* – heads of multinational corporations, petrol men.' But these were 'hard targets', living in virtual stockades, surrounded by armed security. 'I don't want you to feel paranoid, don't think there are guerrillas behind every tree, but from the kidnappers' point of view, you'll do fine.'

Trying to pretend to myself that I hadn't heard this, I changed the subject and asked the security officer about my grandfather's diplomatic career. Leslie had been consular agent at Mariquita for two years. Because of this and the old photographs I had of the Frosts' residences, my sketchy memories of Leslie himself, I couldn't help thinking in terms of Graham Greene's *The Honorary Consul*, 'On the verandah of the rambling bungalow Charley Fortnum sat before a bottle of whisky, a syphon and . . . two clean glasses.' I had tried to find out more from the Foreign Office, its various vaults and depositories in London and the Home Counties. But I was advised that surviving records of the period, if any, would be retained by the Embassy. The security officer said he would have to get the press secretary. But this man's news was disappointing: files

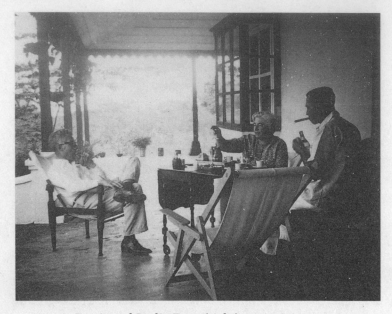

Peggie and Leslie Frost (right) entertaining at
Number Two, Mariquita

were only kept for three years. After that, they went to London.
A few of them. The majority were destroyed.

I was staying in the old town, Candelaria. There, you could
think that Bogota was alpine: the timbered Hansel-and-Gretel
houses and, above them, the mountains, lost in cloud some
chilly mornings. They were the mountains I'd seen with Dom
from the window of the national library.

My hotel was new and well-appointed, but also old and
draughty: the liberator, Simon Bolivar, had once quartered
troops on the premises, and the change of use had happened
comparatively recently in the building's history. It was across a
cobbled street from the Foreign Ministry, a short walk from the

Presidential Palace and the Plaza de Bolivar. The place immediately next door to the hotel called itself a restaurant. But to
all intents and purposes it was a dive, a Soho pub of the sort
which somehow emerges untouched from every phase of modernisation and theming. There was a stag's head on a plinth.
There was a stack of empty beer crates: customers drank beer or
the local firewater, *aguardiente*, a sugarcane-based alcohol
flavoured with anise. (It was clear and sharp and lethal: in
1998, fifteen party-goers went to hospital with respiratory problems, fluttering heartbeats and rashes after sampling a batch in
the city of Cali; five others died.) In the pub, mine host
favoured the kind of clothes worn by men of a certain age,
clothes which eventually turn up among their effects, but
which are sold by no known outfitter. His tie was tucked into
his trousers. His hair was carefully groomed, in an old-fashioned way. He looked like the kind of thrusting Politburo turk
of seventy or under who would be tipped by commentators as
a future General Secretary of the USSR, when that sort of thing
was still done.

I had been reading about Bogota's café society, the *tertulias*,
gatherings of writers and artists putting the world to rights, congressmen declaiming their own poetry. This scene was once
famous throughout the Spanish-speaking world and Bogota was
referred to as 'the Athens of the South'. I looked around the
Stag's Head: it was a Friday night. There were office workers in
suits and ties – civil servants, bank clerks, junior managers –
having a few at the end of the week, always mindful of where
their briefcases were. Beer bottles were their spoor. There was
some kind of *sotto voce* drinking game, not calculated to please
the landlord. A couple came in with their labrador and ordered
Cokes. There was a barmaid who liked to lean on the counter
and chat to regulars and smoke. There was a pub drunk – all
this place needed to be the Coach and Horses in Soho was a few
original *Private Eye* cartoons on the walls. Instead, squatly
mounted, were 'flats' patently recovered from a bankrupt travel
agency, showing the sights of Salzburg, things to do in Trieste.

Ranged alongside these were publicity stills for an ancient film, *Beckett*, starring Peter O'Toole as the turbulent priest and Richard Burton as his sovereign. The drunk bummed a cigarette off the host; I decided he was probably 'artistic'. The landlord himself, asking me if I wanted *una cerveza mas*, had the air of a backstreet abortionist tempting a caller to more gas.

The peak of Monseratte presented views of Bogota laid out in the basin beneath: glittering, scarab files announced the rush-hour; there was the flare of someone welding, and a black army helicopter, of the type shot at while visiting foreign politicians flew over drug-farming areas, seemed barely to clear the down-town skyscrapers. In the foothills of Monseratte, shanties ran into one another in a *barrio* which suggested a tremblingly arrested mudslip. People lived like this on the margins of the city. Doctors saw a thousand cases of eye irritation in 1997 after a *derrumbe*, a landslide, when more than 700,000 tons of garbage blocked a river in southern Bogota. The city might have been expected to be smoggy, but only one or two stacks were a manifest disgrace; at the peak, the air was scented with euca-lyptus. There was a Christ on the adjacent summit, a smaller, less celebrated cousin of the Rio statue, and on this slope, rep-resentations of the stations of the cross endured by '*El Señor de Monseratte*'. As to the agonies of the *bogotanos* below, again, you might have expected the air to crack and split with gunfire. Perhaps Monseratte was just too far above the city for its vital sounds to be audible from there: you couldn't hear the traffic, the sirens. It was disarmingly serene-seeming. Joan Didion wrote in 1974 that Bogota was 'floating on the Andes'. She went on, 'The whole history of the place has been to seem a mirage, a delusion on the high savannah . . . its isolation so splendid and unthinkable that the very existence of the city astonishes.'

Bogota was laid out around a grid, in the American style, and there was nothing to unify it for the citizen on the move.

Instead of a dedicated fleet of cabs, there was a demolition
derby of rival firms; rather than a network of buses there were
chivas and *busetas*, conveyances which varied as much in size
and tariffs as they did in the distances they were prepared to
take you. There was no metro, no monorail, no underground.
There was a train. That's right: train singular. Twice a week, it
ran from the city centre to the suburb of Nemocon. I say 'ran'
but it barely got above walking pace, according to the British
security officer. 'It's just an excuse to get pissed. They call it the
Aguardiente Express.'

I caught a bus, to the Savannah railway station. It was where
the twice-weekly train departed, and where a railway archive
was preserved: I wanted to see if any records survived of
Leslie's career with the private railway companies or the state
concern which succeeded them. As you boarded the bus, there
was a turnstile and an urchin sitting by it, his back to the dash-
board, collecting the fare of a few *pesos*. The bus was full, so I
couldn't sit and I was very conscious of my rucksack, of being a
gringo; of my kidnappability. The headrests were covered in
plastic; set in these clear antimacassars were injunctions against
smoking. My fellow passengers included businessmen, one
with acne and a briefcase; black-skinned men who looked like
labourers; smartly dressed women. The bus driver was wielding
a great gearstick, apparently encased in tan hide: it looked as
though he was about to draw a Winchester rifle from its holster.
His movements were jerky, when you could glimpse them at all.
He was more or less screened from view, the urchin his representative among the passengers.

At the railway station, a kind of elongated Nissen hut housed
more than 100,000 files in near-gloom: you accessed them on
duckboards, for no clear reason. I wasn't supposed to poke
about among the files, but Sra Yolanda Amaya, who was in
charge, seemed to be rather taken with the story of my grandfather. 'Anything to do with the railways makes me impassioned,'
she said, taking off her spectacles. Sra Amaya was a handsome,
middle-aged woman. She had been working on the railways for

thirty years, the last six in the archives. She was supervising a group of pleasant, flirty girls who offered me cherries over the office photocopier. The girls were helping us to look for my grandfather's file. One flipped through a card-index but failed to find Leslie's name: I spotted it, spotted 'F.L. Frost'; it was on a card stuck to the one in front. '*Venga aqui!*' exclaimed Sra Amaya. 'Come here! It's here after all.' There was a look of reproach for the careless clerk. It was an exciting discovery: it was proof of Leslie, his life in South America. There was no shortage of this at home, but this was the first evidence I'd found in Colombia.

Leslie worked for the Barranquilla Railway & Pier Company in his twenties. Barranquilla was a sticky, still city on the Caribbean. The contemporary map I possessed gave no indication of a railway in the area, not even a *ferrocarril abandonado*. But Leslie had carried out a survey of a proposed link between Barranquilla and the port of Cartagena, setting out his findings in a letter to Mr T.M. Priestley at head office in London in November 1925. The letter had been typed in purple ink, or perhaps the ink had faded to purple. The paper was yellow and blotchy like old skin. 'The most feasible and advantageous route,' wrote Leslie, 'would be via Soledad, Polonuevo, Sabanalarga . . . although many other routes were surveyed or reconnoitred, none can be compared with the one chosen from any point of view.' I read my grandfather's report, looking for signs of him, clues to the enigma. 'The passenger traffic would be very heavy and, in my opinion, a service of steam rail coaches would be most suitable. I estimate the number of paying passengers at 200,000 annually.' He described gradients, 'the rapid oxidisation of metals and the short life of timber structures in this country', the possibility of a branch line to Usiacuri in the event of prospectors striking oil. There was a toll road which ran alongside part of the putative railway: '23,840 donkeys pass over the road and it is the custom for the owners to ride them in addition to the goods carried,' wrote my grandfather for the benefit of T.M. Priestley, a world away in London,

adding that these humble equestrians represented 11,920 potential third-class passengers every month. It was a business letter,
a formal communiqué, and it gave no more away about the
author than the reports my father used to write, an engineer
himself.

The reply from head office enclosed a cheque for £100 'voted
to you by the Board of Directors' in recognition of Leslie's
efforts. 'We are, as you know, very pleased with the way in
which you carried out the work of the survey,' said the letter
from Salisbury House, Finsbury Circus – presumably dictated
by Mr Priestley: the signature was unreadable. Priestley, if it was
he, was contemplating a visit to the sharp end of the operation.
'Will you kindly make out and send me a list of what you think
I should take with me . . .' he went on. I thought I recognised
something of my own misgivings about Colombia in the man
from head office: 'I shall spend only one or two days in
Barranquilla,' he wrote, 'and want to take only steamer and
riverboat clothes. Shall I be able to get my dress shirts washed
on the steamer, do you think? Also shall I want a pith helmet on
the river, and what shoes and boots are advisable?

'Please be good enough to make your letter as helpful as possible and remember I have not been into the tropics before and
want all the advice I can get.'

By the time he was twenty-seven, Leslie was acting general
manager of the Barranquilla Railway Company. Barranquilla
today was hot and dreary, noted only for the carnival at Easter.
It figured briefly in the news when a rat closed down the airport. It caused a short circuit, forcing the place to shut for nearly
an hour. Civil Aviation officials found that the rat had urinated
on a power cable. This knocked out communications between
the control tower and incoming aircraft. Ramon Emiliani, civil
aviation director, said, 'The rat was quite frazzled.'

Leslie's contract expired and he left Colombia. He didn't
come back again until 1935, when he joined the La Dorada company and settled his family in Manizales. Apart from brief visits
to Britain on leave, he spent the next twenty-two years in

Colombia: all told, he was there for thirty-five years. By the 1950s, he was earning 1,900 *pesos* a month. Inflation had eaten like worm into the Colombian currency: his paycheck would be worth little more than a dollar now. But Sra Amaya put it into perspective for me. 'It was a lot of money,' she said. When she began working for the railways, ten years after Leslie had retired, she was paid fifteen *pesos*.

A man called Juan Pablo Jaramillo seemed to have occupied a considerable amount of Leslie's time at the La Dorada company. Jaramillo wrote to him on a number of occasions, once asking for a financial contribution towards the removal of his appendix. My grandfather had declined, saying that this was not company policy, but wishing him well under the knife.

When Sra Amaya heard the story of Leslie's Colombian family, she said, 'Oh my God! It gets more and more interesting.' The civic authorities would have details of my half-uncle, she thought; the church would have records of baptisms. 'I want to give you a hug!' she said.

(Above and opposite) the railyard at Savannah station,
Bogota, 1998

Outside the archive, the railyard was a boneyard. There were
four disused steam engines, bleached and rusty, the sun and the
rain vying to pick them clean. One was more than seventy years
old, built in 1927 at the Baldwin Locomotive Works,
Philadelphia, USA; another bore the marque 'The Superheater
Co.' On another, the only bright thing was the bell. In contrast to
this carrion machinery, the Nemocon *Touristren* service was
only a few years old, launched in 1982 'because of the necessity
to preserve a historical *patrimonio* of incalculable value and to
demonstrate the magnificence of a steam locomotive in action',
according to the consortium behind it. After who knows how
many grafts and transfusions, one engine had been brought back
from the dead; it was the only working steam train in Colombia.
As its operating name implied, it was intended to attract
tourists, trippers, and it left on Saturday and Sunday mornings.

A leaflet which came with your ticket quoted, or perhaps mis-quoted, Agatha Christie: 'Travelling by train is to look at the nature, the people, all the little towns, churches, rivers . . . actu-ally it's to see the real life.'

The train got underway without you noticing it, tiptoeing past a convent or school; there was a Virgin in a hollow of a wall, and people asleep at her feet. Slowly, we encountered a man with no feet who was on crutches, and a mule nosing in refuse, and graffiti about *Christo* and *paz*. With colossal patience, the train found its way to a length of track which crossed a main road. It was following the course which had been laid out for it like a bean advancing up a pole.

A conductor came into the rear carriage to announce what was on sale in the restaurant car. By reputation, the passengers on this service were only interested in *aguardiente*. Presumably because it was still quite early, no one on the train was drinking; so much for the *Aguardiente Express*.

We inched across another road. There was no barrier that I could see, no crossing; but cars and trucks were waiting on either side of the line, flying pennants of heat-haze and pollu-tion. A rasp of brakes, a fast-inflating balloon of dust — you wouldn't have thought you could tell but the train had come to rest. Some express! An alarm went off, a shrill tone above the brass section of inconvenienced motorists. Through the door-way in front of me, the carriage preceding ours was shrinking into the distance at an elephantine rate: the train hadn't come to a halt at all. Or rather, only a small portion of it had. The rest of it was going on without us.

Outside the carriage, there were political posters all over a wall — they looked like the building materials: it was as though the wall itself had been made out of papier mâché. This arche-ological layering reminded me of the mummifying of the ancients in Bogota's gold museum, the *Museo del Oro*. The greater part of the train backed up. After a time, a man working for the railway operators came by to see whether our coach could be re-coupled. Another man went past with a pole of

candy floss over his shoulder, like a nurseryman with an exotic
shrub. The sky was in cross-section: from the bottom looking
up, as it were, there was a layer of pollution, of the city's brown
mist; above that, at cloud level, was a clearer strip of atmosphere; and finally the pristine blue of the heavens.

With the train's impetus restored, a metal bucket danced on
the engine tender. In the front carriage was a party of pensioners. Each one had been tagged, like Paddington Bear. Student
helpers were policing their litter while the old-timers themselves sipped juice and effortfully munched sandwiches. At the
first scheduled stop, a wooden halt, a band in matching check
shirts boarded the train: trumpet, two saxes, drummer, cymbal-
ist, and a vocalist who was using a megaphone – why had none
of the punk rock bands thought of that? I asked myself.

Remembering the conductor and his speech about refreshments, I did the cakewalk to the restaurant car. It was designed
like a British one, with a serving counter, the gangway narrower
there. But a uniformed woman said '*No hay café*' through
pursed lips. There didn't seem to be anything to eat or drink at
all, in fact. I sat at a dining table nonetheless, and had a conversation with Sr Gomez Rubio, the travelling representative of
the rail consortium. The train was being pulled by a fifty-year-
old engine, he said. Apart from weekend outings, the *touristren*
made occasional trips for college parties and suchlike groups at
other times of the week. The consortium had been visited by
experts from Spain and Japan, who were helping them to restore
the railway. 'In two years, we hope to have the money to have
four locomotives in action,' said Sr Rubio, referring to the hulks
back at the station. 'It's too bad that the railways are like they
are. Too bad.'

One, two; one, two, went the train. On a grassy bank, a white
hen raced a brown hen. It was too bad that the railways were
like they were. In their decline, the contribution they had made
was forgotten, but it was no exaggeration to say that they had
done more to unite and modernise the country than anything
else. There was a saying that the history of the railways in

Colombia started at the same moment that the *Libertador*, Bolivar, got the idea of building a canal or railway in the isthmus of Panama. Men like my grandfather had surveyed and built and operated railroads over more than 3,400 kilometres. It didn't sound a great deal when you bore in mind the size of the country, the fourth largest in the continent, as big as France, Spain and Portugal put together. But the line had had to be blasted and hammered and flattened through foggy mountains and malarial jungles, against a backdrop of political volatility and civil violence, as unpropitious a set of conditions as engineers had faced anywhere in the world. The railway broke down the isolation of a country which had lived largely in its principal cities, people drawn to them by the need to find work or escape the turmoil of the countryside. For many Colombians, the train was the first means of transport they had experienced which didn't depend on the strength of their own limbs or their livestock. The locomotive was the engine of economic boom, taking coffee to a world with a sudden caffeine craving, connecting the plantations with the rivers which had previously been Colombia's main highways, and indeed subsuming their role in some parts of the country, knocking days off delivery times. It was the only practical means of moving coal, one of the country's greatest natural resources: Colombia had the largest reserves in Latin America.

The *Aguardiente Express* was leaving the city behind. The line ran beside a dual carriageway. You hardly saw a private car outside the metropolis. Was it fear of robbery? Not everyone could afford a car, of course. The government had invested in roads at the expense of railways from the mid-1950s onwards, but lorries clogged the principal routes, and the effect for most Colombians was a diminution of travel opportunities. They became isolated from one another again and the city-states reasserted their power, the two biggest outside Bogota itself, Medellin and Cali, becoming the fortresses of the narco-gangsters. The demise of the railways accompanied, and had a lot to do with, the death throes of the country at large.

We made a stop at a station identified as M.A. Caro, on the route of the northern railway, *Ferrocarril del Norte*, illustrated on my grandfather's map ('*F.C. del Norte*'). We had come thirty-four kilometres from the middle of Bogota and it had taken the best part of two hours. *No hay tinto* there, either, but there was fresh water for the locomotive. The pensioners in their carriage were dancing to the band, wheeling around in the aisle. In an outbuilding, a man was asleep with a hat over his face – he slept like a comic strip Mexican, as though he had just got in from a night of turning tricks on Caracas Avenue.

One, two; one, two . . . as lightly as a cradle, the *Aguardiente Express* was rocking as she passed a turreted folly – it might have been a Hollywood mansion of the 1930s – and a field where glossy, costly-looking horses turned from the train and ran; I suppose that it was out of fear but they looked like they were showing off. The band made their way to the rear carriage but they didn't play. Instead, they put their feet up on the seats and smoked and argued, waving their arms at each other. We had reached the rolling *altiplano*, the high country, outside Bogota. At a crossing, there was a man with a bald head and an empty, metal shopping trolley nodding and blinking, and then market gardens with files of lemon trees. A breezeblock wall, the concrete oozing, was like a badly iced cake. The musicians finished their breather and filed out of the carriage and presently I heard them in the adjoining one, the music just carrying over the noise of the bogies. We were entering open country – the scooped surface of a quarry was like fudge or ice-cream – and I thought about the impossibleness of Colombia. The train allowed you to think; in fact, it more or less demanded it of you, a way of filling the longueurs of transit and the even less hectic interludes of breakdown. There was space to stretch out and cogitate aboard the train, unlike on the buses. In the carriage, each seat had its own foot-rest; there was no trebly, teeth-on-edge radio. The train afforded views. The news that day was of a politician who had been assassinated in Medellin and an attack on a police station in the department of

Bolivar; of helicopters fighting guerrillas and the arrest of a con-
tractor on allegations of graft; there was fresh footage of the
aftermath of a massacre.

I thought about that and then I looked out of the window and
I saw that people loved the train, that they took a pleasure from
seeing it. Their dogs raced it, wagging their tails furiously. Their
children waved at it. A group of youngsters were playing beside
a place for recycling glass; a ruined ice palace. An old man in
blue overalls sitting in the shade of a tree spread his arms and
shrugged, an ineffable gesture which seemed to say something
like, 'We are here, and this is how it is.'

4

Cocaine
Train

The train out of Cali was the Cocaine Train. As if it could be anything else, you might think. It was a big, heavy diesel, and it passed through one of the world's acknowledged hubs of drugs; the clumsy carriages and Neanderthal-browed loco were from time to time a cover for traffickers moving their contraband from the dry heat of Valle de Cauca to the port of Buenaventura. But the Cocaine Train of Cali wasn't the foregone conclusion that it sounds. My general observation was that the city had drugs the way a spa has healing properties, a shrine visitations. They were impalpable, more or less chimerical, sources of revenue, which nevertheless made the place tick. In Cali, drugs were a kind of *devil ex machina*. You probably had more chance of running into them on the train than you did in the city. Running into the people who moved them, too. Did I *want* to run into them? Yes and no. Well, let's be honest about it: no and yes. 'No' is pretty self-explanatory. 'Yes'? It was an interval of fleeting, shamefaced calm on my part. I was here now, and I wanted to take the train: the train was another of the handful of railroads still operating in Colombia which had originally been mapped by my grandfather, as the *Linea Cali*. In blue pencil, he had made a note of *Cementos de Valle*, a reliable supplier near the station of Puerto Isaac. But that was a long time ago.

They didn't grow drugs in Cali: that was increasingly contracted out to farmers in Peru and Bolivia, and it was in those countries and in jungle laboratories in Colombia that the raw *coca* leaves were pharmaceuticalised. What they did in Cali was to sell drugs, to speculate in them. It was a lowland city, a hot city – the first time I saw it, it was on fire, in fact: it was night, and burning columns of sugar cane on the edge of town were like a flaming stockade – but at the same time it was a coolly deliberate stock exchange, a market of mandarin-like ruthlessness, the Dow of drugs. It traded in invisibles, it traded below the line: products you looked for in vain in the average Colombian home, exports which failed to appear on waybills.

On this Wall Street of hustlers, the CEOs were Miguel Rodriguez Orejula and his brother, Gilberto. Colombian racketeers shared with the mafia, and indeed the more august and wasp-y of the Manhattan banks, a habit of keeping it in the family; among siblings, to be specific. High finance at some point shades into politics, even when it's clean, or relatively clean: multinationals wielding enough economic power to change leaders' minds, businessmen bankrolling favoured parties or candidates. This trend had reached its apogee in Cali, where the billionaire Orejulas, who at one time reputedly controlled 80 per cent of the world's cocaine, went shopping for a president. In 1994, they spent $6 million on Ernesto Samper, or rather this sum was secreted in his war-chest, as he glumly conceded on leaving office. By this time, it was already common knowledge: once word had leaked, Samper was a disgrace and a national joke. An *inter*national joke, rather. He was booked to speak to the United Nations in New York in 1996, but the Americans wouldn't let him have a visa. In the end, he had to travel on a diplomatic pass to deliver his lecture. It was about drugs. Appropriately – all too appropriately – eight pounds of heroin were discovered on his plane. Three airforce mechanics were subsequently arrested. (This fiasco uncannily anticipated

an almost identical humiliation for Samper's successor, involving the aforementioned military Hercules and thirteen million
dollars' worth of cocaine at Fort Lauderdale in late 1998.)

Samper's bung, spectacular as it was, was out-of-pocket
expenses to the Orejulas, who disbursed a staggering $500 mil-
lion to favoured politicians, celebrities and journalists. By 1998,
officials had run down 37,000 cheques to 13,000 different bank
accounts and were in the process of working out which, if any,
might be legitimate.

Formally-speaking, the Orejulas were incarcerated in Picota
jail, Bogota, but everyone knew that they were still taking care
of business in Cali. During just three months in 1998, they
found windows in their diaries for no fewer than seventeen
appointments with Fernado José 'Fatso' Flores, a 308-pound
Venezuelan wanted in the United States for allegedly moving
eight tons of the Orejulas' cocaine to Florida inside cement
posts. Like all good busted moguls, the brothers had secured
comically brief sentences – the limo was practically ticking over
outside the prison gates – and they were devoting themselves to
self-improvement with ostentatious humility. Miguel, fifty-nine,
who was known as *El Señor*, or as 'the Chessplayer', on account
of his thoughtful gangland chops, had just received his high-
school diploma, in what was described as a 'small and modest
ceremony'.

The transactions of the money-men didn't go unnoticed in
Cali. There were spin-offs for the average *caleno*, a trickle-down
effect. More than 700 murders and eighteen kidnappings were
recorded in a five-month period in 1997. There was a piece of
the action for everybody: in the space of one year, 1,243 minors
were picked up for offences including murder and robbery. You
could call it a feel-bad factor.

The train – the lumbering, sluggish train outrageously registered as the *Express de Occidente* – was the last place a
hard-pressed police force would think of looking for Cali's
designer products, its white goods. Except that sometimes they
did look. And sometimes they got lucky, and the shipments

would cease for a while. With the same uncertain rhythm of the train itself, they would start up again.

The train was going on Thursday: inland, to the town of El Cerrito, Little Hill, in the Valle de Cauca. On Wednesday night, a card school was in session at my hotel in Cali, a gothic wooden pile run and patronised by ex-pats from central Europe. The proprietor looked up at me from his fanned hand. 'Jazz!' he barked.

I said, 'Jazz?'

'*Jus*,' he repeated. 'It's a Swiss game.'

One of his partners was a pale, Italian dowager. She reminded me of my grandmother. It must have been the cards: bridge was Gran's pleasure. Peggie was the kindly, white-haired granny of children's books. She knitted jumpers and did embroidery and made me a tasselled waistcoat like the one we'd seen Frank Ifield wearing as Robin Hood in *Babes in the Wood*. Gran enjoyed a party, and my dad used to say that he could fine-tune the volume of her voice by how much gin he gave her. After Leslie died, she stayed on at their flat. She worked at a department store and later at the post office in the parade of shops near her home. She was active in a voluntary organisation which helped people who had been bereaved. She seemed as comprehensible to me as Leslie was obscure.

The card school was completed by a man who had maintained a teddy-boy quiff into advanced age. Over a rubber or two, my story emerged, and it prompted the man with the quiff to say, 'Oh, the train! You'll be shaking like this' – and he pitched about on his chair, enjoying his joke. 'Don't have too much to drink before you go on the train!'

I was finding that I had become an apologist for trains – they're green, I told people; they're the most economical means of moving cargo – though what really persuaded me was that they were comfortable, pleasant (the Spanish *agradable* caught the sense of this), particularly in comparison to sweaty, overcrowded *busetas*. I was indignant about the old man with the quiff, a card player with a thick accent ridiculing my grandfather's business:

this was the first time I could recall sticking up for the long-dead Leslie. I asked him, 'When did you last go on a train?'

'About fifteen years ago,' he said, and I was about to pounce and say that I'd travelled by train in Colombia much more recently than that, and it wasn't half-bad, when the old man went on, 'It used to be so beautiful. The ride to Buenaventura — it was wonderful,' and he said it with such a look of contentment that I bit my tongue.

He was Swiss and his name was Nicholas and he had been fifteen in the Second World War — at which point in it, he didn't say. But what was he doing here?

'I fell in love with a Colombian woman, in Switzerland. She had a baby but it died. The doctor said, "This climate is not suitable," so I came with her to Colombia. That was in the month of October. By January, she had another baby,' said Nicholas with a priapic pride. It thrived, and the Swiss thought of returning home. 'But then there was a second baby, then a third, then a fourth. When people say, "How many children do you have?"' Nicholas said, with a wait-for-it expression, 'I say, "Four. In the villages, I don't know!"' In fact, he had remained uxoriously linked to the Colombian. Half of their children were in the United States, the other half at home, helping at the family cosmetics business, exporting lipstick and foundation to Brazil and Peru.

Many years ago, the Swiss had been chief steward on a yacht owned by a British war hero, a man named Cotton. He had once waited on the Duke and Duchess of Windsor. 'She gave me a kiss of welcome on the cheek.'

He steered me to a pair of chairs away from the card table. We got onto the subject of Nazi gold, the culpability or otherwise of Swiss bankers. Nicholas said that Hitler had foolishly considered Switzerland easy meat, to be swallowed up once the Third Reich had taken care of the rest of Europe. 'But he would have found that every bridge, every railway, was mined. Even the dams — water is the capital of Switzerland — the dams would have been destroyed and the Nazis drowned like rats.'

The Germans had allowed themselves to be led – 'like mut-tons,' Nicholas said. But the spell of Hitler had worked on others, too. One in four of the Swiss military was secretly in favour of him. 'This was the fifth column. My father said, "It's a terrible thing, but if the Nazis invade, before we kill a single one of them, we will have to shoot one in four of our own officers."'

Nicholas plucked my sleeve. He said, 'Hitler had been right at the beginning.' Here we go, I thought; and, for a moment, on that muggy evening in South America, the old man with the mittel-European accent and teased coxcomb might have been a well-preserved war criminal instead of a harmless Swiss lip-stick-maker. But what he'd meant, more reasonably than I'd feared, was that the reparations demanded of Germany after 1918, the war Leslie had fought in, had been unrealistic. 'The treaty of Versailles was a dark sheet of history.'

He said that he would love to join me on the train – if he could break an appointment. 'What about your grandfather? It's a mystery, yes? A secret? But this is natural in Colombia, to have children,' said the fecund Swiss.

Unlike the baroque cathedral at the end of the defunct line in Manizales, Cali railway station was like a homage to socialist realism: on one concrete wall there was even a stoic frieze. This was a principal destination on a working route – indeed, a few people were occupying desks in air-conditioned offices – but there was a more profound sense of dereliction than there had been in the redundant terminus on the mountain top. At Cali, you could look out at the platform through thick lozenges of glass; or through the gaps where these were absent. There was a bust of the Virgin of Carmen, minus her scapulary. Encroaching upon the tracks, pressing up to the wheels of the dusty train, was a coarse weed like elephant grass. The ticket hall was deserted. With my friend, the Swiss card player, having appar-ently been unable to break his appointment, I understood that

The Consular Agent

there were no other passengers for the Cocaine Train. It was
eight o'clock in the morning and sunny, and Colombia was
acting on me like a narcotic – to be taking the Cocaine Train
with no other passengers aboard: it was something I couldn't
have imagined myself doing, but my careless boots were finding
footholds in the set of metal steps which led to a carriage. For
better or worse, no *narcos* were taking the Cocaine Train; or
they weren't taking it from Cali, anyway.

The train set off, and went the wrong way: towards
Buenaventura, the fondly remembered run to the sea of the
Swiss. We were reversing; we were *reversing back* – the phrase
was like a snagged nail: it was a line from a television show I
had watched years ago at Gran's flat. Precociously, I had drawn
attention to the tautology, and been rewarded by hearing Gran
say proudly that Leslie had been a stickler for such things. By
today's standards, he hadn't been highly educated. Leaving
school at sixteen and becoming an apprentice on the railways:

on the face of it, this was the record of a young man who had
been pushed out to earn his keep. But Leslie's sister, Babs, told
me that he had been a born engineer. There had never been any
other choice of occupation. I had to remind myself that university careers were rare in Leslie's day, and unsupported by
the state. All he had received by way of higher education was
a stint at technical college courtesy of the Great Western
Railway.

But my grandfather was a well-rounded man, listening to
classical music and Colombian dance bands on the radio in
Manizales, and appreciating books, yarns in particular: Sherlock
Holmes and Edgar Wallace. He wrote well himself, to judge by
his letters. He had a bone-dry sense of humour: an aerogramme
of his which minuted bureaucratic intransigence, inflation and
heavy rains – 'I have been caught with my pants down as all my
construction jobs have been flooded out' – was capped with
the ironic invitation, 'Visit Colombia & see life.' After the
cussedness of South America, the highlight of a spell of leave in
London was luncheon at Simpson's on the Strand. People who
remember Leslie say that he always looked immaculate. He
would stock up at an outfitter's called Langston & Sons Ltd in
Reading. It was in the family, and still trading when I studied in
the town. 'If he saw a shirt he liked, he bought ten or twelve the
same,' Mum said.

The Cali train came to rest in front of an infant school: the
reason for the switchback was that we were picking up a
group of children, their teachers and their pretty mothers. The
party was from *Colegio Adorables Revoltos*, the academy of
little horrors, an institution with a name like a juvenile bou-
tique in Hampstead, this association reinforced by the
matching sweatshirts which the pupils were wearing. They
were on a field trip to a country mansion outside *El Cerrito*
called El Paraiso, a colonial *hacienda* built in 1815 which was
the setting for a love story called *La Maria*. Written by the
poet Jorge Isaacs in 1867, it was considered to be the first
Colombian novel. One of my fellow passengers outlined the

plot for me: boy meets girl; boy goes to England; boy pines for girl and vice versa; girl dies. Shades of Leslie's story, I thought, and frankly not a great deal doomier: as I would discover, Isaacs' narrative foreshadowed my grandfather's more completely than I knew.

We embarked on a low, flat trajectory between palm trees and fields of leafy cane: from the air, the railway might have looked like the zip on a green satin dress. All around the waring business of producing crops was going on. Crops had been keeping Colombians long before the potential of the *coca* leaf had been realised, and I don't just mean comfort foods like rice and sugar. The economy had been built on intoxicants derived from nature of which cocaine was only the latest in a long line, as it were. From one perspective, the history of Colombia was the history of drugs. For many years, the most valuable export was tobacco; then it was quinine; then it was coffee. In the innocent days of the 1960s and 1970s, the illegal narcotic with which Colombia was synonymous was *marimba*, marijuana: it had made the dealers so wealthy that they had built their own *balneario*, beach resort, at a place called Rodadero. In the early 1990s, only Burma and Laos were devoting more land to the cultivation of heroin poppies. Colombia exported 6.5 million tons of heroin a year. In May 1998, the United States Drug Enforcement Administration estimated that Colombia was supplying more than 60 per cent of heroin on American streets, and was edging out Asia's Golden Triangle as a source of the drug.

I sat with some of the school party in the front coach of the Cocaine Train, a refreshment car with a disused galley and peeling lino, and considered the toiling yellow locomotive. This had been the motor to transform life utterly – even more than the white powder which had lent it its name. Cali was among the first places in Colombia to get the railway. Lines were laid from ports to the nearest population centres inland, the train arriving in Cali in 1900, the same year my grandfather was born, the epoch when the locomotive was introduced to

Sulaco, the fictional Latin American province of Conrad's *Nostromo*. Cali was still a remote outpost, more in tune with Quito to the south than with the bulk of Colombia which lay eastwards. For 250 years, the capital of Ecuador had dominated Cali through brute geography: communications were simply much easier in the valley to the west of Colombia's *Cordillera Occidental* mountain range than they were across it – from Cali to Bogota, say.

With the coming of the *ferrocarril*, the city grew into an industrial centre influencing the whole of southern Colombia. This was how things were for a quarter of a century, the railway opening up the territory all around the city but not breaking out of this enclosure to connect with other routes. The railways of Bogota and Medellin were similarly isolated, and there was no link between Colombia's Atlantic–Caribbean seaboard and the south. However, extensive and arduous surveying was taking place during this period, my grandfather in the thick of it, having arrived from England in his vigorous twenties, cabling his reports to Mr Priestley at the London headquarters of the Barranquilla Railway & Pier Company. A map published in 1927 disclosed plans for two great railway networks traversing Colombia from north to south. One route, in the east of the country, began south of Bogota, ran through the capital, and pulled up just short of the ocean at the port of Santa Marta: this was the Atlantic network, the pathway along which Leslie's La Dorada line would eventually be established. The other scheme linked Ecuador with the Caribbean, taking in Cali and Medellin along the way. This was the section of my grandfather's railway map dotted with question marks.

Riding on the Cocaine Train, I read in Peter Pollard's *Colombia Handbook* that 'some of the dream materialised'. Engineers put down 700 kilometres of track between Santa Marta and Puerto Berrio – I knew from Leslie's map that Puerto Berrio was in the centre of Colombia – and built a 'spur to Bogota via La Dorada'. Lines stretched south as far as the cities of Neiva and Popayan, and fanned out to encompass several of the principal towns which were on the way. The trains 'all carried passengers, the *autoferro* (diesel car) was comfortable if unreliable, and the Tayrona Express between Santa Marta and Bogota was an attractive experience in its day.' I had heard an eyewitness account of the Tayrona from Ivan, who had made the journey to the coast as a boy. He had been dragged onto it by his mother, who was afraid of flying. 'It was nice, I suppose. You had a bed and there was a restaurant car where you had all your meals. But it was so slow! I wanted to go on the airplane.'

When the railways were nationalised, the freebooters of the La Dorada company and the Barranquilla company and the rest were replaced by the *Ferrocarrils Nacional de Colombia*. The railway was in decline by the 1970s, the lines mismanaged and underfunded, the government and private enterprise distracted by visions of travel by road and air. What did for the Cali service in the end was not this neglect, however, or the depredations of civil life in Colombia, but the weather: in 1974, a storm broke the link with Medellin, and it was never restored. The limitations of geography and history, transcended for a moment by the railway, stonily reimposed themselves: 'Colombia's life has always revolved around urban centres that functioned almost as city states,' according to Colin Harding in *Colombia in Focus*. The *Ferrocarrils Nacional de Colombia* were wound up in 1988. They were replaced by the present hybrid arrangements, the state-owned *Ferrovias* looking after the track, and the free enterprise *Sociedad de Transporte Ferroviario* (STF) overseeing operational matters.

Beneath our wheels was the River Cauca: we rumbled across a crude wooden bridge, the water turning lugubriously in our shadow. The headmaster of the infant school had been taking the train all his life, he said. 'The workers used it to go to the fields. At the weekend, we would take food and go to Buenaventura.' He was leaning forward in his seat; you could see its slatted planks behind him. He was a large, gentle man, resting himself on his stomach as we talked. 'They call it the

Cocaine Train because the *narcos* use it – they will use anything – though of course they are not able to put a lot of drugs
on the train.'

I asked the headmaster if he knew any *narcos*, if he could by
any chance put me in touch with them. *What was I thinking of?*
Well, I was here now, and this was the Cocaine Train, after all . . .

'I know them, of course I do, they are all around us.' The
teacher leant back against the slats of his seat, considering me.
'After we have returned from El Paraiso, I will be going back to
the school, I will be there tonight. I'll call you.' I'm not surprised that these were the last words I ever heard from him.

We rolled into the town of Palmira and rolled out again
almost at once, among the palms and sugar plantations once
more. The sun having climbed to its zenith, the carriage
window was now a screen with the colour turned up high: for a
time, I was receiving nothing but a green testcard. The train
was travelling within a narrow corridor of dense foliage, or, if
you like, the straightest, least imaginative maze ever erected; but
gaps in this cover allowed you to make out roads between the
paddocks, and trucks, and men at work.

Beside the busy smokestacks of the Manuelita sugar refinery,
one of the biggest in the Cauca valley – noted in red ink on
Leslie's map – the train broke down. 'The railcar was unreliable,' I thought. It seemed I was destined never to complete a
train journey in Colombia without unscheduled interruptions.
We all got out: the schoolchildren, their teachers and parents,
and myself, and we awaited developments. Presently, there was
news about the breakdown: it wasn't our train which had a
fault, in fact, but a freight train further up the line. It had run out
of fuel and there was a delay while diesel was fetched by road:
when the railway was down, *humbled*, the ascendancy of the
newer technology was mercilessly emphasised. The only dis-
traction came from a battery of sprinklers tossing columns of
water into the air at the rear of the refinery, as though an artist
skilled in hydromechanics was rehearsing an elaborate show in
conditions of intense secrecy.

From nowhere, a fleet of buses arrived and the little horrors and their guardians embarked to continue their journey to the tragic backdrop of *La Maria*. And then there was a train coming, the ill-starred diesel coming through on the way to Cali and Buenaventura at last, and the Cocaine Train shunted onto a siding by the refinery to allow it to pass.

I went on to El Cerrito. A changeless agrarian landscape met the eye, and you wondered what it was about invariable prairies like this that made them such fertile ground for violence and crime. The Cauca was as rich in this respect as the straw-coloured interior of Sicily. No, *richer*. A few weeks before my journey, police had made seventeen arrests in the area, smashing a ring which supplied cocaine and heroin to New York. The syndicate was run by another brace of brothers: Julio Cesar and Marco Antonio Ramirez Velez, who had been seized in Cali itself. As well as shipping drugs, the ring had laundered vast sums of money through international financial markets, according to police. The authorities impounded weapons, jewels and gold bullion, cellular telephones and twenty-nine desirable properties.

A black man swept the floor of the carriage with a broom, as though dignitaries had been promised at El Cerrito. The welcoming committee proved to be dark-skinned children on bicycles shouting, '*El tren! El tren!*' The locomotive was moving like a sleepwalker – we drifted past one-storey houses made of brick and roofed in clay tiles; there were squares of cowskin pegged out in a yard like drying handkerchieves – and the children abandoned their cycles and clambered aboard. One boy ran down the carriage towards me. 'Make way! Make way! The guerrillas are here!' he cried.

One of the children was wearing a football jersey. I told him that he looked like Faustino 'Tino' Asprilla, the Colombian footballer who had spent a couple of seasons at Newcastle United. 'But Asprilla is his name!' exclaimed an older boy, briefly awed by the telepathic powers of the *gringo*. It seemed that the star hailed from the Cauca Valley. Not everyone remembered him with affection. Before he left for Newcastle, he'd been involved in an altercation outside a nightclub, in which the headlights of a car were kicked in.

I had a drink at a kiosk in El Cerrito. It had been attacked by arsonists overnight, according to the woman who ran the place. 'Who was it? Let us say it was kids,' she said, scrubbing a blackened grill. The kiosk was adjacent to a cemetery. Masons were sitting in the shade of a tree, cradling stone tablets, finessing details on headstones-in-progress. I asked the woman about *narcos* – how often does journalism come down to asking questions that someone would sooner not hear, that you'd better not ask? The woman said there was a reporter in town, a correspondent for one of the national papers. He had an office in the police station. He might know about them.

There wasn't a correspondent at the police station; either that or he wasn't there any longer; an unlikely posting in any case, I thought. Perhaps El Cerrito was not the kind of place where a reporter put down roots. I had the greatest admiration for the journalists who covered Colombia, a difficult and dangerous patch. More than a hundred of them had been killed in the past twenty years, more than in any other country in the hemisphere. In the course of researching my grandfather's life, researching Colombia, I kept a record of the journalists who were murdered. In October 1997, the dismembered body of Alejandro Jaramillo was found in the southern regional capital of Pesto, near the border with Ecuador. On 11 November, Francisco Castro, the owner of a radio station in the small town of Majagual, was shot to death at his home; later that month, Jairo Elias Marquez, aged forty, the editor-in-chief of a monthly news magazine, *El Marques*, was gunned down by two men on a motorcycle in Armenia. On 2 March 1998, Didier Aristizabel, a former reporter with the Todelar radio station, was shot and killed by two gunmen on motorcycles as he left the university in Cali where he taught. On 16 April, Nelson Carvajal, a radio journalist and high-school teacher, was shot ten times with a nine-millimetre pistol as he left school in the southern town of Pitalito – and so the killing went on, the snuffing out of light in the darkness. I knew a journalist and writer called Edgar Torres, whose own life had been threatened as a result of his stories about the narco-gangsters. He had written a scoop about President Samper, exposing a shady deal which had been offered to the Orejulas of Cali and others: call it a day and we'll let you keep 20 per cent of your wealth, you can make a new start abroad with your families without fear of extradition. Torres' newspaper now supplied him with a bulletproof car. He told me how members of the press discovered that they were targets. 'You might get a warning, someone coming up to you on a motorcycle, handing you a *sufragio*, a card of condolences, with your own name on it. As a matter of fact, this has just happened to a writer I know who covers legal stories,' said Torres. The motorcycle, the pillion assassin: these were such fixtures of the Colombian murder scene that the authorities had taken the drastic step of making crash helmets illegal, because they hindered the identification of killers. Torres went on, 'Another way we might hear about a threat would be from the Attorney General's office, or from colleagues who also have contacts in the criminal world – though any self-respecting *mafioso* wouldn't send you his messages with *anyone*.' He smiled. He was a softly spoken, unassuming man. Easy to miss, you thought. That might have been his strength.

'The dilemma here is not about wanting to be a hero: you have to take a position about whether you want the mafia to continue, or alert the public to what is going on. The criminals have penetrated so many spheres of life, what's at stake here is the survival of our nation. These things have happened because we've allowed it.'

The mafia, as Torres called them, they actually preferred *not* to kill reporters, because they knew the colleagues of the victims would take a personal interest in investigating the crimes and exposing the criminals. 'Some of the *mafiosi* I know respect a factual job of reporting; they don't mind, so long as you are accurate. But things have been bad for the mafia in the past four years or so, I would say. They've been on the front pages more and more. The *narcos* are tired of having to contend with the press. That's why we see these threats starting to flare up again – they feel they have no choice. Of course, the younger ones, they are proud to see their names in the paper!'

Torres estimated that no fewer than 500 significant traffickers remained at large. Under Samper, it had become illegal for reporters to be caught talking to them, using them as direct sources. I asked Torres what his wife thought about the occupational hazards of journalists in Colombia.

'My wife knows I genuinely believe in democracy, and that the press is the screen, the movie screen of democracy.' He leant forward. 'We have to trust that today's corruption and under-the-table business will rebound on those responsible, become *their* suffering, in the future.'

Although I had failed to locate the El Cerrito stringer, my journey to the police station wasn't without interest, because I discovered a rapist in a cave, a narrow cell which was open to the elements on one side. He had been detained the previous day for assaulting a fifteen-year-old. A young woman was crouching in front of him, talking to him, passing morsels of food through the bars: a member of his family, said Officer Rincon. Rincon was young and well-groomed, but the effect was of a school prefect rather than a dashing officer. You trusted that this was the well-documented effect of the police looking younger as you got older, not a sign that their casualty rates were leading the force to recruit from junior high. Rincon reassured me: he had spent ten years in the service. He had clashed with the guerrillas on several occasions. 'In my first month, we lost eight colleagues: blown up in their vehicle.' He had also been present at a police station one night when it came under fire from 160 guerrillas. 'There were only twelve of us officers,' said Rincon, this being the regular complement at a station. The police had been able to call on the 'ghost plane', which scrambled to the scene of such incidents and used powerful searchlights and flares to let the guerrillas know the police *knew* where they were. There had been losses on both sides. The guerrillas' dead included a woman who was seven-and-a-half months pregnant. She was the leader. 'We fear the women especially,' said Rincon.

As for the *narcos* of the Cauca, of El Cerrito, Officer Rincon thought that they were all either behind bars or lying low. It had been a different story while they'd felt that they enjoyed protection at the highest level; their exploits had been something to brag about, to instil fear in others. But now an election was coming, and investigators had launched the '8,000 process', a trawl through the affairs of Colombia's ruling class. That very month, a man with connections to the Cali cartel was arrested over seven tons of cocaine found aboard a ship bound for the United States, and the former third-in-command of the organisation, Helmer 'Pacho' Herrera, told detectives from his prison cell where to find a most-wanted trafficker, the wheelchair-bound José Manuel Herrera, who happened to be his own half-brother. Pacho was a *sapo* in Colombian slang, a toad, an informer. Payback for his betrayals arrived when Pacho was shot six times in the head as he was playing football in the prison yard: a criminal who had invested so heavily in plastic surgery that he had been known as 'the man of a thousand faces', Pacho's posthumous identification was formally confirmed by his fingerprints. At the request of the Drug Enforcement Administration, 'Fatso', the Orejulas' assiduous prison visitor, had been captured in Bogota. If this stocky Venezuelan could be extradited to the States, and offered a plea bargain to tell everything he knew about those concrete posts, the brothers themselves could yet face American justice.

I left Officer Rincon and went into a café. There was football on television, *pollo frito* and *pollo grille* on the menu, a girl with long legs taking the orders. As so often happens, it was when you least expected it, when you had decided that El Cerrito was going to tell you nothing more about the drug smugglers, for example, that the picture changed. I had been thinking of Sicily, as I say, and here was a scene comparable to one I had once experienced in a restaurant in the depths of the Sicilian countryside. A pitcher of moonshine had moved back and forth between my table and one occupied by three men, in increasingly effortful circles. As the other party was leaving the premises, the oldest man, a cataract clouding a piercing blue eye, had held out his hand to me. It had looked as baked and leathery as an armadillo, but the palm was smooth. My fellow diners were absorbed into the sun-bleached afternoon and the waiter murmured, 'That man – in business, in life, he is king.'

The man who talked to me in the café in El Cerrito was hardly a king: sweat oiled the creases of his face and his sports shirt was open to reveal a bosom. But he coined a most Sicilian metaphor when he was telling me about *los narcos*. He had had nothing to do with the bad things, the disgusting things, he wanted me to understand, 'but we all have to eat from the same plate.' It was about knowing that money was crooked but pretending not to know, about looking the other way, not asking questions. I ordered *al muerso*: rice, stewing meat, the dark beans known as *frijoles*. It was the set lunch. The logo of the local gassy water was a soda syphon, a bygone utensil, like the one which had once belonged to my grandfather.

The perspiring man went on, 'The drugs are not grown in Valle de Cauca but maybe they are processed here, moved from here. At this time you have to be careful what you say.' The man had worked for the government for many years, he said, he had his pension to think of.

People did favours, he said – little things, so little they'd hardly be noticed, such as allowing someone to leave something in the storeroom for a day or so, or taking a parcel to a house occupied by somebody's relations – perhaps it contained money, but you didn't know. The television cut away from the football to an ad break. The man said, 'You don't see it here the way we see it. We don't accept the *gringo* view, which says

Colombians must be blamed because they are producing the drugs. We say, "What about the people in the United States and Europe?" They are the ones who are buying them, aren't they?'

An American congressman had coined the term 'narcodemocracy' to describe what was going on in Colombia – the buying of the political process by men like the Orejulas – but he had spoken more sagely than he knew. It was a narcodemocracy in that so many people were involved, government pensioners with part-time jobs in cafés who did favours and watched the wall when *El Señor* went by. So many people were involved and everyone was touched.

I finished my lunch. It was cheap but I left a tip and that was the last of my *pesos* gone. At the bank, the teller wouldn't let me change money until I had given him not only a sample signature, but also a specimen fingerprint. I rubbed my thumb on what looked like a cube of black poster paint, the teller gripping me by the knuckle. Then we pressed my dab onto the necessary slip – 'like a *mafioso*,' I suggested light-heartedly. The teller was expressionless.

I had been given the number of an Englishwoman, Sheila, who worked for the British Consul in Cali. I wanted to meet her because I was curious about consular life, a life Leslie had led. I had his letter of appointment as consular agent in Mariquita:

> 'Be it known to all to whom these presents shall come
> that, by virtue of the powers vested in me, I do hereby
> constitute and appoint Mr Frederick Leslie FROST to be
> Acting British Consular Agent at Mariquita with full
> power and authority, by all lawful means, to aid and
> protect His Majesty's subjects trading in, visiting or
> residing in his district.
>
> 'Witness my hand and seal of office at the British
> Embassy at Bogota, this 15th day of May, 1950.'

The letter had been typed and marked with an Embassy seal and signed by acting British Consul Henry Bartlett. Where Leslie's document of appointment had been folded, it was blotted with rot.

From Bogota, I'd telephoned Sheila, the Englishwoman, and she'd invited me to dinner. Ivan had asked me about her and I couldn't tell him very much, not even broadly-speaking how old she was. But something about her accent, her plan-making, had put me on guard, and when I met her in Cali – a two-piece summer outfit; still-thick bangs – I realised, that is, I *remembered*, who I was dealing with: Posh Aunt. Well, not 'posh' so much as pukka, independent, the sort who had been sent to boarding school, perhaps. Not unduly fussed over by parents. The open house of my extended family had included a number of Posh Aunts on my mother's side.

Sheila and her husband, Jack, a chicken farmer, picked me up in an air-conditioned four-by-four: the locks immediately chunked tight. We drove through Cali making conversation. In view of Jack's occupation, I was anticipating a ranch, a homestead – something out of my grandfather's photographs, I suppose, albeit carpeted in discarded down, and resounding with clucking and scratching. But Sheila and Jack lived near the summit of a tall, fortified condo: the farm – or battery, as it turned out – was elsewhere. We sat on the balcony of their apartment, the city lights glowing and flickering beneath us. I'd bought wine and was regretting that I'd neglected to remove the price sticker. The condo overlooked a *tugurio*, a shantytown built of waste materials. Begun as a few makeshift huts, it had been augmented by brick dwellings; someone had helped themselves to power from the mains, someone else had come by some concrete to lay roads – before long, Cali had been forced to incorporate the *tugurio*, to acknowledge its bastard offspring. Suddenly, there was the unmistakable report of gunfire. I shrank into my chair. 'Squash,' said Sheila, producing nibbles. 'There's a court downstairs.'

Everyone knew someone who had been kidnapped, Sheila

and Jack told me. They seemed eager, Sheila in particular, to tell of the neighbour who had been abducted last year, and of the man taken in January of whom no word had been heard, though six months had elapsed. Jack thought that the man's wife might be keeping mum – the guerrillas liked it that way – but Sheila said she seemed sad whenever she ran into her. One acquaintance had disappeared for eleven-and-a-half months. 'I thought he was dead,' said Sheila brightly. They told kidnap anecdotes the way other hosts might swap horror stories about negative equity or cowboy builders. Jack's view was that you got used to it. He didn't have the same quality of bright-eyed resignation as Sheila. When I asked her how they coped, she looked at me as though I was the kind of go-ahead vicar who wanted to talk about feelings. She said that what she liked was having a maid.

As far as I could make out, the work of the consul and his staff entailed fixing up backpackers and other travellers with temporary ID when their passports were stolen. Sheila had also been involved in a recent visit by Princess Anne. It was safe to assume that no member of the House of Windsor had ever called on Leslie in out-of-the-way Mariquita, to see what use he was making of his royal 'presents'.

After lots of drinks, there was chicken and rice, and microwaved sprouts ('nuked,' said Sheila) which tasted like the day-glo mothballs they put in pub urinals. Sheila knew the security officer whom I'd met at the Embassy in Bogota: 'Very good-looking chap, just the kind you imagine as a bodyguard.'

I myself was never the apple of Posh Aunt's eye. She tended to have a soft spot for clean-cut blokes who had been to good schools (academic distinction optional, but a nice talking point), who married and reproduced reliably, and did well for themselves. Sheila and Jack's son had married a Colombian.

'They're very attractive,' I offered.

'She's not, particularly,' said Sheila. 'But very nice, though.'

Posh Aunt was *fun*: you'd never glimpse a moment's depression, or reflection if it could be helped. That would be *moping*.

Her spouse was a figure of unassuming authority, unstiffened a little by drink: as the evening wore on, Jack told stories of importing chicken feed.

Sheila's parents were both still alive: dad had survived being knocked off his bicycle in London, by a driver from the Colombian Embassy, of all people. I was invited to produce my photographs of Leslie – unenthralling to Sheila, who was more interested in my guidebooks, wanting to see how many of the clubs and restaurants of her friends had been listed.

I don't know why Posh Aunt makes me feel sour: perhaps I feel excluded from the permanent party she would like life to be: people, especially family, dropping in; excursions to beaches, or scratch tennis tournaments, always in the offing, and not much else counting, except the serious business of someone else – Posh Aunt's husband and sons and sons-in-law – making a comfortable living. Certainly not boring things like housework – though I was with her there: had my mother, I wondered, put so much into running a home because her examples were the domestics in Colombia, who had loved and looked after her?

Sheila and Jack knew the tropical *schloss* where I was staying. Three years earlier, a friend of theirs who was a guest there came down to breakfast one day to find a gang sticking the place up. Insouciantly going to get coffee, he rang Sheila, saying, 'I can't talk loudly – there's a hold-up.' She called the police, who turned up just as the robbers were getting into the taxis they'd pre-booked.

'Did they catch them?'

'This isn't a place where people are caught,' said Sheila.

As Sheila and Jack were running me back to the hotel, we passed a house in which one of the Orejula brothers had set up a mistress, a roller-skating queen. But he was in jail and she had a home and rink elsewhere, said Jack, and they were taking the roof off the former love nest, demolishing it. Sheila pointed out the most expensive funeral parlour in Cali. 'When someone really important dies, this street is jammed,' she said, and I thought of a description by Gabriel Garcia Marquez of big-city funerals in Colombia: 'These were the most lugubrious funerals in the world with grandiose ornate hearses and black horses decked out in velvet and black plumed nosebands, and corpses from important families who thought they had invented death.'

5

Railway
of Gold

If there was one thing riskier than travelling around Colombia by rail, it was travelling by road. On top of the robbing and the killing and the abducting that went on – all of which could happen on the railways, too – there was the driving. The Colombians like a conspiracy theory as well as the next man and have a high tolerance of the unlikely, but a cabbie once told me with a hint of scorn that of course the death of the Princess of Wales had been an accident. 'The chauffeur was drunk and he was going too fast,' he said, in what ought to be the last word on the subject, the authority of a living Colombian on speeding and drink-driving being unsurpassable. As if to prove his point, he ran into a cyclist.

Words like 'reckless' and 'dangerous' leapt out of guidebook accounts of Colombian motoring. One Sunday morning in May 1998, five young people died in a car crash in Bogota. The youngsters had been to a nightclub; their car had struck a taxi and they'd failed to stop; four brother cabbies had set off in hot pursuit. After twenty-five minutes of this, the teenage driver had finally lost control and his car had spun into a concrete pile.

Taking the bus wasn't a recipe for long life. When you handed over your *pesos* at the window of the terminal in Bogota, you weren't entering into a contract with the bus company, its side of the bargain being to transport you into the Colombian interior. What you were doing was sportingly underwriting the driver in his high-maintenance pastime of playing chicken with other road users. You boarded: encouraged by your money and by your tacit, pillion consent, the driver would confidently occupy the wrong side of the mountain road, backing his hunch that the bus wouldn't meet anything coming the other way. This was particularly disconcerting on bends.

I began to notice roadside shrines, usually of the Virgin of Candelaria, whom the Colombians adored as though she was their patron saint. Clustered around each one was an incomprehensible seafood tribute, a mound of empty, mother-of-pearl casings. They had the dull lustre of oyster shells. On closer inspection, these offerings turned out to be headlights. Whether these votaries, these highway candles, had been placed by motorists petitioning for *bon voyage*, or plucked from wrecks to serve as their memorials, I didn't discover. The games of chicken, and indeed the shrines, were explained by the state of Colombia's roads. They were often poorly maintained, but a more serious problem was their restrictive gauge. The sclerotic arteries of the trunk roads would become clogged with vast American-made lorries: the only way of passing them was to spend longer than you cared to in the path of oncoming vehicles.

I booked a passage to Honda, a town on the Rio Magdalena, 150 kilometres down the mountains from Bogota. A morning paper in the capital had given over its front page to a lurid photograph of a corpse. It was lying in a field, on a gentle gradient; there was evidence of blood around the waist. An insert picture showed the mortal injury in close-up. Buying a *tinto* at the bus depot, I asked the boy at the bar about the corpse. He looked at the pictures, at the story, and shrugged. 'Around here, somewhere,' was all he said.

The bus was full, or looked full to me, but the driver pulled up several times on the outskirts of Bogota, calling through the open window to people on the kerb: 'Honda! Manizales!' You thought: is he on commission? Does he go to this trouble because it's in his scrupulously observed job description? There were building sites, breakers' yards – illuminated, before mid-morning, by blinding sunlight. A boy in shorts was playing with a hoop taller than he was. A young woman in perfect make-up scowled in the shade of a roadside tree, stood up by her lift. We passed encampments of kiosks, their canopies groaning with mobiles of pork rind.

There was a train, a red loco, brutish and ugly, the sort of thing that ought to have been running on a snow-girt line in Canada. It was pulling three or four wagons, a man in a vest and cap riding on the rear one. It was moving at the pace of a competitor in the Olympic walk. I thought about my grandfather taking the train to Bogota. Company business had required it. So had connections to planes and ships back to England. If ever there was a golden age of travel, this had been it: the dinner menu on the New York flight used to be set out like the *table d'hôte* of a distinguished hotel, and indeed was catered by the head chef of the Myrtle Bank, Jamaica; the names of the Frost family were printed on the passenger list of the M.S. Italia, on her voyage from New York to Plymouth on 4 June 1954, and many of the others aboard wrote their names into my mother's copy of the farewell dinner menu ('P. Thormoehlen, captain'). Two black-and-white photographs survived of this occasion, or perhaps they were of a different celebration during another crossing: anyway, Leslie appears in a highland costume at the base of a grand staircase, which he is sharing with other passengers who are also wearing fancy dress. In the first picture, he is holding a bottle of spirits – scotch, presumably – by the neck. In the second, he is raising the bottle to his lips. For the benefit of the camera, he's wide-eyed like a rumbled drunk.

The bus descended from the mountains and the temperature

A fancy dress party during an Atlantic crossing. Leslie Frost is the tippling Scotsman (third row from front)

climbed. I didn't see another train but the railway line reappeared from time to time at our side. It was peaceful, deserted, surprisingly well-cared-for on its bed of shingle. It was a contrast to the crowded, rutted road. I opened a window: the air was stuffier than the bus, like the draught from a hair-dryer. From where I was sitting, the railway was like the antidote to the highway, which is what it was, or might have been.

I had taken the bus in order to catch a train, the last great train still in service in Colombia. It followed the route of the old Atlantic network, the railway which had been conceived in the 1920s as a conduit between Santa Marta and the far south. The stylish bogies of the Tayrona Express had drummed over its sleepers. In view of what had happened in the second half of the twentieth century, the railway was like a vision of how Colombia might have been, how she might be again – it was the longest uninterrupted man-made link in the country. More or less uninterrupted, at any rate. It no longer extended south of Bogota, as it once had, and you couldn't set your watch by the train smoothly negotiating its 1,171 kilometres: the official journey time was a less-than-Swiss three days, longer in the rainy season, when sections of the line were washed away. Nor had the walnut panelling of the Tayrona marque endured. The passenger service had disappeared entirely; in the general order of things, private citizens couldn't go on it. There was only a goods train now. But it ran over Leslie's old stamping ground, the La Dorada line, the route of the Railway of Gold. That's where I was boarding, in fact: La Dorada itself.

Honda, in the department of Caldas, was the nearest town of any size, a place to pass the night. It was barely 200 metres above sea-level, as though it had been driven into the ground, perhaps by the pulverising humidity. I stepped off the bus and there was a cockroach on my arm. There was a sprawl of a cafeteria, and men, touts, one of them eyeing my wristwatch. He was a pot-bellied man tending a pitch, selling meat and maizey snacks, *arepas*, and wanting to know where the *gringo* was going. A woman was doing her washing by hand in a yard

accompanied by a naked toddler; beyond them was the churn-
ing, foaming brown of the Magdalena. Honda was famous for
its bridges. From one of these, I watched men fishing in
dugouts and a boy on a rock casting an *atarraya*, a net. You
knew that it must be a net, though what it looked like was an
old curtain, or some other stringed refuse that the boy was disposing of.

There was another reason for going to Honda apart from the
Atlantic railway. Birth certificates from all the towns and villages in the area, including Mariquita, had been filed at Honda –
my uncle's among them, I hoped. If Leslie had registered himself as the father, I would be able to discover my uncle's name,
and who his mother was, whether she really was called Isabel,
the name which had emerged when my mother had visited the
hypnotist. I would know when and where my uncle had been
born, and perhaps other details besides: how much he had
weighed, whether he had any birthmarks, how old his mother
had been when she gave birth to him. I found the registrar's
office: inside was the pecking of typewriters; people were waiting to put down in writing the significant events in their lives.
An official warned me not to expect too much of the birth certificates. They had been moved several times over the years, he
said, and once had been stored at the mayor's office. Some had
been lost in transit, others damaged in a flood. The official produced a big polythene sack with a sticker on it saying '1955', the
year in which Leslie's son had been born, my mother believed.
I sat on a bench and began going through the documents. I
couldn't find a record of a Frost, or an Isabel. I went on to the
sacks for 1956 and 1957 – not a trace. Among the fathers, there
were no foreign names at all.

One of the details which had to be filled in on the forms was
whether the baby had been born *legitimo o natural*, the latter a
euphemism for a birth to an unmarried mother: in the event of
a *natural* arrival, the name of the father was seldom listed. In
some of these cases, the circumstances broadly corresponded
with what I knew about my uncle's birth – a male child, a young

mother giving her occupation as domestic service. A nineteen-year-old woman, Dilia Fonseca, had been delivered of a boy, Ricardo, at eight in the morning on 15 January 1955. On 12 June twenty-two-year-old Maria Medina had given birth to José; on 14 December at eight o'clock at night, Blanca Molina, just sixteen, had given birth to Luis Alberto; so it went on. In fact, there were too many cases like these to be of any use. My uncle's birth certificate had been misplaced during a removal, or destroyed by flood water, or else it languished in one of the polythene sacks at the registrar's office, unrecognisable to me without my grandfather's name on it. I surprised myself at how let down I felt. It wasn't only a sense of my own failure. While it was perfectly possible that Leslie *had* registered his son, had done the right thing by him, and the proof had simply been mislaid, the suspicion took hold that Leslie had kept his name out of it; that the son he'd thought he would never have, had been disowned by him.

'Is it very hot?' my mother asked me later by telephone. 'Lovely!' What did she remember of Honda? 'The river. And the markets. I bought some jewellery there once.' I marvelled at the fact that she and Leslie had thrived in the soupy heat, that he'd actually got work done. 'Isn't it a lovely country?' she said.

My trip on the Atlantic railway had been arranged in advance, a letter to the Colombian Embassy in London securing offers of cooperation from the rail operators, STF. They would be delighted to take me on the Santa Marta train, they said. Embarking me at La Dorada, the place which had lent its name to my grandfather's company – that was their thoughtful touch. Dr Manuel Lopez of STF had informed me over the telephone that the train boasted an excellent safety record. 'It has never been attacked by the guerrillas,' he said.

I put this to one or two officials at western embassies in Bogota and one man said, 'But it runs right through guerrilla country – they must be paying them off.' At the STF office, I brought up some of these diplomatic reservations with Dr Lopez himself. 'Of course,' said Lopez genially, 'as I said to you on the phone, there is a risk.' I didn't recall him mentioning a risk. In the flesh, he was of medium height, smartly turned out, keen to please. He repeated that the train had never been attacked. As if he was reading my thoughts, he went on, 'We don't have an agreement, nothing,' meaning an undertaking with the guerrillas. I asked Lopez to explain how STF had been so fortunate. He drew my attention to a map on the wall, as the security officer at the British Embassy had once done. Here was the Magdalena river, and here the railway, said Lopez. Here was the highway. 'And, you see, the guerrillas –'

'– are on the highway?'

'– are on the *river*,' Lopez corrected me. 'These three things look close together on the map but the railway is maybe fifteen kilometres from the highway, it's ten kilometres from the river.'

In other words, the guerrillas were ten kilometres from the railway. Listening to Lopez, you could be forgiven for thinking that they paid no attention to it. Except that they did. They rode on it! 'Sometimes they go over the train,' admitted Lopez, and I thought for no clear reason, though a psychologist might have called it denial, of those sketches you see sometimes on television using a time-elapsed shot, in which hordes appear to disgorge from Minis or black cabs. 'They ride maybe on the last car, but they don't bother the train.'

There was nothing for me to worry about in any case because STF was taking special measures. 'I have some good news for you,' said Lopez. The company was laying on the presidential carriage for my trip. 'It's the one we use when the president of our company goes on the train.' Indeed, the president himself was deliberating whether he was free to accompany me. The carriage was being transported from Bogota. Perhaps STF was going to this trouble out of respect for Leslie's contribution to the railways, or because the Colombian Embassy in London had scented some publicity which didn't dwell entirely on the country's problems; perhaps the company was simply glad of a visitor and was dusting off the

presidential carriage like a hostess looking out the best china.
Dr Lopez assured me that I would be safe in my prestigious
conveyance because it was designed to look like all the other
wagons – the guerrillas who might or might not hitch a lift on
the train wouldn't even know I was there, though in reality the
carriage was equipped with all mod cons, including beds and a
WC.

The truth of it was that the railway, though less often targeted
than the highways, was not spared by the guerrillas: things
hadn't changed since Leslie's time. A few months before my
proposed trip, two trains had been blown up on the Santa Marta
line within a few days of each other. In one blast, dynamite
ripped up seventy yards of track from under the wheels of a
freight train, derailing seven wagons. The other explosion was
similarly triggered as a train was rolling over the bomb. This
time, no less than a thousand feet of railway was damaged and
twenty-seven wagons uprooted. I thought of something the journalist Jeremy Harding had written after covering civil wars in
Africa. 'The roads and railways were the rebels' noticeboards.
Here they scrawled their views in a profane language of sabo-
taged track and crumpled cars . . . On the rail lines, they had
their presence down to an art, clinging to the bush like some
obscure species, emerging now and then to shed blood and
tamper with the track. Yet the railway seemed to braid a strange
goodness into the ground; the further the repair work went, the
more confidence it gave to villagers living near the line.'

At first light in Honda, I took a *colectivo* taxi to catch the
Railway of Gold. Rising from the green river basin, a church at
La Dorada was like a chess piece left out in a garden. At the railway station, the presidential carriage, Dr Lopez's inconspicuous
hidey-hole on wheels, couldn't have drawn more attention to
itself if it had indeed been decorated in gold leaf. It was finished
in drab grey-green, as it happened, and in due course I discovered that its exclusive extras were tucked away well out of sight,

as promised. But it couldn't have looked less like the other
wagons with which it was supposed to blend in: ten bare
flatbeds, daisy-chained behind it. There were no prizes for
guessing where any robbing, killing or abducting action was
going to be. The president of STF would not be joining me.

The sun was buffing the rails, the eight-cylinder loco was
humming: I couldn't wait to get on board. It was the effect of
Colombia: in that drug-addled country, the strongest intoxicant
was turning out to be the country herself. A railway worker
told me that the La Dorada line took its name from a fish, a
sprat which passed for gold in the right light. It was the Railway
of Little Fish; not even this discovery stripped the gilt from the
moment.

The presidential carriage was done out in blond wood, with
a vinyl floor of the type found in Portakabins. Sets of grey,
upholstered chairs faced each other across tables. These were
inlaid with what you might call sunken coasters, to prevent
drinks from spilling while the train was on the move. The
Bogota newspapers had been laid out, perhaps by the overalled
employee who was busying himself in a galley which would
not have disgraced the swankiest mobile home or cabin cruiser.
A pot of *tinto* kept hot on a gas ring while the STF steward,
behind his counter, was familiarising himself with the contents
of two huge ice-boxes. I didn't want to spoil any surprises but I
noticed drink and sandwiches between the chilly bricks of the
ice-packs. There was a dining table, with more glass-sized
craters in it. You might almost have been in a ship's mess. The
table was in a nook behind a pair of cabins, which slept four
apiece: it was the presidential *wagon-lit*, really. There was not
one WC but two: in one of them, a shower had been installed
and, a homely touch, a mirror in a wooden surround which
might have come from a residential cloakroom. I thought of
Conrad's *Nostromo* and the fictional South American territory
of Sulaco, where another Santa Marta was also located on a
railway line: the chairman of the railway board had come out
from England and 'the journey from London to Sta Marta in

mail boats and the special carriages of the Sta Marta coast-line
(the only railway existing so far) had been tolerable – even
pleasant – quite tolerable.'

A pair of STF engineers were making the trip, reading the
papers and sipping *tinto*, grateful that the presidential carriage
had been hitched to the train. They were going up the line to
attend to problems with the track and would otherwise have
been crammed cheek by sweaty jowl on the narrow footplate.
One of them was an old boy in blue denim workman's trousers
and small brown shoes. The train was going as far as Puerto
Berrio: it took eight hours, he said. (By car, it took three.)

Despite the comforts of the carriage, I couldn't resist the
Huckleberry charm of seeing the railway from the cow-catcher.
The train went over a tributary of the Magdalena, over a bridge
as rudimentary and insubstantial as a divan, my feet dangling
over the side of the loco. There was fruit the size and texture of
basketballs, and pale, humped cattle in the shade of a tree. Thin
chickens scratched at dry earth. *Campesino* huts beside the
tracks, consisting of thatched roofs and flimsy walls, couldn't
have changed much since Leslie's day. I looked back at the artic-
ulated flatbeds: STF had posted a man on the last one, as a
lookout. In the news that morning, the guerrillas had planted a
booby-trap bomb on the corpse of a soldier: four of his comrades
had died as they attempted to remove the body.

The La Dorada company had managed both the railway and
the aerial ropeway, and in the course of my grandfather's long
career with the firm, he had migrated from the heights of
Manizales and *La Oficina del Cable* to the railway engineering
works at Mariquita, in the humid Magdalena basin. There were
several digressions along the way. Leslie, the former air ace,
had volunteered for action during the Second World War – not
once but twice, judging by the letters of refusal sent by the con-
sulate in Bogota in September 1940 and November 1942. A
'certificate' from the consul in March 1943 said, 'It has been
decided that he will render the best services by remaining in his
present employment with The Dorada Railway Company

Limited. A record has been made of his offer, and if it is desired at a future date that he should travel to the United Kingdom he will be informed accordingly.'

Leslie, entering his forties, had failed the medical, my mother said. 'He smoked like a chimney.' The other engineers returned to Britain to join up, and the Frosts set up home in a place called Fruitillo. There was a workshop at Fruitillo in which machinery for *El Cable* was repaired, but apart from that, almost nothing at all. Fruitillo was in the mountains; it was engulfed in cloud for days at a time and the rain rang on the corrugated iron roofs. It was five miles to the nearest village and three-and-a-half hours' hard riding to the closest road, and the peasants walked through Fruitillo on their way to market with their shoes over their shoulders, to preserve them. There was electric light as long as the workshop was in use, but a wood range was the only cooking to be had and a local woman who did all the chores at the Frosts' place lived in a house with an earth floor. (The only conveniences in the woman's house were chamber pots: when after long service one sprang a leak, it would be filled with soil and converted into a hanging basket.) What gaiety there was came in the shape of *fiestas*. Leslie was referred to as 'doctor', in the South American style, and was on the same social footing as the mayor of the village. On the day of a *fiesta*, the Frosts would be sent for, shown to their seats beside the priest in the plaza, and plied with drink.

An American called Frank Bradley left my mother his polo pony and his dogs when he joined up. Leslie made her sell her own horse, Lucero. 'I remember crying all the way home. I saw Lucero a few days later and he tried to follow me.' It was a wretched life for Gran, and the loneliness of it was punctuated for my mother by the heartbreak of parting with her animals. One day Leslie's favourite mule died of colic: Mum was astonished by her father's reaction. 'Nobody else could ride Reina. My father was so upset. Unbelievably upset.' The only other occasion on which Leslie's upper lip visibly unstiffened was when he heard of the death of his mother. 'He was extremely fond of her, though he hardly ever wrote to her from Colombia. He actually sobbed – it was the only time my mother saw him cry.'

After the war, the Frosts came down from the mountains to Mariquita and the house at Number Two. 'I remember Pop coming home from work. He loved to sit down of an evening and have his two or three drinks before dinner. He had pipe dreams about retiring to Canada – I don't know why, he just liked the idea of it. He sometimes exaggerated things. It was only when I got older that I realised it, I realised that you couldn't believe everything my father said. He talked about telling people where to get off but he was very polite, he would never say boo to a goose.'

The Frosts' neighbours were Leslie's colleagues. Mr Blackett, managing director of the company, used to put up at Number One, Mariquita, though he was based in Bogota. On his visits to Mariquita, he would entertain the staff on Saturday evenings to drinks, dinner and billiards. Ana and Isabel Cruz, local girls who worked in Mr Blackett's house, were my mother's friends. In time, they were the ones who wrote to her about Leslie's affair. There was Mr Kippen, a man in his fifties who married a woman he met in Havana. He was general manager of the railway. My grandfather was his deputy, and also managed the ropeway. He later took over from Mr Kippen, and replaced him as consular agent. There was Mr Cooper, the accountant, and his wife and two daughters, and Mr Crease and his wife, and a West Indian called Mr Nicholas, who was in charge of the stores. There was Mr Birchall, who ran the workshop. He had a Colombian mistress. She was always elegant, my mother said. She stayed in the background. She had a deformed hand – she was missing two fingers – and kept it out of sight in a pocket of her skirt.

My mother remembered the La Dorada as a braying, dust-raising railway moving cattle to market, coming through Mariquita at eight o'clock in the morning, regularly interrupted by breakdowns and floods and landslips, and by strays loping

The railway station at Honda

fatally into the path of the locomotive. It was like the *ferrocar-ril* that Gabriel Garcia Marquez recalled in conversation with the Colombian journalist, Plinio Apuleyo Mendoza: 'The train – a train he would later remember as yellow, dusty and enveloped in suffocating smoke – crossed the vast banana plantations and arrived in town every day at eleven o'clock.' In a place as turbulent as Colombia, the railway brought with it a nerve-soothing predictability.

The Dorada line charged farmers by the head for transporting their livestock, plus a fare of four Colombian cents a kilometre. Domestic animals went for half a cent. The tariff on coffee was up to four *pesos* per ton: there was a machine for threshing coffee in one of the railway buildings. It wasn't clear when work on the line had begun, but by 1891 the stretch between La Dorada and Honda was complete, and two years later, there was a railroad as far south as the town of Ambalema, passing through

My grandfather's train set

Mariquita. It was built and run to move freight and livestock and there was no regular passenger train for Mariquita at first, though VIPs such as government officials, foreigners and the company paymaster were accommodated aboard a special rail-car like STF's presidential carriage, and the public were allowed to use it whenever it was put on. Later, there was a scheduled service with first-, second- and third-class coaches, and a good seat from La Dorada to Mariquita cost fifty-five cents. Government employees on official business and military personnel travelled for half price and prisoners and warders went for nothing. The stretch of the La Dorada between Honda and La Dorada itself was still functioning, but the Honda–Ambalema link, taking in Mariquita, was represented on my contemporary map of Colombia by the undertaker's stitching which told you it was a *ferrocarril abandonado*.

The STF train drew onto a siding near a bend. We were waiting for another loco, coming the other way. The second of the two STF engineers, a man dressed as though for the country club, introduced me to the *brujita*, the one-man peasant train. A *brujita* was a wooden cart, a Winter Olympic luge with castors, propelled gondola-style along the railway line. A *campesino* who was gathering firewood, for example, might use a *brujita* in order to save himself time and effort. The engineer had discovered one under a tree; I took a piece of wood and went for a spin. The name *brujita* was vaguely onomatopoeic – deriving from the action of snatching up the *brujita* at the sight of a train, although it also contained an echo of *brujeria*, black magic.

There was the lowing of a horn and the STF engineers were waving, shouting at me to get out of the way. Coming into view was the awaited loco. It was pulling a column of goods wagons. I grabbed the *brujita*, suiting the action to the word. As the last wagon emerged from around the bend, I saw that there were men riding on the roof. Some of them had white bandanas tied around their faces. I stood beside the track and watched the train coming towards me. The STF engineers, the overalled steward, the men on the footplate – they were all thirty yards away, up the line. There were perhaps eight or ten men sitting cross-legged on the last wagon of the oncoming train. They were simply dressed. They wore hats and boots, like men who spent most of their time out of doors. Now the loco was level with me, and the wagons were going by – there was the creaking of the wood and the dull ringing of the wheels on the tracks – and I was looking into the eyes of the masked men. 'They ride maybe on the last car,' Dr Lopez had said. This was how the guerrillas travelled on the railway.

'The majority are on the *carril* of Jaime,' a graffito announced a short distance up the line. Most people were on Jaime's track. This was a reference to the Jaime Bateman Cayon guerrillas, otherwise the Jaime Bateman Front. They were based in the countryside and had been responsible for kidnapping a British diplomat, Timothy Cowley, in 1995, and holding him for four months. Perhaps the people along the line, the men in the bandanas, were supporters of the front.

The majority *weren't* on Jaime's track, as it happened. The front was inconsequential in terms of Colombia's conflict, capable of raising a militia no bigger than, say, all of the gunmen and all of the bombers that the Provisional IRA could muster at the very height of the Troubles. By contrast, the leading guerrilla factions were the size of feudal armies. In 1998, it was estimated that 20,000 Colombians belonged to one cause or another, and that between them they enjoyed de facto control of an astonishing 40 per cent of the country. The Revolutionary Armed Forces of Colombia (FARC) was perhaps the largest formation of irregular soldiery in the world, with up to 12,000 committed to the struggle. It grew out of peasant militias formed at the time of *La Violencia*. It had officially been Marxist since the mid-1960s, but diversification into drug-trafficking, extortion, kidnapping and cattle-rustling had helped it to turn over $530 million a year by 1997, according to the government's calculations.

FARC had a reputation for audacious stunts. In March 1998, in the municipality of Pena less than fifty miles outside Bogota, they seized a helicopter which was delivering cash to a bank – itself a sign of how firmly the guerrillas controlled the local roads. The raiders stole the money, killed a policeman and three civilians, and set the helicopter alight. Staging an assault on the town of Vista Hermosa in Meta province, FARC rolled out their homemade tanks: farm tractors stripped down to their chassis and fitted with extra-thick tyres; the drivers' cabs protected by thick sheets of steel and with M60 machineguns mounted on top. These engines of war rumbled through the town at about twenty-five miles per hour and razed the bank to the ground. One crashed into the police station, where it was abandoned. 'It was a sophisticated machine and could have destroyed an entire army,' according to a quakingly impressed council official who had witnessed FARC's extraordinary weapon in action. Police conjectured that the rebels were trying to form their own 'armed cavalry division': a couple of years earlier, an army patrol in Bolivar province had discovered two dumper trucks reinforced with steel sheeting.

The National Liberation Army (ELN), the second biggest guerrilla movement, had a headcount of 5,000. It was led for twenty-five years by a Spanish priest, Manuel Perez, who was excommunicated in 1986 after the ELN was blamed for the murder of a bishop. The ELN wasn't as close to the *narcoticos* as FARC, largely financing its activities through kidnapping instead. In 1997 alone, it collected a staggering $112 million in ransom money.

Like FARC, the ELN espoused left-wing causes, taking its inspiration from the Cuban revolution. In Louis de Bernières' Colombian satire, *Señor Vivo and the Coca Lord*, a general observes, 'Who would have believed that in this day and age there would still be Maoists and Stalinists? But there are, and the armed forces have sustained terrible losses in the struggle against them.' The army's worst reverse at the hands of the rebels came in March 1998. At least sixty-two troops were killed in a three-day battle in jungle along the Caguan river in the south-western department of Caqueta, an area described by one journalist as 'a lawless frontier where FARC rebels guard cocaine labs'. The guerrillas took forty-three infantrymen prisoner. It was five days before soldiers dared reclaim the bodies of their comrades; by then, DNA tests were required to identify them. Manuel José Bonett, commander of the armed forces, was as despairing as de Bernières' general. 'Any aid from any country would be welcome.' He would even accept atomic bombs, he added blackly.

There *was* aid from the United States, theoretically directed towards the 'drugs war', though there was a good deal of mission creep, on the analysis that drugs and guerrillas were mixed up with one another. General Charles Wilhelm, chief of United

States Southern Command, based in Miami, described Colombia as 'the most serious challenge facing the United States military in Latin America'. America's top brass privately voiced the fear that Bogota was losing the battle. Officially, about 200 United States military personnel were in Colombia – operating two jungle radar stations, and providing the security forces with counter-narcotics training.

Human rights campaigners were concerned that Washington was becoming involved in another Vietnam. An organisation called Washington Office on Latin America cautioned against the Pentagon using connections between *narcotraficantes* and rebels to justify stepping up military support. A similar warning came from Felipe Torres, an imprisoned cadre of ELN, in March 1998. He said, 'If the United States gets involved, there will be generalised action. Colombia's insurgent groups will become true armies and this will become another Vietnam.'

In the region where the massacre of Colombian infantry occurred, the Colombian state was effectively a foreign power; the nightmare of five-star *gringo* generals appeared to be realised already. There were no hospitals, no schools, no courts. It was in Caqueta in 1984 that United States agents uncovered *Tranquilandia* in what amounted to the biggest drugs bust in history. Like an aircraft carrier stationed just over the horizon, *Tranquilandia* was Escobar's secret weapon, fourteen fully equipped laboratories which were sustained by their own water and electricity supplies, roads and an airstrip. They were capable of yielding more than 3,500 kilogrammes of cocaine every month. After the raid on *Tranquilandia*, a crop-substitution programme offering peasants alternatives to *coca* was introduced – and given up as a bad job in short order. Generally speaking, there were no roads to bring goods to market. Gasoline was taxed because it was used in the manufacture of cocaine: presently, only farmers making the sort of profits that went with cocaine could afford to buy it. Clouds of herbicide released from government aircraft to destroy *coca* crops tended to go astray, blighting legitimate harvests, pauperising the peasantry. The poverty of many ordinary Colombians was the guerrillas' strength. They demanded a fairer distribution of wealth, land reform, an end to unbridled free-market economics.

In many parts of the country, the word of the rebels was law. If a *campesino* fell ill, FARC ordered his employer to pay the doctor's bill. The group distributed property when marriages failed, ran child-care centres and imposed summary justice on petty criminals and anyone accused of collaborating with the military. In June 1997, President Samper had confirmed what everybody knew, by demilitarising – that is to say, handing over to the guerrillas – 5,000 square miles of Caqueta, in exchange for the lives of seventy captive soldiers.

FARC had let it be known that they weren't interested in peace so long as Samper was in power. But there were signs that the various renegade movements were willing to treat with a new government. Prior to his death from hepatitis in 1998, Father Manuel of the ELN had indicated that he might be prepared to come to terms. And Felipe Torres said from his cell: 'We all have a historic responsibility to join together to search for a way out of this common grave.' As I was travelling in Colombia, tentative talks had begun in Europe between emissaries of the state and spokesmen for the rebels.

The modern history of Colombia was of unstinting violence driving the country to the absolute last resort: peace. And then the peace failing and the cycle beginning all over again. The slaughter of *La Violencia* was finally arrested in the late 1950s by a unique power-sharing agreement involving the two leading political forces, the Liberals and the Conservatives. Under the *Frente Nacional*, as it was known, the parties supported a single presidential candidate at elections, and shared out political offices between them. There followed sixteen years of almost undreamt-of administrative stability: no coups, no martial law, no governments of national emergency. But this wasn't to say that the system had eliminated unrest; on the contrary, the cosy arrangement had failed to accommodate appreciable forces within Colombia. One of these was the *Movimiento 19 de Abril*,

or M19. They took their name from the date of an election in
1970; the reason this meant a lot to them was that their candidate, General Rojas Pinilla, who had already served one
presidential term in the 1950s, failed to be returned, amid allegations from M19 of ballot-rigging. The movement advocated a
democratic socialist society, and went about promoting this in a
cerebral way at first, placing itself in the tradition of Bolivar.
Their first public gesture was to steal Bolivar's sword from a
Bogota museum. But then in 1976, M19 kidnapped José Rafael
Mercado, a trades union leader, accused him of fraud and mis-
conduct, subjected him to a trial under their own cognizance,
convicted him and executed him. The head of the communist
party was also abducted. The embassy of the Dominican
Republic was taken over during a reception, and fifteen ambas-
sadors held hostage for two months.

In 1982, faced by escalating guerrilla campaigns and waning
support for the established parties, the president, Belisario
Betancur, announced a 'democratic opening' of political insti-
tutions. He acknowledged that poverty, unemployment and
inadequate state services had encouraged the development of
insurgent forces. An unconditional amnesty was offered; 400
political prisoners, including many guerrilla leaders, were
freed. Two years later, the government signed ceasefire accords
with four guerrilla outfits, promising land reform and an all-
embracing political process. But the effort failed. By 1986, all
the factions had taken up arms again, and Colombia was
embroiled in a blood-drenched 'dirty war'. Pardoned guerrillas
who had reinvented themselves as congressmen and mayors
were themselves the victims of assassinations and kidnapping.
In 1989, after everything else had failed – there was peace. A
new president, Virgilio Barco, reopened dialogue with the out-
laws and, within a year, M19 were surrendering their arms to
international monitors, a flash of their old wit in the stipulation
that the weapons be melted down and modelled into a statue
dedicated to peace.

Within weeks, M19 entered electoral politics, as the *Alianza*

Democratica M19. Their candidate for president, Carlos Pizarro, was on his way to address a rally when he was murdered aboard a plane. Mourners stopped traffic in Bogota on the day of his funeral; the killing of Pizarro produced a huge surge of support for the former guerrillas, and their new representative went on to garner 12 per cent of the vote, an unprecedented showing for a third-party candidate. *Alianza Democratica* M19 built on this popularity a few months later at special elections to a constitutional assembly; there it was joined by a number of other factions, which had also signed peace treaties with the government. Events suggested that the Colombian state would only treat with rebels after the option of violence had been exhaustively explored; if so, then a settlement with FARC and ELN was surely overdue.

The train passed through the cool darkness of a clay tunnel. I had settled myself in the presidential carriage. I was drinking *tinto* and looking out of the window. There was a man's face in the trees, under a camouflage cap, and a glimpse of another figure gripping a machete. I could see three men in all: they were poised on branches level with the slowly moving carriage. They were in combinations of combat fatigues and had a pair of machetes between them. What the men were doing, I saw with relief, was cutting back the forest which pressed down to the line. Who they were exactly, no one in the carriage was able to say. One man had been wearing leaves under his cap, a recommended method of keeping cool. How did Jeremy Harding put it? 'They had their presence down to an art, clinging to the bush like some obscure species, emerging now and then to shed blood and tamper with the track.'

The train came upon a station. The ticket office was an impressive affair, or had been: doric columns and primary blues, now faded, and a great lurid tabernacle devoted to the Virgin and Child. Breezeblock huts bordered the line and washing was drying on a barbed-wire fence. This was Puerto Triunfo in the department of Antioquia, Escobar's former domain. Puerto Triunfo was the stop for Napoles, Escobar's place in the country, a combination of ranch and criminal theme park. He had named it in honour of the Italian mafia. Impudently erected within sight of the main Bogota-to-Medellin highway, the crowning glory of the imposing main gates had been a single-seater plane: it was the one Escobar had used when he was a struggling racketeer, and he had memorialised it the way another sentimental self-made man might have commissioned busts of his pets.

There had been a thousand feet of runway for operational air-craft at Napoles, and a rash of mortar emplacements. Escobar had put together the 15,000-hectare spread between 1979 and 1982. He had established a zoo, importing species including elephants, ostriches, antelopes, buffalo, gazelles, camels and zebras. There were possibly apocryphal stories that their exotic excrement had been used to throw sniffer dogs off the scent of cocaine smuggled into the United States. Hippopotamuses had bathed in some of the sixteen artificial lakes which Escobar had sunk. Statues of dinosaurs had been dotted about like plaster gnomes. An abandoned, crumbling *casona*, a mansion, had room for a hundred guests; half a dozen overspill cottages could accommodate even more visitors. There was a swimming pool drained of all but a few inches of murky water.

In 1991, Escobar had sold up, emptied the zoo, all from his prison in Medellin. Now the government was intending to use Napoles to house internal refugees, under a law entitling the state to the assets of narco-gangsters. Cesar Manuel Garcia, pres-idential adviser on the displaced, said, 'What we wanted was to send a symbolic but very clear message to drug-traffickers: "no land is sacred".' Those helping the dispossessed pointed out that not even Escobar's posthumous hospitality was equal to the task. Within days of Garcia's remarks, 3,000 people had fled disturbances in Cordoba, a department bordering Antioquia.

I had Leslie's railway map with me. The STF engineers admired it, the smartly dressed one calling it a jewel, an ancient jewel. 'You must look after it well because it's impossible to replace.' He was disdainful of the steward in the presidential carriage, who was bringing around meat sandwiches and glasses of *gaseosa* (pop) with his overalls open to the waist because of the heat. Butterflies kept pace with the train and a smell like liquorice came through the open windows. The sun was at its height. There were some trees, perhaps ash, around a lake. The trees had no shadow; shimmering streaks of silvery-grey, they were almost without substance, too.

The engineer in denim trousers and brown shoes, whose name was Guillermo Villamarine, said that in the 1960s, most freight was moved by rail between Buenaventura and Santa Marta, all the way through Colombia, because businessmen didn't like paying to use the Panama Canal. It was a great pity that the line along the River Cauca, the one which used to connect Cali and Medellin, had not been repaired after it was flooded. 'No one understands why the government refuses to put up the money for it,' he said. 'It's a superb opportunity to link up the different areas of Colombia much more easily than can be done by road, but instead the policy has been to concentrate on roads.'

The pocket of Villamarine's shirt was a baggy quiver of ballpoints. 'Men like your grandfather were pioneers,' he said. 'They were the people who really built Colombia because the railways united Colombia as one country. At that time, it was hard to do because the terrain was very difficult. You know, I have great admiration for him.'

How my mother would have loved this trip, I thought, how proud she would have been of her Pop. I was proud of him, too, proud that the railway people had made the generous, ridiculous gesture of laying on the presidential coach for one of his relatives. For the first time since coming to Colombia, I felt close to my grandfather. I had been on his railway line at La Dorada. I had been on the trail he'd blazed. Like him, I'd stalked the big game of the mud-striped Magdalena, as mesmerising as a tiger, at the voluptuous speed of an elephant chair. I watched

Villamarine snoozing after lunch. He was nothing like Leslie Frost to look at. But he was a resourceful man, a man with Biros in his top pocket, an engineer – like my grandfather, after all; like my father. Villamarine was like family.

A memory surfaced of being on a train with Dad when I was very young. Despite the well-known magnifying effect of child-hood recall, the train I remembered was small. But then it really had been *small*, a scale replica of a steam locomotive pulling dwarfish carriages on a shrunken line. In the Midlands some-where, if I wasn't mistaken: while Leslie was still alive, then, before we moved to the house where he and Gran came to stay with us when he was ill. Being on that train with Dad was almost as far back as I could remember. In the presidential car-riage, I belatedly registered (though of course I had always *known*) that I was writing my notes on Dad's old memo pads, left over from his days as an engineer.

Beyond a *campesino*'s corrugated roof, I saw the eggshell dome of a tiny church. We had reached a place called Cocorna. It was a stronghold of FARC. A few months earlier, a captain of police had moved into the mayoral parlour in Cocorna, FARC having abducted the rightful incumbent. Similar emergency measures had been taken in three other towns on the orders of the governor of Antioquia. Mayors had been going missing in the run-up to municipal elections. In twenty-five townships, the poll had to be abandoned altogether because of sabotage, and in Simiti, in the northern province of Bolivar, the entire town council – nine officials, including the treasurer – was seized by the ELN on the way to a meeting. Since the previous round of municipal elections, in 1994, no fewer than twenty-eight mayors and 150 town councillors had been killed.

I went into one of the cabins, read for a while, had a lie-down. I listened to the modern jazz percussion of the bogies over the track. Lulled by the rhythms of the train, I thought I saw what Leslie had seen in this life: the sheer lark of messing about on trains all day, in the sun, out of the office; the perhaps unconscious sense that what you were doing was of worth in the development of Colombia, that it gave heart to people for whom the train was a constant in the middle of uncertainty – not to mention the irresistible fertility busting out all around you, overwhelming to Europeans like the Swiss of Cali, like my grandfather himself . . . By the time I woke up, the train was lost in a sugar plantation. There was cane next to, and as tall as, the carriage. It was late afternoon. Thinking to freshen up, I went to the bathroom and popped my head under an invigoratingly scalding shower, not having considered the effect of Magdalena valley temperatures on a train-lagged water tank. Elsewhere in the carriage, the steward was serving whisky, beakers of Old Parr with ice, wrapped in napkins.

Herman was driving the train; he'd been driving trains for sixteen years. Did he enjoy it? *'Claro, claro.* The best locos are the large ones, with wider cabins, to allow more air in. Otherwise, it gets very hot.' I squeezed past Herman on the footplate, slid onto his seat. There were *campesinos* on the line, a pair of them riding a two-man *brujita*. I thumbed the button that made the horn blow – on the train out of La Dorada, my grandfather's old railway-set. The *campesinos* looked up; shamblingly, they removed themselves from the path of the train. The biggest problem was the state of the track, said Herman; that's why we would be stopping at Puerto Berrio and the engineers going on by road, to see if they could get things fixed.

The rebels were an obscure species as far as Herman was concerned, so obscure that he didn't notice them. Didn't talk about them, anyhow. 'Possibly some of the other drivers know about them but I don't personally. They are mostly up in the mountains.' But driving a train, Herman had met some interesting people. Two months ago, he said, he had been in the driver's seat when the presidential carriage was occupied by the president, the *real* president, Ernesto Samper himself, and his retinue of ministers and flunkies. They had gone out into the countryside. 'It was only for a few kilometres, not a long journey like this,' said Herman. 'They had a special waiter. There were bodyguards everywhere – in the carriage, on the roof.' I wondered what might have gone on during this mysterious journey, in the carriage where Engineer Villamarine was now taking a whisky after a run up the line, in the traditions of the La Dorada railway. The journey in the special carriage of the Sta Marta line had been tolerable – even pleasant – quite tolerable. Yes, I thought, quite tolerable.

6

Inside
Escobar's *Baño*

Gran was saying, 'Your grandfather is wonderful with children, apart from little boys who come into the room and
steal the meat.' Next I was on a train over water, and the wheels
were picking their way between bobbing logs. And then it was
a leaden morning in Puerto Berrio, and there was a helicopter
buzzing the hotel, and a rare and baffling dream involving my
grandparents was evaporating. Puerto Berrio was a military
town, it was an edgy town. It was a close, dusty, two-storey
cowboy town – notwithstanding that the herd, when you
encountered it, looked so scraggy you thought it could barely
support a cowboy *hamlet*. There were *vaqueros* everywhere,
men in cowboy hats, drinking *tinto* and gossiping at cafés
around the plaza. There was an army patrol and stalls of black-
ening bananas.

In a restaurant the night before, Engineer Villamarine and I
had been drinking beer which was warm before our glasses
were half-empty. A party of slightly sinister young men –
pagers, suspicious looks – had occupied the next table.
Villamarine told me the uncanny story that he'd once come
across plans for the Manizales-to-Mariquita ropeway, the cable

operation across the Andes which Leslie had run. He had admired the plans so much that he'd had them framed and they'd hung at the STF building in Bogota, the offices where I'd met Dr Lopez, though they'd gone missing a long time ago.

Thinking of Leslie's railway map, I said, 'Could my grandfather have made them, I wonder?'

'It's possible.'

The sinister party got up from its table and went out into the street and got into a jeep. As it slid beneath a streetlight, I saw that it was the property of a gas company.

Puerto Berrio had once been a prosperous town, where the men lit their cigars with *peso* bills – that's what Villamarine said. This was when the *peso* was worth something, he wanted me to know. The good times began before the coming of the railroads, when rivers were still the main means of transportation in Colombia, and Puerto Berrio enjoyed the natural advantages of being on a bend in the country's mightiest causeway, the Magdalena. Like the speculators they were, the townsfolk got out of rivers and into railways: the shippers were always moaning about that stretch of the *Rio Magdalena* in any case, saying it was an uncertain transit, that low water interrupted navigation in the middle and upper courses for long periods of time. They 'complained of inventory tie-ups, high losses through pilferage, and the costly cargo transfer at Puerto Berrio,' according to *Antioqueno Colonization in Western Colombia* by James J. Parsons. The people of Puerto Berrio thought they saw a good thing coming in the railroad: they watched it inch over the horizon towards them. It was more than eight years in the making, an American engineer of Cuban birth named Francisco J. Cisneros having been commissioned in 1874 to build exactly 100 miles of line between Puerto Berrio and a town called Barbosa. It was single-track, with a gauge of a yard, and it cost $61,999 a mile, the government of Antioquia and the national congress meeting the costs between them. Eventually, this stretch formed part of the *Ferrocarril de Antioquia*, running to Medellin in the west, and when this was joined to the Atlantic railway in the 1960s, the junction was the fortunate Puerto Berrio, set fair to be the most important axis in the country. River traffic duly tailed off: once-crowded wharves emptied, and by the time the last paddle steamer on the Magdalena was destroyed in a fire, it was already a museum-piece. But Puerto Berrio's charmed existence hadn't prepared it for the impact of roads, and the preference of Colombia's decision-makers for this option. 'The expected volume of rail freight movement failed to materialise,' wrote Parsons. 'Cargo handled at Puerto Berrio declined more than 50 per cent in the decade 1955–1965 and there have been further drops since.'

By the time I got there, Puerto Berrio's reputation had nothing to do with commerce. It had been called the birthplace of Colombia's right-wing paramilitaries. The authorities were closing in on a leading paramilitary while I was in town – he was arrested within days – and it can't have been a week later that a further eleven suspects were rounded up in Puerto Berrio and relieved of machine guns, pistols and grenades. The paramilitaries were the people who decapitated their victims with chainsaws – and ate their brains, or so it was said.

From a distance, the paramilitaries appeared to be the opposition to FARC and ELN and the other revolutionaries, and that's how they liked to present themselves. In fact, there were striking similarities; they were the image of the guerrillas seen in a grotesque hall of mirrors. If anything, they were even more brutal. At least the guerrillas here and there offered some benefits to the peasants who found themselves under their tutelage. The paramilitaries, who also went by the unambiguous style of 'death squads', only visited suffering on them, and any interest they had in the welfare of others was reserved for the landowners and *narcos* to whom they sold protection.

The best-known paramilitary was Fidel 'Rambo' Castano. His gang murdered country people accused of collaborating with the rebels. It called itself by the black-is-white title of the 'Peasant Self-Defence Force of Cordoba and Uraba' (ACCU): in May 1998, gunmen identifying themselves as members of ACCU killed at least seven peasants outside Medellin. The bearded, stocky Castano claimed that the abduction and murder of his father by 'Marxists' when he was a boy was what had launched him on his 'crusade'. He had also lost four brothers and a sister, and had a bounty of $1 million on his own head. He regarded himself and the men and women of ACCU as patriots, once issuing a statement saying, 'I'm proud of what I'm doing. It's a duty and an obligation I had to fulfil.'

The many criticisms levelled at the paramilitaries by Amnesty International and others included the charge that they seized lands abandoned by frightened peasants, either keeping them for themselves or selling them to big landowners. Castano admitted coming into many thousands of acres, and disposing of them in order to fill his war chest. He didn't deny levying *boleteo*, protection, from landowners (some of them, he agreed, cocaine-traffickers) though he touchingly protested that he only charged half as much as the left-wingers.

One way of telling the paramilitaries apart from the rebels was that the former enjoyed a close relationship with the Colombian security forces. These links were confirmed in 1998 when five former army and police officers were imprisoned over a massacre in north-west Antioquia. A 'faceless' judge in Bogota, his anonymity preserved for his own safety, heard that gold miners in the town of Segovia had joined a national strike in November 1988. Three four-wheel-drive vehicles pulled up in the middle of the town and their occupants opened fire indiscriminately with rockets, grenades and automatic weapons. The toll was forty-three: men, women and children. Two journalists from *El Espectador* who went to Segovia to do a follow-up story fully three years later were forced to kneel in the town square by gunmen and shot dead at point-blank range.

The men who had pulled the triggers weren't caught; four civilians accused of playing a direct role in the butchery were handed down prison terms of thirty years each in their absence. But the former officers were found guilty of acting in complicity with the killers. Each received eighteen years. Standing in the dock was a former lieutenant colonel who had led the Bombona army battalion, based in Segovia.

The connection between the paramilitaries and the armed forces was confirmed by Castano of ACCU, who claimed that he and his brother had acted as 'guides' for the Bombona battalion before setting up on their own. A shadowy army unit, the 20th Intelligence Brigade, was accused of involvement in political killings – by, amongst others, an outspoken American ambassador, Myles Frechette. The unit was officially wound up in 1998. In the last days of his presidency, Ernesto Samper publicly apologised for the deaths of forty-nine people at the hands of security forces in separate incidents between 1991 and 1993 – before Samper himself was in office – expressing shame for what he called 'these deliriously violent events'. Perhaps it was no coincidence that Puerto Berrio, cradle of the death squads, was also an important military base.

The STF engineers and I had disembarked from the presidential carriage in marshalling yards at Gracia, a mile or two from the town, where FARC graffiti on a station building proclaimed *Muerte a los Paramilitares*, Death to the Paramilitaries. As we had pulled in, a passenger train was being made ready for departure. I'd climbed into it: wooden, slatted seats in standard-class accommodation, and a man in a darkened *baño*; a *restaurante* attractively liveried in cream and mint; and a more comfortable carriage, with padded banquettes. There had been a few people aboard, though the train wouldn't be leaving for hours – 'There are no timetables, only rumours,' wrote Charles Nicholl, author of *The Fruit Palace*, about Colombian railways. This was the passenger train from Puerto Berrio to Medellin; the *Ferrocarril de Antioquia*. I wanted to take it and go to Medellin. There was a metro system there – it was the only place in Colombia which had one. It was the second biggest city in the country. It had achieved notoriety, or had notoriety thrust upon it, as the murder capital of the world. It had been the home of Pablo Escobar: I wanted to see the prison where he had been held, to see if it was as fabulously cushy as I had heard.

Medellin was a crucial part of the story of what had become of Colombia. But at the restaurant in Puerto Berrio, Villamarine and his smarter colleague, who had arrived late after going to hospital with a migraine, had expressed reservations about the train. This was partly due to its excruciating slowness, partly to the fact that it was chiefly patronised by very poor people – what reason but poverty could there be for choosing the train over the quicker, more expensive *buseta*? Life being what it was, very poor people might be tempted to rob me. The other thing on the engineers' minds had been *securidad*. It was known that *los guerrilleros* were active in the mountains on the line, the *Cordillera Central*. Mostly they left the dirt-poor passengers alone – they were *their* people, after all, or that was the idea – but a wealthy *gringo*, well . . .

'If you are determined to take this train, you should remain at all times in the restaurant car,' the smart engineer had instructed. It wasn't clear to me how this would help.

It seemed that the road was little better. Though the journey would be speedier, there were similar problems of security. The latest ruse, the smart engineer had explained, was for paramilitaries posing as election agents, canvassers, to board the buses; to abduct the passengers or, more commonly, to shoot them by the roadside.

Before elections in October 1997, the death squads not only killed left-wing politicians in some areas, but also frogmarched the entire population out of certain towns before the polling booths opened. Some candidates were elected with a handful of votes because of the abduction of the electorate. Mayors in at least nine towns were returned with fewer than twenty votes; considerably fewer, in some cases. When gunmen swept through the town of Murindo in Uraba province a fortnight before the election, most inhabitants fled and the new mayor collected the chain of office on the strength of a solitary ballot paper. Gloria Cuartas, the independent mayor of Apartado in Uraba, said, 'The paramilitaries' strategy has been to wipe out the left-wing political force and create a new style of elections where voters can only choose those parties that the death squads permit.' Democracy brought out the worst in Colombia's killers. In the south of Colombia, FARC and ELN had seen to it that campaigning was banned; in the north, the death squads had driven out left-wing parties.

It was all pretty lowering: the antics of the paramilitaries hadn't come up in Bogota, with Dr Lopez. On the other hand, the engineers were the men on the ground; they, of all people, ought to know what was happening. They had proposed giving me a lift back to La Dorada by car. I could catch a bus from there to Medellin, along a safer road. Better still, one of them had said, why didn't I go *half*way back to La Dorada and pick up a bus there? I thought: if I don't take the train into Medellin, I can always take it out again instead.

First, in the morning, the engineers had to make their recce up the line. I had been ill in the night – perhaps that had something to do with my dreaming about Leslie and Gran, something I couldn't remember doing since I was a child. I felt like going back to bed but there was a need to find a bottle of scotch, as a thank-you to the engineers. Pretty girls were scooting about on mopeds. There were hardware stores, outlets where cowboys could stock up. There was a place with a dusty-looking tombola of spirits in the window: Teachers, Remy Martin. But it was a bar, not a shop. The bottles were purely for show and might have contained anything. The off-licence choice was restricted to the local poison – *aguardiente* – or Colombian brandy or something with a red cross on the label called, without art, 'Alcohol'. There was also a brand of gin named after 'Lady Di', bearing a silhouette of a familiar profile in an Ascot hat.

The engineers didn't come back for me until the middle of the day. The problem with the line wasn't something that could be fixed immediately, they said. They would think it over in Bogota. We left Puerto Berrio through the main square: languishing behind a mesh fence in the middle of the plaza was locomotive No. 502, a real old steam engine like the ones I'd seen at the railway station in the capital. It was unregarded by

the gossiping cowboys. A loose branch had caught on the
handrail of the cab, the black and gold engine was dusty. If it
symbolised the role of the train in unifying the country –
Engineer Villamarine's argument – then its neglect seemed to
stand for more than the disrepair of the railways alone.

We drove out of town, mostly in silence, odd questions pop-
ping up from time to time (how tall was I?). There was an
Ecopetrol plant where lethargic soldiers were on duty, and, for
a time, a steel pipeline running alongside the car. Villamarine
was the lead engineer, I decided; he was addressed as '*señor*'.
I'd thought at first that this was larky, ironic, but then I doubted
whether the term would have been used in that way. Having
said that, his smartly dressed colleague pulled Villamarine's leg
about his origins, claiming that Colombians from Villamarine's
rustic corner of the country affected blankets as coats.

We came upon a rubble-strewn bridge. There were warning
notices: it looked as though the road was up, the road was
closed. Where to now, I wondered? Back to La Dorada and the
long way round to Medellin? Or right back to Bogota with the
engineers? As we pulled up, I saw men working on the bridge,
a contraflow of traffic. The road was passable, after all. A *clima-
tizado* stopped behind us, an air-conditioned coach which was
going to Medellin, and the resourceful engineers immediately
bagged me a berth. I was sorry to say goodbye: I would miss
Engineer Villamarine, a man who was nothing like my grandfather but who had made him come alive for me. I felt that having
met him I had unexpectedly accomplished some part of the
purpose of coming to Colombia.

A television set hung behind the coach driver's seat, though
the driver himself was invisible, obscured by a partition or mod-
esty hatch – this was to prevent light from the windscreen
obscuring the picture on the set. The windows of the coach
were tinted, down to about head height. Many had curtains
drawn across them. The television was showing an action film
with Spanish subtitles. Impervious to the magnificent mountain
scenery through which it presently passed, the coach was a

travelling cinema. The passengers – the audience – relaxed in their tilting seats. There were plastic buckets hanging over the armrests of the aisle chairs. These were for rubbish. The man across the gangway leant towards me and hawked into his. At first I thought that being unable to see where I was going would make me nauseous, though there would have been precious little to be nauseous on: a piece of bread at breakfast was all I'd had since a hearty evacuation the night before. But I found I was all right if I divided my attention between the window and the film.

I wasn't sick so much as scared. I was thinking about what bogus election agents got up to on roads like this one in Antioquia, a road which was empty of other traffic for mile after mile, with only a shack every once in a while, displaying a glass case of fried food, to remind you that people actually lived in these parts and tried to make a living. I was thinking about chainsaws. Not under attack, not threatened with kidnap, I was merely on a road where either of these things was possible and I was thinking of Garcia Marquez's 'thunderous truths that seem ridiculous to anyone who has not lived through them'. I began saying to myself, not least during the sustained farting of a passenger identifiable only in terms of his rough proximation, 'Everything's all right so long as you're not being kidnapped.' A month after this coach trip, about forty paramilitaries, in camouflage and armed with machine guns, dragged ten passengers off a bus in a part of Antioquia about 180 miles north of Bogota. They forced the passengers to lie face down on the road and shot them. According to reports, the gunmen 'went on a killing spree that stretched into the next day', leaving a total of twenty-one people dead. Some of the bodies were piled side by side into the back of a pick-up and driven to the local morgue. The survivors fled, under the impression that the killers would be returning to burn their homes, according to a local priest, Father Diego Rivera. In the course of their enquiries, police came across the cadavers of three people who had been abducted some days earlier from the nearby town of

Bello; five remained unaccounted for. Bello was a destination on Leslie's old railway map. It was also at one end of the highway that the coach was travelling on; it was at the end we were travelling towards.

There was a minor family connection with Medellin. It was the base of Coltejer, Colombia's biggest textile manufacturer. Leslie had had shares in the company, and it was assumed that these and other assets would be surrendered for their cash value before he finally came home. In 1948, Mum left Colombia to go to college in Bristol and her parents accompanied her, Leslie taking six months' leave. On their return, Leslie and Peggie moved into Number Five, Mariquita: that was their home until 1955. It was only after another spell of leave in England that Leslie went back to Number Five to live on his own; on his own until Isabel moved in.

The running down of the La Dorada line and the ropeway, the handing over of these concerns to government agencies: it was all attended and delayed by bureaucracy and union unrest, wild weather and civil disturbances. Gran was for long periods a house guest of her mother, and of her sister and brother-in-law. She missed Leslie dearly. Writing to her on 21 March 1955, my mother observed prophetically, 'I really do think it's a pity now that you didn't go back with Pop.' She went on, 'I am pretty sure he could do with your assistance out there especially now. Goodness knows for how long he will be stuck out there all on his own and it won't be any joke getting things packed up and sent to wherever it is you will be going next. However, as I said before, it's no use worrying about what might have been.'

Leslie's own letters to Peggie weren't calculated to encourage her. On 9 July, he wrote that he had no news about the hand-over or whether or not he would be staying on after it; the chairman of the company had been looking out for jobs for Leslie and the others, 'but can hold out little hope of worthwhile appointments in view of our ages.' Leslie was by now fifty-five. 'It looks as though matters are going to be somewhat

My grandfather, with his wife and daughter

tougher than was anticipated unless the National Railways come along with an offer.' Friends had suggested that Leslie strike out on his own as a consultant, and indeed, he had had offers, he wrote. 'But once embarked on a stunt of that sort one would have to settle here. Money could be made, quite probably in plenty, but one could not leave a private business of that sort except for very short periods and, apart from family reasons, it has never been my idea or wish to become a permanent resident of Colombia.'

There was a presumably unintended ambiguity in this last remark: at the time of writing, Leslie was living with his mistress; his son, if not already born, was on the way. He now had 'family reasons' for contemplating Colombian citizenship, though there is no sign that he ever did. As he was writing, my grandmother was anxiously awaiting word from him: she was planning a journey to Colombia to see him. With hindsight, his letter was clearly intended to put her off. He was sorry that she was feeling so fed up, he wrote; 'I am even more so but, as there is nothing I can do about it, at any rate for the time being, I just have to curse and bear it.' Leslie steers Gran firmly towards 'a seaside holiday' in Britain in August or September. 'Frankly, I cannot see much hope of leaving here before then and it is doubtful whether I shall know even if I shall be going home or staying in Colombia by that time. Until that is known I can make neither arrangements for my passage home or yours out, so the holiday is clearly indicated, Darling – it will probably do you lots of good anyway and may make you feel a bit more cheerful. What the heck!!! Something has to bust soon, even if it's only the seat of Salcedo's pants.' (Who was Salcedo, I wondered. My mother didn't know; a Colombian politician, she guessed.)

The gravity of the family crisis may be judged by the actions of Leslie's father, Major Frost. There was still no clarification about my grandfather's departure from Colombia in the spring of 1956. *La Violencia* was raging; Leslie's son was being nursed in secret at Number Five by his mother, Isabel. The picture was so uncertain that the Major took the extraordinary paternal step of withholding Leslie's biannual necktie. As he wrote to Peggie, 'I have bought the usual tie for his birthday but I do not think it safe to send it so if he is still there I must just write a few words of birthday greetings by air mail.' (Was Leslie aware of an act of revenge upon the Major, who he felt had abandoned the family himself in Leslie's youth?)

The family in England waited, oblivious to the fact that Leslie was living with his family in Colombia. Though my grandfather eventually came home, the best pieces in the house and the Frosts' investments, including the value of the Coltejer shares, never did. He wrote to my mother in April 1957, 'Lots of things, especially our books, will have to be dumped or sold but it is a bad time for selling, as nobody seems to have any money. The rate of exchange is so bad that my *cesantia* [redundancy settlement] and a spot of money I have saved out here will be reduced to next to nothing when converted into pounds . . . I am thinking seriously of buying tobacco and brewery shares with it and leaving it out here to earn money.' My mother suspected that, in the end, he'd sold up and left the money to his mistress and her child. I already knew that I would get nowhere with Leslie's shares in Medellin: this was a man who had apparently not registered his own son.

A lorry passed the coach, coming the other way; later, two buses did, travelling close together. This seemed hopeful – they had not been sacked up the road. The *Cordillera Central* was towering: vast, partly terraced slopes and mountain tops obscured by cloud. Other peaks were so brilliantly lit by the strong afternoon sunshine that you struggled to make them out distinctly. I was looking down on birds soaring over ravines and it felt as though we were in a plane rather than a coach. At the kerb, there was a madonna set in a plinth which was shored up with pebbles. Then a school, the pupils playing in a field, though it was by now well past four o'clock.

The coach stopped and two young men got on. They began gabbling at passengers near the door. I was feeling calm – the nearer we were to the big city, the lower the risk of kidnapping, surely? – but all the same I eyed the newcomers uncertainly. Was this how it happened, youths boarding in broad daylight, no attempt at concealment, brassily yelling their piece at resigned passengers? Well, no; or no, not this time, at least. The two were vendors, selling fried snacks, brown, greasy parcels of food.

Like Bogota, Medellin was well-found among mountains. According to its publicity material, it was the city of eternal spring, and it occupied a pleasant, well-situated valley. In practice, as with Bogota again, Medellin had expanded up the surrounding slopes, the poorest parts of the city the most far flung and the least favoured, so that the appearance was of red-brick shanties slipping towards the metropolis, as though the heat of expansion had cooled above the tree-line, and the groundswell would shortly be returned as precipitation. On one hillside, the word 'COLTEJER' was spelt out like Hollywood's famous hallo.

I liked Medellin immediately, happy to be in temperate climes after the tropical *Magdalena Medio*, to be in a city rather than the country. Crime was worse here, without doubt – common or garden car-jacking, rucksack-rifling, wallet-filleting crime – and the statistics mocked my intuition that the incidence of abduction declined as populations grew denser. But the thing about a city was, you knew that there were *things* there, things you needed, things you wanted: a reasonable hotel, say, or a taxi cab. I selected a hotel at random from the guidebook and, by the same principle, a cab from the rank. The hotel, when we reached it, had been closed for two years. The cabbie, who said he was *nuevo* though he was well into middle life, didn't know where it was. He stopped and asked a fellow driver, neglecting to put his meter on hold – perhaps he wasn't as *nuevo* as he made out.

Fortunately, there was a man standing distractedly in the middle of the traffic outside the closed hotel who was able to direct us to another one, perhaps for commission. At this place, rooms were about £15 a night and there was a comely *colombiana* in the lobby who gave you the eye over a corner of *El Tiempo*. Naturally, there would be hookers circulating in a joint like this, I thought: outside was a kind of Times Square, adult movie houses and a tiresome music store with a speaker in the street. A shoeshine whose name was Austin removed all traces of the road for a thousand *pesos*. The success of men like Austin – here, as in other Colombian cities, the trade of bootblack was thriving – was due in part to their deep understanding of the newly fashionable precepts of reflexology. A dextrous *lustrabota* like Austin knew that the shoe was a membrane of the foot – that shameful, hidden extension, so neglected compared to the hand with its more regular launderings, its jewellery, its symbolic importance as the first portion of ourselves that we thrust forward in greeting. Austin was providing a service almost as relieving as the one offered across the lobby by the student of *El Tiempo*.

Of the two cathedrals in Medellin, the one in Parque de Bolivar has by far and away the lesser association with murder. It's the largest building made of brick in South America and its confessionals are open-plan. You see the priests – frowning, ears cocked – twiddling the cords of their vestments. The bricks had given shelter to many mourners in the days when the city was ruled by Escobar. But if you wanted a cathedral with a *past*, you made for the mountains. The second great building in the Medellin see had been founded on a prime slice of real estate which distantly overlooked Parque de Bolivar's central location. Actually, *La Catedral*, as it was known, wasn't a cathedral at all. Or if it was, then only in the same way that the expression 'at Her Majesty's Pleasure' refers to a royal palace. The title was conferred by the people of Medellin upon the soaring gaol in which Escobar served his debt to society. That is, until he got fed up and escaped. Presumably, this had nothing to do with the situation and layout and fittings of the place, upon which the principal inmate himself had been consulted. The Lonely Planet's doughty *Colombia Survival Kit* described *La Catedral* as 'a huge hotel complex with sports facilities including a football ground and a swimming pool, all surrounded by barbed-wire fences and several guard towers. There is a marvellous view over the Aburra valley . . .'

Escobar was the best-known and most charismatic figure in the Colombia of modern times – he would out-score even bubble-permed soccer favourite Carlos Valderrama in focus-group samplings. In terms of legend, and the fear this was capable of transmitting, he was a low-life reincarnation of Bolivar, to whom Escobar was wont to compare himself. He was born a *paisa*, one of the ordinary people of Antioquia. He is supposed to have embarked on his life of crime by hustling headstones: stealing tablets from cemeteries, sanding them down to obliterate the dedications, and re-selling them. Next came a career as a car thief: Escobar formally came to the attention of the police for the first time when he was arrested for stealing in 1974. He became an experienced contract killer while he was still in his teens, and then one of the first Colombians to ship cocaine into the United States in volume, clearing $10 million on a trip to Florida in the single-seater aircraft which later hung over the entrance to his Napoles mansion. This was at a time when unsophisticated smuggling methods still held sway, unhappy *mulas* travelling to the United States on scheduled flights with cocaine packed into the heels of their shoes, or stitched into the linings of coats and suitcases, or secreted internally. To emphasise his pretensions as much as his new-found wealth, Escobar bought himself a car which had once belonged to Al Capone.

The slopes around Medellin, the *piste* of shanties – Escobar came from these surroundings, the son of a local schoolteacher, and he made them his base. A Colombian film-maker called Victor Galvira has aptly observed, 'The only law which holds true on the hillsides of Medellin is the law of gravity.' As the most exceptional of the new cartel *capos* amassed an illicit fortune estimated to be worth $2 billion, he was building a *barrio* to house 200 of Medellin's poorest families. He gave them social clubs and sports grounds and invested in the city's beloved soccer teams. He bought a newspaper and entered Colombia's Chamber of Deputies in 1983. He was a substantial, if vulgar, man of affairs, repellent to the respectable *antioqueno* establishment but toasted in the *communas*, the poor neighbourhoods, where he was known as *Robin Hood Paisa*. 'At the height of his splendour, people put up altars with his picture and lit candles to him in the slums of Medellin,' wrote Garcia Marquez in *News of a Kidnapping*. Of course, there was more to Escobar's rise than a woozy charm and the altruistic outlay of a few million dollars. He was a corrupt and ruthless man, buying or scaring off any judge, general or politician who gave the merest hint of standing in his way. Those who wouldn't be bought or scared were killed – sometimes killed anyway, killed instead, killed first. Even in a country as soused in blood as Colombia, there was a peculiar horror in the story of Escobar.

His first, unsuccessful foray into politics had seen him rejected for the emerging New Liberalism movement led by Luis Carlos Galan, who denounced him before a crowd of 5,000 on his home turf of Medellin in 1982. Though his formal political career was underway within a year, Escobar had not forgotten this humiliation, and set in motion a personal war against the Colombian state. Rodrigo Lara Bonilla, justice minister and luminary of New Liberalism, was assassinated in a drive-by shooting in Bogota. He was succeeded by Enriqué Parejo: he was followed to Budapest by a hired gunman and shot in the face. In 1989, seven years after his public humbling of Escobar, Galan himself was cut down by machine-gun bullets, notwithstanding the ministrations of his eighteen bodyguards.

As much as revenge, fear had been the spur. Escobar and other notables were afraid of extradition, having seen what had happened to a *narco* by the name of Carlos Lehder. He had been dabbling in newspapers and politics, just like Escobar, when the Colombian government signed a treaty making extradition possible for the first time. The Americans got hold of Lehder and sentenced him to life plus 130 years. Escobar wouldn't get off so lightly.

It wasn't just Washington that Escobar had to worry about: the up-and-coming Cali cartel was snapping at his heels. If he was to stay alive, and stay out of an American jail, he calculated that his only hope was to strike a deal with the politicians. An election was approaching, and the New Liberals were firmly pro-extradition. But the murders of their main spokesmen appeared to have the desired softening-up effect: Cesar Gavira, who had been Galan's campaign manager, assumed the leadership and advocated a policy that criminals who surrendered and confessed to at least some of their offences would receive non-extradition in return. This still wasn't good enough for

Escobar and his cronies. The Extraditables, as they became known, embarked on a series of kidnappings, principally of well-known journalists and broadcasters, in order to get their own way: a watertight undertaking that they could not be removed to the United States. Put on their mettle, legislators found themselves discussing urgent connundra which would not have been out of place in the magic realism of *One Hundred Years of Solitude*: they had to impose a closing date on the extradition honeymoon, otherwise the deterrent power of this weapon would be forfeit: they had to set a deadline after which extradition once again became active in the case of certain offences. But someone pointed out that as soon as this deadline expired, so too would any incentive to the underworld to cooperate with the state, viz the chance of avoiding extradition.

I cut a deal with a taxi driver called Mario to visit *La Catedral*. He wanted 3,600 *pesos* for the round trip. This was getting on for £20 but it didn't seem out of the way because we had to go out to Envigado, as far as the Medellin city limits, where Escobar had grown up. When the authorities had finally made him an offer he couldn't refuse – he would have been *mad* to – i.e. avoid extradition by pleading guilty to a single offence, he had unaffectedly chosen to remain in his hometown to do his time. The specifics of his incarceration were agonised over as though the business in hand was finding a palace for a potentate: there was a high-security block at Itagui, but it might be a target for car bombs; there was a convent in El Poblado, but the nuns weren't selling. What about Medellin prison? The city fathers wouldn't wear it. Moreover, the prison guards had to be Antioquian; the police mustn't be left in charge of security outside the prison gates, for fear of reprisals against the inmate who had been responsible for the deaths of so many officers. At last a place was settled on. It was owned by one of Escobar's hangers-on. By a very Colombian irony, it was a rehab centre for drug addicts.

Alone among the cabbies I encountered in Colombia, Mario liked to drive without the accompaniment of the car radio. Also unusually, he wasn't particularly interested in discussing football and his country's chances against England in France '98 – perhaps because the citizens of Medellin were sick of thinking about Andres Escobar, the *capo*'s namesake, who was shot dead in the city after scoring an own goal during the World Cup finals of 1994. Most people seemed to think the player had been killed out of peevishness by a gambling syndicate, who had taken a bath on a bet following his error. It made me think with an unexpected tenderness of the match-fixing trials of Bruce Grobbelaar and the others which I had covered at Winchester Crown Court, the judge's limo drawing past Moss Bros at the end of each day's proceedings, the flashier barristers chatting up local girls in the wine bars.

Mario's taxi was leaving the city behind, winding up a hill lined on its lower slopes by single-storey houses with terracotta roofs. It might have been southern Italy. There was a brace of tethered mules, each with wooden boxes tied to its flanks. Presently we reached a fruit stall at a fork in the road. A man in a gigolo moustache recommended the right-hand turn. We travelled for perhaps a mile or so on an unmetalled road before arriving at high, red gates. The guidebook had talked about a police post outside the prison, the second-best of long-range photographs. But Mario seemed to know that these were the wrong gates. We backtracked to the fork, selecting the other turn this time, and found ourselves on a twisting route into the mountains. Greenery grew densely at the roadside, and it was only where this cover was broken that you could see how it otherwise masked a sheer drop. A truck laden with logs came down the hill towards us, pulling up dust from the road. Mario let the truck pass, a manoeuvre which involved reversing until my rear window overlooked the very lip of the precipice.

I felt quite safe. I mean, I felt *quite* safe. Excepting a brief brush with a boy on a push-bike in the suburbs of Medellin,

Mario seemed to know his stuff, but road safety wasn't upper-most in my mind in any case. It came down to mathematics: notwithstanding the departure of Escobar, as many as eighty people a week were meeting unlawful deaths in Medellin, a city of fewer than two million inhabitants.

It was a hot afternoon and all you could hear was the taxi rattling over stones, and birdsong. And then only the taxi. There was a couple mending a fence and, on the next bend, a line of children standing cheek by jowl against the sheer side of the mountain. They looked like characters from a nursery rhyme. I assumed I would know *La Catedral* when I saw it but just in case, there was a description in *News of a Kidnapping* to refer to:

'The basic construction displayed an elementary simplicity, with cement floors, tile roofs, and metal doors painted green. The administration area, in what had been [a] farmhouse, consisted of three small rooms, a kitchen, a paved courtyard, and a punishment cell. It had a dormitory measuring four hundred square metres, another large room to be used as a library and study, and six individual cells with private bathrooms. A common area in the centre, measuring six hundred square metres, had four showers, a dressing room, and six toilets. The remodelling had begun . . . with seventy workers who slept in shifts at the site for a few hours a day. The rough topography, the awful condition of the access road, and the harsh winter obliged them to do without trucks and carriers, and to transport most of the furnishings by muleback. First among them were two fifty-litre water heaters, military cots, and some two dozen small tubular armchairs, painted yellow. Twenty pots holding ornamental plants – araucarias, laurels, and areca palms – completed the interior decoration. Since the former rehabilitation centre had no telephone lines, the prison's initial communications would be by radio. The final cost of the project was 120 million *pesos*, paid by the municipality of Envigado.'

Mario's taxi rounded a corner and into sight on a far slope came what appeared to be a concrete-built motel. Or perhaps the remains of one. Even separated from it by a valley, you could tell that *La Catedral*, if that's what it was, was no longer the rosetted gulag of the early 1990s. There was a gatepost but no gates, and no sign of the police. A former guardhouse had been prettified and was now used by wildlife conservers; hanging baskets featured. It made me think of a stationmaster's house on a disused branch line. Were any of the plants reclaimed araucarias, laurels, or arecas?

There was nothing to stop Mario and me from driving up to the sacked-looking *Catedral*. It was largely horizontal, a pile of rubble and timber, the parts which remained upright boarded up and covered with half-hearted graffiti, the cleared ground printed with the tracks of heavy vehicles. I got out of the taxi and stepped over a barbed-wire fence. There were people in the ruins. At first I thought that they must be contractors, demolition men, but then I saw that two of them, in shorts and singlets, were doing their washing, pounding clothes on a board, working up a lather while a jet of water played from a hosepipe. A boy sharpening a knife was standing at the doorway of what was now evidently a squat. Inside, a pot simmered on a gas ring in a kitchen – perhaps the kitchen of the administration area. It had an 'elementary simplicity' now, all right: no lights, beachcombed furniture, a 'cement floor'. Two dark-skinned men ignored me, not looking up from a card game. They weren't at all put out: a *gringo* was no threat compared to Medellin council and a metal ball on the end of a crane. In the room next to the kitchen were homemade bunk beds, and a length of cable protruding from the cracked ceiling – all that was left of a light fitting. What had once been windows were now unglazed, the glass replaced with wood, to keep out the evening chill.

The only real indicator of *La Catedral*'s former grandeur beyond its considerable floorspace was what must have been the bathroom. It was next to the room with the bunk beds. The toilet facilities had been a point of bitter contention in the early days. A politician named Alberto Villamizar, whose wife,

Maruja, had been one of the Extraditables' hostages, had taken exception to an 'Italian-tiled bathroom' proposed for Escobar. 'He recommended changing it – and it was changed – to more sober decoration,' wrote Garcia Marquez. Looking at the bathroom, I wondered. As smallest rooms go, it was a good size, an impression heightened by the fact that the roof was missing – I liked the thought of Escobar in there, the man whose cocaine had been consumed in so many water-closets and lavatories: kings had their counting houses, but a powder room was surely the right surrounding in which to contemplate a drugs lord. His gaolers had allowed him to carry on his racketeering, his profiteering – in a word, his *laundering*. Water was spilling from a ruptured pipe but it was impossible not to notice that Escobar's *baño* remained sumptuously tiled throughout – in mocha, I would have said.

When even these italianate furbishings palled, Escobar and his crowd had escaped from *La Catedral*. Well, that was the official version: there had been a nod and a wink about it, according to any *medellino* you spoke to, the guards not about to stand in the way of the mighty *capo*. Or perhaps he had offered to make it worth their while, or perhaps even *they* believed that the man in the penthouse cell was *Robin Hood Paisa*. After 499 days at large, he was run to ground in 1993 by a force of 1,500 men. The somewhat portly fugitive – less Robin Hood and more Friar Tuck, by now – was disastrously glimpsed through the sights of police marksmen as he struggled over rooftops, and shot dead . . . He hadn't left Medellin; a call on his mobile phone to one of his children had undone him.

I considered a hand basin. The taps had been removed – had they been coated in something precious? Escobar had been a scourge, but Colombians like Garcia Marquez were entitled to apportion blame more widely, to talk about the 'primary responsibility' of the consuming nations. People killed each other in Colombia regardless of cocaine – they had been doing so in an unbroken line since my grandfather had been there, from *La Violencia* to the murderous excursions of the guerrillas and the paramilitaries – and the evidence appeared to be that drugs-related violence lagged behind other causes of summary morbidity, including out-and-out lawlessness. But it was difficult to travel through Colombia, to see what life was like there, without feeling a prickling of nausea about the careless recreational abuse which contributed to it all, a flare of contempt at the dreary glamour of it.

The authorities had pulled down *La Catedral*, or at least they had made a start. It was their solution to the always ticklish question of how to dispose of a monster's effects and familiars. They didn't want the people whom Escobar had helped, the families from the *barrios*, coming up to the prison, mooching about, missing him. It occurred to me that I would be one of the last people to see it intact, or still standing, at any rate. Colombia was still haunted by Escobar's ghost. The papers that morning carried reports that half a dozen of his former associates and henchmen had been convicted of an exhaustive slate of offences. They received jail terms totalling 206 years.

Mules were tethered in Escobar's old quarters. You could stand on top of this makeshift stable and gaze out across rolling agricultural land, the coveted *fincas* belonging to the prisoner's former neighbours. The spire of the redbrick *Catedral Metropolitana* in Parque de Bolivar was a distant, hazy surmise.

7

The Dry
World Cup

Was there always a full house at the Teatro Colon, I wondered, or did it have something to do with the new *ley seca*, the dry law, which banned the sale of alcohol in Bogota, but made allowances for the thirsts of respectable theatre-goers? Certainly, you couldn't fully appreciate the meaning of the term 'crush bar' until you'd seen them storming the deceptively amateurish trestle-table of drinks during the interval of *Las Leandras*. It wasn't as if the evening of traditional Spanish *zarzuela* entertainment was a surefire hit in its own right: imagine Gilbert and Sullivan, minus the social comment.

Faced with the rare conjunction of a presidential election and a World Cup match involving Colombia over the same long weekend, the authorities had imposed emergency restrictions on liquor. Looking in at my old haunt, the Stag's Head, I found that the snap temperance obtained even there. I watched Holland thrash South Korea over a mineral water. I was in one of the most notorious countries in the world, unable to buy a glass of beer, while in Europe, the cradle of law and civilisation, my drunken fellow countrymen were terrorising the hosts of France '98.

At the British Embassy, there was a new man in charge of issuing blood-chilling advice. He had a crew cut, and a manual for a Sig Sauer pistol on his desk. 'Have you been taking notes?' he asked me after he'd been out of the room for a moment. 'If you've been taking notes, I'll have to shoot you.' Colombia were playing Tunisia over the weekend, and England four days later. The advice from Our Man in Bogota was to beware of a backlash if English fans clashed with Colombians in France. There was a report on television warning that English hooligans, on the run from the *gendarmerie*, might turn up in Colombia: this was illustrated by mugshots of supposed trouble-makers, and what was claimed to be their fingerprints. The serious coverage and analysis, by contrast, concerned the national disaster of the 'Tino crisis'. This was the departure of 'Tino' Asprilla from the Colombian camp after he'd criticised the coach for substituting him during the team's 1–0 defeat by Romania. There had been a row in England after supremo Glenn Hoddle omitted an overweight Paul Gascoigne from his pool of players, but that had been a tremor besides the earthquake of Asprilla's exit. The hordes of Colombian media at the World Cup, who had hitherto confined themselves to rushing members of the national squad every time they stepped out of doors, abandoned this restraint where Asprilla was concerned, and rushed him indoors as well. On one occasion, the bulletins showed him walking along a French railway platform with his hand around one of the many microphones which had been thrust in his face. At first you marvelled at the player's composure: not only was he putting up with astonishing harassment, but he was going out of his way to make sure that the TV crews were picking up good sound. Then it dawned on you that he was holding on to stop himself from being swept under a train.

The outgoing President, Sr Samper, called for Asprilla's reinstatement. This enraged the man who had dropped him in the first place, Hernan Dario Gomez. Gomez announced that he would be throwing in the magic sponge as soon as the championships were over. As he must have known, Samper could not have got himself bigger headlines if he had walked off the job early himself.

The campaign to replace Samper as president was outstandingly tense. At a time when elections in stable Europe increasingly concerned themselves with the question 'Whose hand on the tiller?', the contest in Colombia came down to 'Who looks like he could fix a bilge pump and shoot a mutineer?' To pursue the maritime analogy, Colombia appeared to be in danger of sinking, dragged to the bottom by its crew of smugglers and brigands, the rest of the world not hastening to rescue the cartels' murderous barque under Samper's flag of convenience. In contrast to western polls, the battle in Colombia was glaringly ideological, and the ideologies couldn't have been more starkly ranged against each other. It was nothing less than a match between good and evil – though it was another thing to say that these ideologies found perfect representation in Colombia's two major parties, both of which looked and sounded and indeed behaved like centrist, catch-all political machines. A vote in one direction would tend to propel the country more steeply towards Davy Jones' locker; a vote the other way would tend to halt the slide. That was about the size of it. But at the turn of the millennium, after half a century of violence and upheaval, one prospective outcome offered a chance to travel in the right direction. The other offered nothing.

Hoping to keep Samper's Liberal Party in office was Horacio Serpa, a man who was never seen in public without his improbable disguise of thick glasses, bulbous nose and moustache. Serpa's big problem was that he had done Samper's dirty work for him, attempting to cover up the slush money from the Cali cartel. Serpa's rival was the Conservative, Andres Pastrana. His big problem was that he had been born with a silver spoon in his mouth. Both candidates had seen off the one conspicuous success of the process, the independent, female candidate, Noemi Sanin, who had come a close third in the first round and been eliminated. Her supporters had been going around town, updating pro-Noemi graffiti with an injunction to the electorate to vote *blanco* – there were also professional-looking posters along these lines. It wasn't a call to boycott the poll or an appeal to apathy. Strictly-speaking, there were three options on the ballot paper. Voters could either place a cross for Serpa, or for Pastrana, or say 'no' positively, so to speak, by registering a blank vote, by leaving a non-cross in a pristine space. It was assumed that even the long-suffering voters would eventually return a flesh-and-blood entrant of one affiliation or the other. All the same, it was an election with a touch of the scratchcard about it, and Colombians could, if they chose, stick or twist for a president.

Ivan, the simultaneous translator, drove me out to the offices of *El Tiempo*: I was going to see Ernesto Cortez, one of the paper's political correspondents. *El Tiempo* was as fortified as a military base or a mint, encircled by a high metal fence. At the guardhouse, they swept under Ivan's Twingo with a mirror, as though we were at an RUC checkpoint. This would have happened even if a presidential election campaign hadn't been at its height. In September 1997, a bomb of no less than 550 lbs was left in a car outside newspaper offices in Medellin. It was claimed in the name of the Extraditables, who had evidently survived the loss of their most famous member, Pablo Escobar – for a long time, it was assumed that the Extraditables *were* Escobar. The group released a letter saying the device, which was made safe, had been planted in response to moves to lift Colombia's ban on the extradition of drug-traffickers and others. The Extraditables signed off with the rubric: 'We prefer a tomb in Colombia to a jail in the United States.'

Ernesto Cortez was fresh from organising an office ballot: among the journalists, Pastrana had trounced Serpa, seventy to forty-four, but there had been many blank votes. The editorial staff were out of line with the leader writers – it was a Liberal paper so it backed Serpa, Cortez told me. He was young, curly-haired, with a button-down shirt over a T-shirt: you might have taken him for a journalist, but you would probably have made a stab at an American one; a preppy op-ed columnist, perhaps. The election campaign proper had been very emotional, he said, the links between the outgoing government and the *narcos* had seen to that. Serpa had been playing the populist card for all he was worth, Pastrana struggling to maintain a more outward-looking, internationalist position. 'He has a lot of the world in him,' was Cortez's singular expression.

'But does the result matter to the outside world?'

'Yes, very much. If Pastrana wins, a much more optimistic message will go out from Colombia. He has allies in the United States and Europe.'

'And if Serpa wins?'

'You will see a big crisis. Many investors will pull out, I think.'

I thought I would spend some time with Serpa's chief ghost-writer – that had to be a tough job, I thought, a hard sell. What was left for the candidate to say, other than 'Sorry' or 'I quit'? Sr Huber was a young man with his teeth in braces who was responsible for putting the jokes into Serpa's campaign publication, *Mamola*. *Mamola* was either an ironic way of saying 'Sure!', or a straight up-and-down way of saying 'Screw you!', and the publication was comparable to a student rag-week magazine. It drew its inspiration from the coarse rhetorical style of the candidate, who had once called the United States ambassador *gringo maluco*, which might be translated as 'evil foreigner'. When I called on Sr Huber at Serpa HQ, he was looking up from a word processor and asking an aide, 'How do you spell "shameful"?' I asked him how could he put such crude stuff into the mouth of his boss.

'Colombian culture is full of refrains, something we have inherited from Spain,' said Sr Huber. 'A sentence uttered by a *campesino* might have one of these refrains in it. Sr Serpa has made use of this language and people like it; it's a different way of doing politics in Colombia.'

'But "Screw you"?'

'Serpa is a statesman,' said Huber. The hutzpah would have been breathtaking even without the teeth braces. 'He's manifested that. He's also a man of law. He's contributed a serious and coherent discourse –'

'– haven't you got *anything* nice to say about him?'

Huber smiled. He could produce trashy copy when it suited him, and talk highfalutin, too, when that suited him. I asked him which of Serpa's dubious one-liners and off-colour zingers he was most proud of.

'That would be disloyal,' he said with a trained simper. 'All merit should go to the candidate.' Some merit had clearly been rubbing off on the candidate, the rough-diamond stuff going down well in the countryside, some opinion surveys giving him a thin edge over Pastrana, and all sorts of people queuing at campaign HQ to get involved, to get a little piece: amid the vital swirl of student gofers and Dunkin Donut boys, there were *mestizos* wrapped in blankets and a retiree in houndstooth wanting to write out a cheque.

But the second ballot lay ahead. Like the professional that he was, Huber rehearsed the problems the Serpa side was encountering: the other man had all the media contacts, the friends in high places; the Liberals had reached out to the ordinary people of Colombia instead, but a money-raising drive, a 'Serpathon', had proved a bit of a disappointment. This was the party's Achilles heel, of course, campaign finance.

'That's something that's part of the past,' said Huber. 'The nation has learnt the lesson. We've taken every precaution to prevent any infiltration of drug money into our campaign and so have the other campaigns.'

Other precautions had to be considered in a Colombian election. If anything went wrong in the next couple of days, Sr Huber could find himself a ghostwriter to a ghost. I gathered that Serpa had a bulletproof vest – his actuaries would have insisted – but that he didn't care for it. 'He tends to break with security arrangements. He trusts the people,' said Huber.

'You're his spin doctor as well, aren't you?'
'Let's just say I'm his image adviser.'

Bogota felt like a city cut off. Many people had left town for the weekend. Hotels were empty; where I was staying, Bolivar's old quarters, the porters had wrestled with each other to carry my bag. Telecommunications workers, opposing moves towards privatisation, were threatening to pull the plug on international and long-distance phone links; the government was putting armed police on the picket lines. Travelling out of the capital by road was rated extremely dangerous by the British Embassy; there would be high tension, said the man with the crew cut. In Bogota itself, there was the unrelieved here-and-now of the *ley seca*. What to do on Saturday evening except go to Mass at the St Ignatius Church, wander the Plaza de Bolivar, where notices about the hustings had been pinned up under the arches of the wormy Edificio Lievano, gatecrash a wedding at the candy-striped Iglesia del Carmen? The bride and groom attended the priest on chairs, hers draped in white cloth. Apart from what looked like a bustle over her backside, her dress might have been seen in any parish church any Saturday. Had Leslie's woman longed for a day like this?

The tolling of the St Ignatius bell woke me on the day the president would be elected. There were armed police beneath my window, and strolling *tinto*-salesmen in white overalls, gleaming urns on their backs like jet-packs. The *bogotanos* called them the Ghostbusters. As I was dressing, there was a knock at my door. When I answered it, there was no one there. There really *was* no one there – I was the only guest for breakfast and the waiter whose job it was to keep the coffee cups topped up relinquished the jug to me. The knock at my door had been a movement of air around the empty central courtyard of the hotel.

From the Plaza de Bolivar, I watched the mountain tops go in and out of cloud the colour of cigarette smoke. It was drizzling, and voting was taking place in little green tents at the edge of the square. There were detachments of *Policia del Congreso* and *Policia Nacional Explosivos*, and two nuns, and a nut-brown man in a jacket and tie going on with the business of persuading people to have their picture taken as though it was any other day. An inscription on a wall in the plaza said, 'Guns gave us independence, laws will give us liberty.'

It was busy in the centre, *bogotanos* on their way to vote, or taking the chance of stretching their legs before the curfew of expected lawlessness. The polls were tipping Serpa, though no one you spoke to was for him; everyone was afraid of what would happen if he got in. There would be trouble, and after that something even worse: nothing, nothing changing. The shops were shut. Only the news vendors in their bathing-hut stalls were at their station, and the men selling things on the pavement – posters, utensils such as scissors and pliers.

The Stag's Head was full of policemen eating lunch. They watched an Iranian score a goal against the *gringos* of the United States and turned to each other and laughed. There was a line of cars going past the window of the restaurant all afternoon long, horns blaring, and voices crying 'Serpa! Serpa!'; and from somewhere in Candelaria, the sound of a gunshot. And then after voting had ended at four o'clock, and the website graphics on television began telling the story of Serpa's defeat – the defeat of the Liberal Party which had treated with the *narcotraficos* – the people driving past the Stag's Head were cheering 'Pastrana! Pastrana!' The winner appeared on television with his family to say that he intended to serve all Colombians, a speech which was heard in the capital against the crack and rumble of fireworks. More than twelve million people had turned out to vote, an unusually high proportion. Pastrana had beaten his rival by about a million and a half votes, admirers of Noemi Sanin apparently transferring their support to him in the decisive round. The number of *votos en blanco*, representing citizens who had chosen to stick rather than twist, was 372,749.

With Ivan, I drove to the north of the city. It was nose-to-tail Pastrana supporters, some of whom presumably had an allegiance stretching back even further than the four or five hours since his triumph had been confirmed. They were in new-model sports cars, four-by-fours – or, in several cases, out of them: leaning from windows twirling flags; springing from doors to samba deliriously in taillights. 'Can you imagine what this would be like with alcohol?' said Ivan. It was the voice Truman Capote would have had if he'd had a Latin American upbringing; the voice if not the sentiment. Generally speaking, the *ley seca* appeared to be holding, although at one intersection we watched a driver hand a chunky bottle of spirits through the window of the landcruiser pulled up alongside his.

By the flashing light of an ambulance, medics were cradling a figure who was half on the road and half off it. The ambulance's hatchback door was open and the medics were trying to lift someone inside. A group of teenagers were looking on anxiously from the kerb. As we got nearer, it was clear that the figure was struggling, flailing its legs – and that those weren't medics, they were the police, the ambulance a Black Maria, only painted white. The last we saw of the police, they were trying to cram the door down on a pair of shoes, like people who couldn't fit everything into the car when going on holiday.

Ivan and I went Dutch at a place that did crêpes. At the next table, a boy was leaning across to his girlfriend, so close that their foreheads were almost touching. Ivan, the dentist's son, said, 'He wants to be an orthodontist.'

In contrast to the atmosphere earlier that night, Bogota was silent by the time we returned to Candelaria. The right man had won, but the self-imposed curfew obtained anyway. A car had been abandoned, its lights still on, at a crazy angle in the middle of the road. Everyone was off the streets; everyone who was anyone. Leaving only people who were nobodies: a woman was on her haunches, sifting through trash, panning refuse; there were hoboes, destitutes, desperadoes, sometimes singly, sometimes in groups – but Ivan piloted the slight and lonely Twingo in complete unconcern; the same Ivan who'd once resisted counting *pesos* in a bank on safety grounds, who'd shuddered at the hazards of transporting them to his own bank (it was the money he had been concerned for, I saw now, rather than his own personal safety), who had struggled with himself at the crêpe restaurant before settling the tip of 1,000 *pesos* – say, 50p – out of his own pocket. The odd thing was that Ivan came from a well-to-do family. His father had pioneered dental braces for the offspring of Bogota's elite; his brother did the teeth of the children of the president-elect; there were maids.

There was a news flash on the car radio: a comment on the election result from ex-president Betancur. 'Is he still around?' I said. 'You don't hear much about him.'

'He's like Nixon,' said Ivan.

Betancur was in office in 1985 when a terrible conflagration at the courts of justice, on one side of the Plaza de Bolivar, consumed an entire generation of judges. They had been held hostage in the building by thirty-five members of the guerrilla faction, M19, but had been in contact with Betancur by telephone. 'They said, "For God's sake, make a deal",' Ivan told me. But the military warned the president that if he caved in to M19, the generals would overthrow him. 'He wouldn't even come to the phone any more after that.' The army went in, backed by tanks, rockets and helicopter-gunships, and the building went up. Officially, about a hundred people died, including eleven supreme court judges. Perhaps the purposes of a number of people were served by the extermination of Colombia's judicial class. Ivan said, 'None of the relatives would allow anyone from the government to go to the funerals.' No one was ever tried and an official inquiry claimed that most deaths were attributable to the guerrillas rather than the army. These findings were contested by a prominent human rights lawyer, Eduardo Umana Mendoza, who also alleged that the true death toll had been 150. He claimed that at least sixty bodies had been buried in a mass grave; it was opened in 1998 after he won a court order for exhumation. On 18 April, Umana was murdered in his office in Bogota, shot twice in the head by gunmen, posing as TV journalists, who had bound and gagged his secretary.

Ivan was an admirer of the revolutionaries of M19 – Ivan with his exclusive health club and his bank account in Philadelphia. They had done 'bold, innovative, creative, daring things,' he said, citing the theft of Simon Bolivar's sword. 'They said they would hold on to it until Colombia was governed for the benefit of the people.' The Twingo rounded a dark and pot-holed corner. 'Many of my friends were in M19,' said the scion of Bogota's first family of dentistry.

There was no more gunfire in Candelaria, and no disturbances in the night, but in the morning there were armed men under the window for the third day running – the third day of the *puente*, the long weekend of elections and the World Cup, the third day of *ley seca*. On its front page, *El Tiempo* said, '*Hoy es el dia definitivo*' but it wasn't referring to the change in government. '*Colombia debe ganar o ganar a Tunez si quiere mantenerse con vida en el Mondial.*' In the World Cup, Colombia had to win or *win* against Tunisia to have any life. Here was the nation's paper of record solemnly honouring the insight of the late Liverpool manager Bill Shankley, that football wasn't a matter of life and death – it was more important than that.

Countries with economic problems, galloping inflation, had more banknotes than you could keep up with; every time I looked, the Colombians, struggling to put a lid on runaway violence, had issued a new militia. One identified as the presidential guard had taken up a position outside the Stag's Head that morning, presumably because it was the nearest place to the presidential palace which had a TV set. They wore olive

tunics boasting many flashes and patches, webbings and belt-
ings, epaulettes and brooches. But during the country's
hyperinflation of violence, no two military characters had the
same face value: so this guardsman had a CS gas cannister on
his belt; that secured the holster of his pistol around his thigh
with a bootlace. As they were relieved, troopers took off their
helmets and joined us in the pub: ironically, I was better protected in Bogota than I had ever been in my life. President-to-be
Pastrana could not have been more densely thicketed with
muscle. The soldiers ate crisps and savoury biscuits. One
frowningly stirred crunchy cereal into a pot of yoghurt.
Uniformed troops somehow looked absurd dining on these
rations: I thought of a day trip I'd once made to the Great Wall of
China in the company of the formidable Red Guard, who had
passed high-smelling hard boiled eggs around the coach.

On the television screen, a Tunisian forward headed against
the post. There were cries of 'Oooh!' from the presidential
guard. 'Wheesh!' went the soldier next to me. The guardsmen
who were still on duty followed the action through the windows of the pub. Bright sunlight caught the decoration on one
battledress lapel. It appeared to be a foil-wrapped after-dinner
mint.

In France, Colombia's Valencia shot over the bar. 'Wheesh!'
repeated my neighbour, a bottle of Coke suspended on its way to
his lips. There were disparaging remarks about the *negro* who
had missed, and laughter as a cut-away showed him contritely
slapping his forehead. What the crowd in the bar seemed to
enjoy most was the sight of their stars suffering calamities. It
had been the same in a cinema at Manizales, where I had gone
to see the blockbuster *Titanic*: the audience cackled as each gur-
gling death was reenacted.

Somebody brought a radio into the Stag's Head for the second
half. I had thought the television coverage of the tournament
was hysterical, commentators demonstrating the Latin talent of
'singing a goal', but it was nothing compared to the radio output
I heard: forty-five minutes of shouting fire in a crowded theatre.

The television set stayed on, and by the time the picture cut away from the action to reveal the pundits in their moustaches and headsets, you were ready to think of them fondly, perhaps as the coolly monosyllabic flight crew of an airship which was unhurriedly circling Montpellier. You could almost forgive the steady march of commercials around the edge of the screen: a cheery beer ad aired as a Tunisian was stretchered in pain from the field. I never saw a commercial clash with a goal – a credit of a sort, I suppose, to the wretched director who was playing in the sponsors' stings and jingles. The crowd in the pub was slower to warm up than the broadcasters, but they stirred themselves as a Colombian scrapped with an opponent, and there was a cry of '*Solo!*', go it alone, as a yellow shirt was put through on goal. The chance was missed – 'Aiee!' went the guardsmen – and moments later a shot trickled past the Tunisian posts: applause, sardonic laughter. Aristizabal put a free kick wide, to growls.

Carlos Valderrama, that busy hippy, passed to the substitute Preciado, on for the tiring Valencia. One touch from Preciado, holding off his man; then another, a shot – and the ball was in the net! The presidential guard sprang to their feet, cheering and clapping, shouting Preciado's name, muffling the operatic confirmation of his goal from the television, which cut to the Colombian dug-out to find coach Gomez looking like a man on death row who has just received a letter from the governor. Outside, the car horns began singing the goal, and they went on all day and into the night, celebrating Colombia's 1–0 victory, and heralding the match against *Inglaterra*, which suddenly became the crunch game for both countries after England's 2–1 defeat by Romania. The jubilation was wilder than on Sunday night for Pastrana's election, the continued lack of alcohol failing to prevent *bogotanos* happily flour-bombing each other's cars, a traditional expression of joy. Another way of looking at it was that the win in the World Cup prolonged and intensified the euphoria of the long weekend, which had turned out in a way Colombians had scarcely dared hope for. In the Plaza that

afternoon, there were children's rides and a man blowing bub-
bles, and at the presidential palace, they were changing the
guard. The chancellery responsible for producing new denom-
inations of armed Colombians, for minting new insignia, had
reached the zenith of its presumption with a batch of enlisted
men who were clearly counterfeit even to the naked eye – they
were wearing spiked helmets, as though they had been cos-
tumed by a wistful, fugitive Nazi, as perhaps they had. There
were drums that mimicked gunfire, drums that mimicked rain,
to mark the passing of the rainy season, the end of the dry law.

Ivan and I were going to be in Medellin on the day of the big
game. That ought to be interesting, I thought: Medellin, where
the independent-minded Antioquians weren't inclined to go on
the wagon just because the *bogotanos* couldn't handle their
drink; where the defender Andres Escobar was shot dead after
his own goal put Colombia out of the previous World Cup finals
of 1994. If England beat Colombia or even drew against them,
they would be out again. What would it be like to be an
Englishman in Medellin if *los ingleses* were responsible for
sending them home in disappointment?

The murder of Andres Escobar had never been satisfactorily
cleared up. There was some suggestion of a row outside a nightclub, and the dismal truth of it was that getting shot in Medellin
was just one of those things, international footballer or no. But
most people thought drug dealers had been involved – the real
shock would have been if they hadn't – perhaps paying Escobar
back for inadvertently costing them a number of their narco-dol-
lars in bets. There appeared to be a precedent, in the 1993
murder of Omar Dario Canas, a striker with Atletico Nacional
and a protégé of Pablo Escobar. Many Colombians suspected
that the Cali cartel had killed him in order to hurt their rival.

The *narcos* had penetrated soccer wherever you looked,
either directly or through their proxies. A government survey
concluded that the cartels owned 80 per cent of the top five

clubs: Atletico Nacional and Envigado of Medellin; America and Deportivo of Cali; and Millonarios of Bogota. The national side was made up of the past and present stars of these clubs, though no blame clung to anyone in the proud *amarillo* of the national jersey.

Professional football had proved an ideal environment for laundering money. The druglord Gonzalo Rodrigo Gacha, otherwise known as the Mexican, was the owner of the Millonarios: after he was ambushed and killed by security forces, it emerged that he had been paying the players' wages and bonuses in (undeclared) drugs money. The former head of Colombia's soccer federation, Juan José Bellini, was sentenced to six years in jail for laundering cash for the Cali cartel. He was a friend of the Orejula brothers and an ex-director of the America club. Before a championship decider in December 1997, the crowd observed a minute's silence for the death of the Orejulas' mother. It became a joke in Cali that the safest time to walk the streets was when America were playing at home, because all the villains would be sitting innocently in the stands. In September 1997, a Bogota swat team on the trail of kidnappers who had seized a businessman waited until Colombia scored in a World Cup qualifier, and burst in to find the gangsters off-guard, celebrating.

The goal which had secured Colombia's place in France '98 was scored by a one-time America player, Anthony de Avila, who dedicated it live on television to the Orejulas. A former prosecutor-general called Alfonso Validivieso, who had shown an interest in the presidential race, criticised de Avila's remarks, only to see his popularity plunge: he promptly ruled himself out of the hustings.

Knowing the passions that football aroused, and the unhealthy company it kept, I wasn't about to go to into the Uzi-bristling streets of Medellin as a supporter of Colombia's *gringo* opponents without taking precautions. I would have Ivan with me, it was true. But you learnt something about a man when you watched him scuttle across a street with a bag of your money under his arm, something that didn't necessarily fill you with confidence – I can't explain it. All I knew was that I couldn't rely on Ivan to save my neck. The International Committee of the Red Cross had launched an appeal to Colombians to bury their differences with a 'Fair Play' campaign, tied to the football championships. All very well meant, no doubt, but in the circumstances, a little self-defence was called for. By the time Ivan and I took a *colectivo* into the city, I'm not ashamed to admit that I was packing a piece. And when we sat down at a crowded bar on *La Setenta*, Seventieth Street, to watch the match, the first thing I did was to produce my piece, putting it right out on the table in front of me where everyone could see it. I had everybody's attention immediately: I could tell by their faces. I knew smirking when I saw it.

'Excuse me, why have you got a statue of Valderrama?' managed the mother of a boy in a Colombian headband.

I held it up so that she could get a better look: my piece was a somewhat crude affair, certainly; not the acme of the potter's art, the famous coiffure rather lifeless, you could argue, the eyes a little dull. I had only paid a few *pesos* for it at a souvenir stall in Cali, after all. But the Colombians could tell who it was meant to be, and that was the main thing. The doorstop Valderrama was in his familiar No. 10 top, and holding a clay football. I said, 'It's to protect me.'

The boy's father said, 'But the hooligans are all in France.'

'That's right,' I laughed. That was a bit off, wasn't it? The man was smiling, but that didn't tell you anything. By 'hooligans' he meant the English, I supposed. *I* was English, though I had my bust of Valderrama as a sign of my lightly worn internationalism. I remembered what the security officer at the Embassy had told me about a backlash if there was trouble between England and Colombia fans. I hadn't heard of any. It was England's third match and the *gendarmerie* had already had a good look at our hard cases – perhaps they had all been locked up or sent home; perhaps the defeat by Romania was concentrating their minds on the *other* reason for being in France: the, you know, football.

But the father of the boy in the Colombia headband had alerted me to the true precariousness of my position. I had always known that I had to worry if Colombia were sent packing – look what the *medellinos* had done to poor Andres Escobar, and he was one of their own, for pity's sake, not a supporter of the other side. Now I had to worry if Colombia *won*: England would be out of France '98, more than enough provocation for the nutters at the fixture to vent their disappointment on any Colombians they could lay their hands on. That could all come back on me in Medellin. I had to hope for an outcome in which everyone's honour was satisfied, such as a flood.

But that would come too late to prevent the kick-off: on the television set visible from our sunny sidewalk, the game was about to get underway beneath the floodlights of Stade Felix Bollaert, Lens. Everyone in Medellin had stopped what they were doing and come down to *La Setenta* to watch. The people who would have been on *La Setenta* anyway, because that was their place of employment – the police, the road sweepers, the shoeshines, even the men selling the supporters their flags and horns – they had all stopped what they were doing as well. The cafés and bars were lined so deeply that the people at the back were standing in the middle of the road, but it didn't matter because all the traffic had stopped too. I wasn't so full of my own problems that I didn't feel for the bank customers standing in a long line at the Caja Agraria – imagine being stuck in a queue at the bank when Colombia were playing England in the World Cup! The ref blew his whistle. There was a roar along *La Setenta*. I glanced round at the bank: the customers were stationary. My heart went out to them. An earringed Colombian called Rincon was on the ball: he looked like a pirate, I thought. The queue at Caja Agraria hadn't moved. I shook my head at this and Ivan said, 'They have TV at the bank.'

We had picked one of the most crowded bars on the street, *Las Reminiscencias*: football fans and families and office workers yelled and clapped every time a Colombian touched the ball. Agog, a bevy of meaty blondes chewed gum with their mouths open. A beauty in a shiny vest blew a perfect, involuntary smoke-ring. The barmaid, a woman with curly ginger tresses and a halterneck pants-suit, brought *aguilas* to our table. I was cheered by the beer, and by a man in a wheelchair who was watching the game in a custardy fright-wig clearly inspired by Valderrama. I had been right to identify with this exotic character: I almost didn't care that the bust on my table made me look like an exam candidate with a favourite gonk. On the screen, the real Valderrama was trying to impose himself on the play. He was as old as me, I thought, probably older, having admitted in various preview articles and scene-setting interviews to different ages in the upper thirties. The Colombians guyingly called him *El Pibe*, the Big Kid. I studied that hair. It was more like a mane, or even a coat. No question, Valderrama had the look of a world champion about him, although you felt more than ever that the stage on which he ought to have been proving this was Cruft's.

The game was going well for Colombia; that is, it wasn't going badly: they were the underdogs, so it came to the same thing. And then Darren Anderton scored for England.

One–nil! England were ahead! Surely we were going through!

I did what any red-blooded Englishman would have done in the circumstances: I swallowed hard, and looked at the table, and held on to Valderrama by his china jersey. Provocatively, I pretended to take no interest in the action-replays of the goal, giving my full attention to the label of my *aguila* bottle instead. I was expecting a bar brawl out of a Hollywood western – drinks swept from tables, chairs cracked across shoulders, bulletholes in bat-wing doors – only gingered up for the Medellin milieu of the late 1990s with *aguardiente* and automatic fire. But the bar was silent. The most dramatic reaction was that of a bald man standing by our table, who died of shock: his body underwent immediate rigor mortis; his hands clamped themselves to his thighs; he emitted a low, gargling noise, which was interpreted by the waitress as a plea for another drink. Never mind the bar, the street was silent: *La Setenta* where Andres Escobar had partied his last night away. The only sound came from the television sets in the bars and banks: an ad was airing around the margin of the picture. I considered developments in France: the comforting thing was that the odds on the *medellinos* beating me up in revenge for English fans beating up Colombian fans in revenge for Colombia beating England – these had lengthened. The less comforting thing was that the reverse was true of the odds on the *medellinos* beating me up in revenge for England beating Colombia. The father of the boy in the Colombian headband asked me a sinisterly innocuous question. 'Which team does Batty play for?' he said. His wife attempted to lull me into a false sense of security with a delicious slice of green mango.

The Colombians kicked off again. After seeing their side go behind, the crowd at *Las Reminiscencias* were slow to warm to the action. It was only relief that made them applaud when Farid Mondragon, the goalkeeper, plucked the ball off Alan Shearer's head. While they were doing this, I celebrated the English goal by demanding more beer from the barmaid with an uninhibited nod. As long as the result stays like this, I thought, registering the award of a free kick in England's favour; as long as we don't rub it in – after all, we are supposed to be the stronger side: what did the Colombians seriously think was going to happen? It must have been a foul on the edge of the area, I thought. Yes, I might still be all right here, provided England don't go and score – another goal! A David Beckham special, a chip over the wall by the other bottle blond on the pitch: I *never* liked him, I thought, replacing my hand on Valderrama's plaster garment, certain this time of a blizzard of swept drinks, cracked furniture, ammunition.

Instead, the father of the boy in the Colombian headband said, 'The British are superior', and everyone who could hear him nodded ruefully. Leaning against the handlebars of a parked moped, a policeman thoughtfully stroked his chin. The

man who had died took a long draught of *costena*. The waitress
came round with *empanadas*: hot potato snacks. It was half-
time, and many of the people on *La Setenta* were finishing their
drinks and going away, going home. There was the sound of
crates being stacked, and of fireworks being let off – someone
had paid money for them, after all, and what was the point of
fireworks if you didn't let them off? Colombia had to score three
times to stay in the World Cup, but I thought the *medellinos*
were being a little defeatist, myself. I didn't think it was all
over for the *amarillos*. That was the view of a cautious England
fan – and an anxious Englishman. I *hoped* it wasn't all over for
me, did I mean?

Colombian TV brought us the grim insights of the mousta-
chioed, ear-muffed commentary team in their zeppelin over
Lens – pilot and co-pilot with some bad news to tell us involving loss of altitude. I imagined what the pundits were saying
back home – in all the replaying of, and wallowing in, the
England goals, would someone find a moment to talk about
'temperament', I wondered, to expound forgivingly on the lack
of 'character' in the Colombian side? Was this what I was seeing
on the emptying *La Setenta*, a lack of character?

Gomez, the Colombian coach, rang the changes in the second
half. He withdrew *Chico* Serna, Leider Preciado, who had
scored against Tunisia, and Anthony de Avila, whose goal had
enabled Colombia to qualify for France '98, and who had dedicated his effort to the Orejula brothers. On came Victor
Aristizabal, *Tren* Valencia and Hamilton Ricard, who played
his club football near me, at Middlesbrough in the north-east of
England. The remaining audience at *Las Reminiscencias* voiced
its confidence in Gomez's tactics. 'Ten–nil,' said a pawky, grey-
haired man.

Valderrama got bogged down in the English box. 'What an
idiot!' said a woman. The father of the boy in the headband
covered his eyes. His wife said, 'We've got to score at least one
goal, for honour's sake.' In Lens, there was a Mexican wave,
and hearty England fans linked hips in a conga. In the bar,

someone cried, '*Gol, gol, gol!*': the TV was showing England's
Michael Owen on the ball, bearing down threateningly on the
Colombian defence – the *medellinos* were now rooting for *us*. It
must have been the bloody-minded *paisa* individualism I had
read about. 'When will a Colombian run like him?' said the
father of the boy in the headband. 'The only one we have is Tino
and he's out.' The boy in the headband himself was no longer
looking at the screen at all, but drinking Coke and drumming
his shoes against his chair. A Colombian striker essayed an overhead kick. The commentator went mad but the crowd at the bar
weren't fooled. The meaty blondes didn't even look up from
their conversation: the shot was off-target. England's Lee came
on for Anderton. Shearer and Palacio bumped into each other:
they sat and held their ears.

A glum man appeared at my side wearing a hat-cum-brolly in
Colombian colours: it was the *empanada* salesman. A camera-
man offered a close-up of a labouring Valderrama. '*El Pibe se
esta derretiendo!*' someone said, 'The Big Kid is melting!' and
the *empanada* salesman nudged me and said: 'Why do they
call Valderrama "Viagra"? Because he holds everything up for
ninety minutes.' There wasn't a lack of character on *La Setenta*,
I decided, but a fine display of it, defeat accepted with mocking
humour. The father of the headbanded boy said, 'If Colombia
had won, the whole street would be blocked,' and I saw that an
England win was a good result for me, after all, and that the
most dangerous outcome would have been a Colombian victory, not out of any malice, but the exuberance of the
celebrations; it would have been a *fiesta* to top the revels after
the Tunisia game, the presidential election – even the lethally
high-spirited Love and Friendship Day, 20 September, the day
when Colombians love the most and kill the most.

In the closing moments, Owen was unsophisticatedly
brought down. One of the commentators came through from
the gondola of the winded dirigible over Lens: 'This is the reality of our football,' he said, all bluster gone. Shearer took the
free kick. Mondragon saved – no thanks to his defence.

'*Hijodeputa!*' exclaimed the father of the headbanded boy, 'Son of a bitch!'

The whistle went. A group of fans at their table entered the final result uncomplainingly in their World Cup logs, and the waitress came out onto the street and removed a Colombian flag from an awning. The television commentator whose job description included singing goals went into a Wagnerian passage: 'We've been eliminated . . . we leave sadly. The goalie alone has shown that we have soccer. He's saved the day. We would have gone down ten–nil but for Farid Mondragon.' Mondragon had taken over the national gloves from the eccentric René Higuita, who was known for his dribbling and trademark 'scorpion' overhead clearance. Higuita had visited Pablo Escobar at *La Catedral*, and was briefly jailed for his part in a kidnapping, thought to have been connected to a cocaine deal. His replacement, Mondragon, was weeping as he left the field in France, carrying on the tradition of colourful Colombian custodians. It was an exit which would do for Mondragon's career what the tears of the absent Paul Gascoigne had once done for his, though in the *Las Reminiscencias* Restaurant and Bar, it was met with a round of ironic laughter and applause.

The next morning, the headline in *El Tiempo* was *Que Horror!* and one columnist was likening *los ingleses* to the mighty TGV train in France, the Colombians to the *Aguardiente Express*. In my hotel room, I knocked over my bust of Valderrama and the clay football broke off.

8

Naked Parade

There were bras like motorcycle helmets in the market at Plaza Bolivar, Medellin, and a stall selling rodent poison – on the lethal sachets lay the corpses of a rat and a mouse, by way of testimonials. There was a metro stop at Plaza Bolivar, although it wasn't the first one I'd come to: a taxi driver had dropped me elsewhere along the line, but there a soldier was barring the way to the platforms, also a woman in what were presumably metro colours – a fetching two-tone tie, the longer stem green, the shorter, yellow. She'd explained that there was a *problema industrial* at the next stop. I'd been obliged to pick up another cab and vault over the strike-bound section of the system.

This probably wasn't a very representative experience of Medellin's mass transit scheme. In the heart of the city, you heard it swishing overhead like a curtain rail – it looked like Escobar's most audacious attempt to launder his dirty money in public, and it was evidently the most modern thing in the country. The stations were clean, the platforms broad and shady and paved in a matt marble or granite. When I finally boarded a metro train, it was fast and smooth and air-conditioned and there was no graffiti, only polite notices injuncting the wearing of loud headsets. It was as good as, better than, anything in Europe. And, as far as I could make out, there was nothing funny about the money, after all. It cost $1.8 billion, half of this sum borrowed by the Colombians from Germany and Spain and other overseas creditors. Extraordinary local taxes on tobacco and petrol were chipping away at the debt. The *medellinos* were hopping on and off more than 130,000 times a day and their fares were helping the metro to pay for itself. Work had begun in 1985 but the network had been ten years in the making: it floated above the city on concrete pillars, reducing disruption of city traffic to a minimum (fares were pegged slightly above the *buseta* rate, to avoid putting bus drivers out of work); engineers had had to lay some thirty kilometres of track for the two lines, which met each other in a textbook right angle; the precincts of the metro had been enterprisingly landscaped to make room for pedestrianised areas, parks, cafés and street markets like the one at Plaza Bolivar; according to the *Colombia Handbook*, sections of the route were distinguished by trees with different coloured blossoms – red flowering near Berrío station, yellow erupting between Alpujarra and Exposiciones, pink busting out at Prado – though I regret that I didn't detect any evidence of this splendid finishing touch.

Medellin had a history as a go-ahead city. There had been horse-drawn trams in the 1880s, and electric trams in 1921, and trolleybuses in the 1930s – *medellinos* loved the idea that they had trumped Bogota by getting a metro. The project had been a live one since the 1950s, since Leslie's day. It wasn't the sort of railway he was used to, a sooty loco dragging freight wagons to port and back again. But perhaps he read about it in the newspapers, thought about getting involved – any excuse to put off returning to the cold and damp of England – mulling it over with a whisky on the veranda at Mariquita.

I sat on one of the green benchseats of my metro train, listening to the conductor calling the stations over the public

address system, watching the people of Medellin as they went
about their pursuits. The city came to life as if in a child's sto-
rybook: *See! People play tennis, on the smart, clay, country club
courts! Look! Boys play football!*

The city was in the throes of *La Feria Taurina de la
Candelaria*, the bullfight season. On *La Setenta*, the boulevard
where *medellinos* of all descriptions spent at least part of any
good night out, musicians with trumpets and tubas formed up at
restaurants to play the preposterous Latin oompah which was
meant to stir the blood for the bouts of the coming day. There
was nothing Antioquians liked better than a tune with a good
martial rhythm and lyrics dwelling on bloodshed: nostalgic
bambucos – ballads; *carrilera* music which spoke of treachery,
revenge, bitterness; romantic airs like *La Cuchilla* – 'If you don't
love me, I'll slash your face' – the kind of thing you were liable
to hear when people went out to get drunk, even if they happened to be respectable businessmen. Among the diners on *La
Setenta*, the men all had cowboy hats – they had them the way
actors have props: these weren't the shapeless working *sombreros* of the Puerto Berrio *vaqueros*, but a range of impeccable
accessories aimed at the ranch-hand inside every Medellin
executive. Pert women, much younger than the men, sat at their
tables, and the atavistic Antioquian scene was completed for
them by the arrival of possees, to the clanging of hooves on
tarmac: these were other weekend cowpokes like themselves, in
hats and chaps, jovially extorting tribute from the restaurateurs
in the form of slugs of *aguardiente*. Everyone was getting in the
mood for *La Feria*.

I had once been to a bullfight in Madrid. Nothing I'd seen or
read had prepared me for the shock: I'd had no idea it was so
civilised. The *madrilenos* watched proceedings from leather
cushions, and high-concept event-catering – baguettes boasting
a ham so laboriously cured it was practically distilled – reinforced an impression that you were attending opera rather than,
say, speedway. Would it be like that in Colombia? I was curious
to see how the local event compared. At *La Plaza de Toros La*

Macarena in Medellin, one familiar feature of the spectacle was the extraordinarily diverse crowd. Men in working clothes queued for cheap seats – they were to be found in the section which is referred to as *son*, because it was exposed to the heat of the day. But it was not out of the ordinary to see well-to-do families and ash-blonde *colombianas* with exquisite profiles. A helpful marshal led me to the ticket counter. When the queues there proved sluggish, he escorted me past them into a courtyard where a man enjoying his golden years was taking the air in the spangled catsuit of a *toreador*. The marshal persuaded another man to fix me up – perhaps because I'd asked for a *sombra* ticket (one in the shade), and he had mistaken me for an *aficionado*.

My seat was a hard granite bleacher in the gods, not ameliorated, as in Spain, by a hide cushion. The action was about to begin and, below me, everything was being made ready. Stewards were in the ring, clearing away gas-filled blimps promoting various sponsors. Members of bullfight fan clubs, *Los Manchivoros Pona Taurina* and *Pena Taurina Femenina de Antioquia*, were unrolling their banners.

Suddenly, shots echoed around the arena. On the second burst of fire, spectators began shinning up the stands towards the row in which I was sitting. A prosperous-looking man dropped onto the seat beside me.

'What's going on?' I said.

'*Agua*,' he said, with an indifferent expression.

'*Agua?*'

'*Si.*'

Water? This was no help at all – was a crazed gunman on the loose or not? Violence at the Medellin bullfights wasn't always confined to the ring. During the 1991 season, twenty people died when a 150-kilo car bomb went off outside *La Plaza*. I thought, where were all those heavily armed soldiers when you needed one? Then the picture cleared. One of the sponsors' inflatables had burst: a winsomely humanoid bottle plugging *agua, aguardiente*.

A horseman came on, the warm-up act, doing tricks, making his mount play doggo. I recognised him by his costume as the man whom I'd seen when buying my ticket. But for the absence of padding on the horse, he might have been taking the role of *picador*, I thought, the fighter who jabs the sharp *pic* between the bull's shoulders to weaken the animal – or test his mettle, according to Ernest Hemingway in *Death in the Afternoon*.

As the crowd applauded, the horseman removed his hat, divulging a bald spot. I was interested to note that matters were formally inaugurated, as in Madrid, by the appearance of the *alguazils*, men in cockaded millinery whose largely ceremonial role appeared to consist of declaring the games open and seeing a good, clean fight. They were piped into the ring by a trio comprising horns and drums. According to the nineteenth-century bullfight-goer, Prosper Merimee, the *alguazils* accompanied a herald who would read out the rules on behalf of the crown. These deputations were regularly barracked; a whiff of republicanism surrounded the Spanish bullfight, or had done. In Colombia, a sovereign republic, the *alguazils* were indulged as colourful relics of a colonial past. A ceremonial key, lowered to these flunkeys to enable them to admit the bulls, looked like a twenty-first birthday souvenir, or a gameshow gimmick.

Beauties toured the ring with cards, as at a boxing match. The name of the fighter was supplied, and a brief bloodstock biography of the bull. To my surprise, the first animal was released to chase the mounted entertainer, perhaps in some cockeyed acknowledgement of his local popularity. He protected his mount and himself with supreme horsemanship.

The longer the fight went on without the introduction of a *matador*, the firmer grew my suspicion that the horseman was the bullfighter in the Colombian scheme of things. Ringside attendants held out what looked like furled parasols – deadly *pics*, tied with streamers of many colours. The rider collected a pair. The next moment, the crowd was cheering as he drove one into the bull's neck: he was the *picador*, after all. People rose to their feet and the horse curtseyed. This was the bull's Hemingway moment.

For sixty years, even if you could overcome your qualms about bullfighting, there has been the obstacle of *Death in the Afternoon*, that primary source of the writer's legend – nowadays perhaps unread – and its message of annihilation redeemed through manly courage. Bovine courage, too, come to that. In Spain, I had lugged my copy to the *corrida*, thinking to cringe behind it during the gorier episodes. (My companion, who had been dipping into the volume, announced that the hired cushions had a secondary use besides the obvious one, and I was briefly cheered by the image of Papa crushing his face into the obscuring pouffe: in fact, according to Hemingway, fight fans used to pelt unsatisfactory *matadors* with their pillows.) Two things had emerged fairly swiftly from *Death in the Afternoon*. One was that it stood up surprisingly well, or at least a lot of it did; the other, not unconnected thing was that the author admitted a fundamental truth about bullfighting, i.e. that it wasn't really on. 'I suppose, from a modern moral point of view, that is, a Christian point of view, the whole bullfight is indefensible,' he wrote, 'and I should not try to defend it now, only to tell honestly the things I have found to be true about it.' This was good news, I'd felt. Hemingway was surely right to call bullfighting indefensible, yet he went to bullfights, he loved bullfights. Maybe it was possible to hold such apparently conflicting views simultaneously. After all, I thought, I had never attempted to make a case for eating meat to my vegetarian sister – on the contrary, I agreed with her – but I went on eating meat all the same. Admittedly, Hemingway was rather dodgier a page or two later (in what may be the most Hemingwayesque sentence ever written, by Hemingway or anyone else). 'So far, about morals, I know only that what is moral is what you feel good after and what is immoral is what you feel bad after and judged by these moral standards, which I do not defend, the bullfight is very moral to me because I feel very fine while it is going on and have a feeling of life and death and mortality and immortality, and after it is over I feel very sad but very fine.' So long as it works for you, Ernesto.

Taking *Death in the Afternoon* to the *Plaza de Toros* in Madrid had turned out to be a smart move, because one of the ways in which it stood up was as a kind of match programme. The action was largely unchanged since Hemingway described it – indeed, since well before his day. It was a tableau out of Cervantes, or something even older, something like Greek mythology.

In Medellin, the balding rider had the immemorial honour of administering the *coup de grâce*. The crowd squealed; I heard someone shout 'Bravo!' The bull lost control over its hind quarters. It wasn't dead: you would want to say that it was sitting, though what looked like red emulsion was spreading across its shoulders. Now it toppled, and a sideman appeared with a knife like a mafia executioner and stuck it between the horns. This man didn't look as though he cared for the work; although having said that, he didn't look as though he didn't, either. The fighter himself milked his applause with a sentimental expression which seemed to say, 'What a good boy am I!' Someone in the crowd threw him a skin of *aguardiente*: he tipped it over his mouth and directed a jet of liquor between his lips.

The second fighter on the bill was younger, with the looks of a dull romantic lead, and an eye-catching outfit suggesting an out-and-proud pearly king. But he lacked the equestrian tricks of his predecessor: theatrically eyeballing his bull, he almost tipped out of the saddle. It was apparent, as it had been in Spain, that the creature wouldn't attack unless goaded. A drum roll and a blast on the cornet and a fighter entered on foot, to distract the bull while the good-looking man changed horses. Now he was aboard a chestnut which had been made ready as though for a dressage competition, with what looked like a bride's headdress in its mane. The fighter lost his hat – I think that was all part of the fun. The band built the tension and you wondered idly whether this accompaniment had been the origin of the score for an action sequence, now a commonplace of films. Flamboyantly, the bullfighter broke his *pics* in half, so that he had to get closer to the bull before he could place them, increasing the risk to himself.

According to custom, the spectators entreated the president of the fight to award the coveted honour of the animal's ear to the successful contender. The fighter himself savoured his victory with a walkabout. People tossed flowers. Some threw hats. These were gathered up and thrown back.

Juan Rafael, the third man up, was fighting a breed of bull called a *peloncho*. He was wearing brown leather chaps, the stitching highlighted by what might have been rhinestones. His horse stumbled – Rafael was dumped! Fighters ran into the ring (the reverse of what happens in Spanish bullfighting, in which the *picadors* relieve the *matadors*). The incident was presumably a setback to Rafael, the equivalent of an ice-skater grounding during a triple axel. But he resumed, on a majestic Arabian-looking horse, to a generous hand from the fans. He shortened his *pics* even more drastically than the second fighter had done – soon, you thought, somebody would be attempting to kill a bull with cocktail sticks. Things didn't improve for Rafael and he gave way to a fighter on the ground. Before the latter could strike, however, the bull dropped to the dirt – Rafael blew out his cheeks with relief. The kill would be chalked up as his, after all. Another Joe Pesci figure in leisure shirt and slacks, a man for doing dirty work if ever there was one, came on to perform the vital task uncelebrated in all the feudal theatrics – chopping through the bull's cerebral cortex to end its life.

Mouthing '*con much gusto*' in the direction of the presidential box, the first contender, the ageing crowd-pleaser, made a reappearance: evidently, the fighters faced two bulls each, as they do in Madrid. The bull wouldn't be persuaded to take an interest in developments. The crowd entreated the president to

void the fight (this course of action much the best for the bull, if
it did but know it. Hemingway says somewhere that the bullfighter would never win if the bull had the opportunity to go
around a second time). In order to provoke the listless animal,
the veteran took the greatest risks yet. Just as you were sure
that he had allowed his quarry too close to the horse, he accel-
erated away in the nick of time. He trimmed his *pics* so much
that he might as well have fought the bull with a pair of tiepins.

Taking a taxi back into the centre of Medellin, I saw an advertisement on the wall of an underpass for a helpline run by
Narcotics Anonymous. You pictured a horseshoe of unshaven
young men in dark glasses, grounding their automatics and
rising to their feet one after another in a church hall, huskily
identifying themselves, admitting that they had a problem with
drugs. It struck me that the people with a drugs problem in
Medellin, the people who had *given* a drugs problem to
Medellin, the 2,000 or more who had worked for Escobar in his
pomp, were largely unknown: they were the *narcos* anonymous.
Even after the big names had all been killed or jailed or usurped,
the drug business was thriving and the gunslingers went about
their business with the dispatch of bullfighters – murder was
the most common cause of death among young males; the homicide rate had actually risen since the days when Medellin ruled
the world, and was continuing to climb. It wasn't as if this could
be explained by unmitigated poverty. As Colin Harding has
noted, 'The violence of Medellin is not the violence of decline.
The city is booming economically, even as the murder rate spi-
rals.' As so often with Colombia, drugs had created a heady
illusion: put simply, violence had pre-dated the well-publicised
excesses of the Escobar period and had survived him without
interruption.

Medellin – the department of Antioquia as a whole – had
always been a frontier place. The city was founded in 1661,
probably by a community of Spanish Jews, and was almost

entirely cut off from the outside world until the nineteenth century. There were stories of comely black divers attaching weights around their necks so that they could sink to river beds in search of alluvial gold. Prospectors of an agricultural bent were slashing and burning the undergrowth to carve out small farms. After coffee emerged as a lucrative export, Antioquia was the only part of the country where it was grown on smallholdings instead of sprawling plantations. "This provided the economic foundation for the subsequent image, or myth, of the sturdy, hard-working *paisa*,' according to Harding.

The railway made a decisive contribution to the Medellin story. The *Ferrocarril de Antioquia* first ran in 1893, cleaving a path through the *Cordillera Central* to the Magdalena valley and the Atlantic railway, upon which I had travelled in STF's presidential carriage. The result was a boom in coffee exports: Colombia was established as the world's leading producer of *arabica* or mild beans, many of them grown in Antioquia. Nor did expansion end there. The first big textile mill opened in Medellin in 1900, and within a few years, the city was full of cotton factories. By the end of the Great War in Europe, when my grandfather the fighter pilot was being demobilised, Medellin was the industrial capital of Colombia, employing 6,000 textile workers, with migrants from far and wide arriving all the time. This was crucial to subsequent events. In the 1950s, the textile industry went into decline because of cheaper foreign competition, and although other industries took its place, a large working class was now exposed to the effects of cyclical unemployment and instability. In the 1970s and 1980s, a pool of idle, poorly educated young people in the *communas* was a ready source of labour, not for Escobar – at least, not at first – but for guerrilla factions including M19. The army drove the rebels from Medellin and many of their protégés drifted into crime. It was only then that they fell under the influence of the nascent drug cartel. Escobar, who had been a petty crook himself, of course, was recruiting for a hit squad called *Muerte a Secuestradores*, Death to Kidnappers, following the abduction of a member of a drugs family called the Ochoas.

A Colombian sociologist, Alonso Salazar, compiled a study of the street hoodlums of Medellin and found that they saw violence as the only means of improving their lot. It was an everyday occurrence, of which political and drug-related killings represented only a minor part. At the bottom of the hierarchy were the *pedalos*, the kids, who were already learning their craft at the ages of twelve and thirteen, knowing that few crimes were detected or punished (on the government's own estimates, 95 per cent of offences never came before a court). Salazar observed the remarkable phenomenon that these children were regarded even in their own communities as *desechables*, disposable. Their older brothers were the *sicarios*, the teenage hit men, inexpressibly fatalistic in the face of likely early extinction. Some of them had perhaps carried out contracts for Escobar himself; others used their weapons for crime and settling personal scores. Some offered their services as vigilantes, protecting their *barrios* against their more reckless peers. In the 1990s, there were said to be 190 corps of vigilantes in the city.

Salazar's research threw up cameos like the deathbed scene of a pubescent gunman called Antonio, who claimed that he and his cronies bought their weapons and ammunition from the police. Antonio had a recipe for a tonic to suppress butterflies before a hit. 'I've found a trick which always helps me: I get a bullet, take out the lead, and pour the gunpowder into a hot black coffee. I drink the lot, and that steadies my nerves.' And there was Antonio's mother, whose faith was of an eye-for-an-eye dispensation: 'I've made a vow to the Fallen Christ of Girardota to make sure my boy gets well quickly. That's what I want, I want him to get well and go and find the coward who shot him.'

Salazar himself commented, 'God's pardon for killing is something that has been assumed throughout the long tradition of violence in Colombia. The Church itself has taught it. A rich businessman prays to the Virgin that a deal in which he will be cheating a neighbour goes well for him. And in the neighbourhoods they pray that a stabbing or a shooting will be successful. It is the culture of the rosary and the machete, which nowadays have become the religious medallion and the mini-Uzi.'

Finally, there was Don Rafael, the creator of a neighbourhood self-defence committee, reminiscing about the early flowering of Colombia's troubles during *La Violencia*: 'In those days, there was violence and there was magic. There were people who knew secrets, who turned themselves into animals to escape their enemies, so even bullets that had been blessed had no effect on them.' Now Don Rafael and his kind were associated with violence of a less enchanting quality, the tragic realism of Colombia.

I wanted to see the neighbourhoods which had bred the awful world-weariness of the *narcos* anonymous. The receptionist at my hotel told me that she had grown up in one of the *comunas*. A beautiful *medellína*, tall and dark, Constanza came from a place called Bellen Saffra. Her family still lived there. Would I like to see it? She made a call from the desk, and then we were going, going in a taxi to Bellen Saffra. We went under the stanchions of the metro and through the traffic and up into the red-brick slums which grew on the mountainside like terraces of crops. Constanza said that we were going to the house of her uncle, who was a nightwatchman at a fast-food restaurant. The family were looking forward to meeting me, she said, but it was better if I went straight into the house, if I didn't take photographs. That would draw attention to the family. There were vigilantes in the *barrio*, members of a neighbourhood self-defence committee. The taxi driver said, 'The vigilantes here are the same as the paramilitaries in the countryside.' In April 1998, in a *barrio* of Medellin just like Bellen Saffra, hooded men armed with automatic assault rifles and pistols had kidnapped eight people – 'all of whom were presumably marked for death,' as an agency report put it.

Bellen Saffra was probably in line for one or two civic amenities. Sixty per cent of Colombians were living in poverty, and they were the sort of people who lived in a place like Bellen Saffra. The government had pledged to raise living standards through public sector expenditure, and by bringing in private enterprise on infrastructure projects. The policy was to decentralise spending and decision-making away from the capital. Departmental and municipal authorities were given more money for health, education and sanitation. Inflation interrupted this process in the mid-1990s, when Colombia was simultaneously rocked by strikes and the disclosure that the cartels had underwritten President Samper's bid for office. Foreign aid and investment dried up. The president was reduced to issuing compulsory war bonds just to pay for fighting the guerrillas. In January 1997, he had declared a state of economic emergency, only for the constitutional court to countermand this, ruling that the budget deficit of $4 billion was merely chronic – rather than 'extraordinary'. There followed a rough passage of high wage settlements, inflation, a slump in the coffee and banana markets, and an over-valuation of the *peso*. But in September 1997, the value of the currency had fallen, helped by lower interest rates, and decentralisation had been resumed in a limited way.

I'd been reading that the local and national governments were putting money into rehabilitation schemes for Medellin gangsters, setting up training courses, creating jobs. And the newspaper *El Colombiano* was reporting that one of the non-governmental organisations active in the country was running a firearms amnesty, with the young gunmen of the *barrios* in mind. But these encouraging trends were left far behind on entering the street-corner tyranny of Bellen Saffra.

There was a dusty football pitch and lines of drying clothes. 'There was a shoot-out outside this house not long ago,' said Constanza, pointing to a shack to our right. Bullets had drilled themselves into a wall – three or four, perhaps. There had been others, said Constanza, but the houseproud occupants had already made good the damage, the desire to keep up appearances tenacious even here. I wanted to get out and have a look but Constanza said, 'It's better not to stop.'

An old boot of a woman was watching from a doorway as the taxi arrived outside the house of Constanza's uncle. The uncle greeted us, a spare man not as old as he looked, and introduced his wife and grown-up daughters. There were articles of underwear in polythene on coat hangers, and a Singer sewing machine with a pedal, and a glass counter. The front room of the house was also a shop. I asked the aunt about the shot-up house. 'That's not the only shoot-out we've had here, there have been many,' she said. '*Muchas muertes.*' Many deaths.

'We've been here for about ten years and to begin with, things weren't too bad. But then came a period with a lot of problems due to violence, so much so that we lived in fear and there was a high level of anxiety, and I even got sick because of it.'

Lawless young killers had turned Bellen Saffra into a corner of Hell, according to Constanza's uncle. 'The neighbourhood was in the hands of criminals and drug dealers. Some times, there would be two murders in a week, just in these few streets. It went on for six or seven years and in that time 150 of our neighbours and friends were murdered.'

Within the past twelve months, the scene had changed utterly; though the cure didn't sound much better than the disease. From the uncle, I heard the chilling story of how life in Bellen Saffra had been transformed almost overnight. 'The militia came a year ago. They arrived hooded and armed. Did you pass the soccer field? Well, the militia rounded up some people – they claimed they were drug pushers – and they took them down there. It was broad daylight. They pointed guns at them, machine guns. They ordered them to strip naked while they had their guns on them. The so-called drug pushers were terrified. Watching all this, we were expecting a massacre. The children would see and hear everything! But the militia made the people walk round the field, round and round, in a parade. They were naked, scared and humiliated, walking round and round the soccer field with guns at their backs, and all of Bellen Saffra seeing this parade. This was their one warning to the pushers. You could say it's been totally successful.'

Surely everyone was frightened of the militia?

'Well, it's good, it's done some good things, but it's also created a reign of terror,' said the uncle. 'As we say in Medellin, they are sharp people. The ones we see, they are rotated by the leaders. They're not necessarily from around here.' An informal curfew was observed in Bellen Saffra. The uncle said that when his girls came to see him and his wife, they had to keep an eye on the clock. They couldn't afford to set off late when getting home to their families. One of the girls told me that her boyfriend had had a gun put to his head in the street and been ordered to explain himself. Constanza's husband, who was not from Medellin, had not been recognised when he tried to enter the *communa*. 'He was taken in a car in the dark up the mountain and asked for his papers,' she said. 'They wanted to know what business he had here.'

The uncle looked at me. 'You're lucky they didn't stop you,' he said.

I asked his daughter why the family hadn't left. She rubbed her thumb and forefinger together – money was the answer.

Where were the police, I wondered. 'They're as scared as the pushers about coming in here,' said Constanza. 'Many a policeman has been killed in here.' Her uncle said that he had only managed to survive by being neutral.

Not even the absolute power of the militia, the shame and fear of the naked parade, had suppressed the craving for drugs irrevocably. There were signs that drug abuse was returning to Bellen Saffra, said the uncle, all youngsters were tempted. Thinking to offer Constanza's family a gift, I slipped next door, to a neighbour who also kept a shop. I bought beer in a front room where sausages hung like washing and the sound of chickens clucking and high-stepping came from behind a curtain. In the street, no hooded and armed vigilantes were to be seen; only the old boot of a woman, now holding a shopping trolley as though it was a dog on a lead.

At last I was riding on the *Ferrocarril de Antioquia*. It was the line I had been going to take from Puerto Berrio to Medellin, only I was travelling in the opposite direction now. This was *el paseo*, the weekend train. I had boarded all of the railways still running in Colombia. This was the last survivor of the routes recorded on my grandfather's map; the one that went through Villa and Bosque and Acevado and Bello . . . This was the line through the long, dark tunnel. This was where I came in.

Drawing away from the city, the 1969 diesel loco was comfortably outpaced by two metro trains. They made for vast, impressive, brick marshalling yards, where far more metro trains than you could ever imagine being necessary were at line abreast. Aboard our service were vendors from every generation and they came through the carriage like a piece of theatre, like a cautionary tale, the *tinto* man handing on to the tic tac boy who in turn gave way to the *chiclet* toddler. For younger passengers, there was a real actor, a mummer got up as a cat: black nose and whiskers, black body-stocking. He looked apologetic as he embarked on songs *por los niños*, but they went down well, and this had the effect of rallying him. A man in blue overalls appeared with beakers of juice on a tray held above his head, and slices of unbuttered white bread on another. Another salesman was circulating with English language guides sealed in polythene. There was a man in a green shirt with a thick neck reading a newspaper.

Outside my window were silent forests, and the brown, fast-flowing waters of the *Rio Porce*, a tributary of the Magdalena, capped with clods of white foam. A man who had been drunk in the ticket queue at Medellin found his way to the rear of my carriage. Above the sibilance of the bogies, he could be heard making water from the footplate. I was interested to see that the conditions printed on my *ticket especial* outlawed drunkenness, though they were dumb on the subject of micturition.

This was the railroad that engineer Cisneros had founded, at $61,599 a mile. He seemed to have been something of a visionary, correctly anticipating that coffee would swiftly put the new *ferrocarril* in the black, and that opening up land outside Medellin would consolidate the expansion of the department as a whole. According to Parsons' *Antioqueno Colonization in Western Colombia*, 'Cisneros is still honoured throughout Colombia as the father of the railroads, having provided the initial impetus and overcome the formidable obstacles of malaria and politics.' He went on to involve himself in bids for railway projects including the one at La Dorada, and a streetcar in Barranquilla, but unrest in 1885 led to the temporary abandonment of these enterprises, and Cisneros sold his interests to the government. In Antioquia, it was left to a junta composed of the governor and two private citizens to complete the railway. Contractors converged from both ends of the line: fifty-eight kilometres of track were laid heading east out of Medellin, alongside the River Porce, the direction in which I was travelling; coming the opposite way, the line reached a terminus named after Cisneros, 108 kilometres west of Puerto Berrio. The two sections were bridged by a twenty-seven-kilometre road, over the implacable mountain of the Quiebra de Santo Domingo: for twenty years, completion of the *Ferrocarril de Antioquia* foundered on the stumbling block of this 1,650-metre granite barrier, engineers contesting the relative merits of tunnels, aerial cables and funiculars. Finally, a contract was awarded in 1926 to a British company, Fraser, Bruce Ltd, for a tunnel through the rock. Parsons wrote that, 'The first train passed through the 3,742-metre tunnel on 7 August 1929, to set off celebrations throughout the department. Medellin was now only eight hours distant from the Magdalena.'

In the dining car, there was an old woman with no teeth. A pan was simmering on a grimy stove. A man selling tumescent sausage warned me that we were only five or six minutes away from the tunnel. A boy was playing a guitar in second class and there was a woman with a poodle. People sat sideways on to the engine on wooden slats and I spotted the drunk from the station, now asleep.

More than twenty years after Leslie came to Colombia on the La Dorada commission, he was still there. He wrote to Peggie on 23 July 1956. 'If you could only know my state of mind,' he said. But how could she? His aerogramme might as well have been in code. Encrypted in neat pencil (and reproducing the thrifty single-spacing Leslie favoured at the typewriter), it included what might well have been a number of red herrings, to keep the pot boiling. The other ex-pats were away in Bogota, Leslie said, and he was temporarily in sole charge of railway and ropeway. The natives were restless. 'I have sacked quite a few men for misdemeanours, including the stationmaster at La Dorada, the Doctor and both dispensers . . . but the National Rlys. just pay them off, uphold my decision and make no comment.'

My grandfather had received a visit from someone called General Beyamo, who 'arrived at the house suddenly, last Wednesday afternoon' with a view to asking him to stay on with the nationalised *ferrocarrils*. These agencies were to have been signed into being at about the time of the general's surprise house call, but 'I heard unofficially that the deed in question had been mislaid in the Ministry of Public Works and that the signing couldn't take place until the next Cabinet meeting – on the 26th. Goodness only knows whether this is truth or rumour but anything can happen out here.' The general appears to have gone away under the impression that he had won *Señor* Frost round: the radio presently reported that the National Railways had contracted his services to complete the training of Colombian engineers. This premature announcement caused 'quite a spot of embarrassment': the people responsible for booking Leslie's passage home queried whether it was still

required. 'In any case, I shouldn't have rated my services as
worthy of public notice over the national radio – the company
certainly doesn't.' I think he was secretly quite tickled to hear
the item on the radio, though like the practical man he was, he
didn't have a great deal of time for paper-shufflers and politicians. I once asked my mother how he voted. 'Probably Tory,'
she said. 'I don't think he was very bothered.'

I've no doubt Leslie was telling the truth in his letter. But I
wondered how much Isabel and the boy had to do with the
delay in his homeward journey. In his mid-fifties, he had had an
adventure, sexual if not necessarily romantic: his son the proof
of this. Gran had gone through the change of life at an early age,
according to my mother, 'and after that Pop never went near her.
She was very hurt. He didn't have anything more to do with her
sexually at all. Years later, they discussed it. "Oh, I didn't think
a woman could have sex after the menopause," he said. This
was so ignorant and yet we had been surrounded by sex!' Leslie
had been very much in love with Peggie, my mother thought,
but not very good at sex. 'Perhaps the Colombian girl brought
out the animal sense in him.'

The *Ferrocarril de Antioquia* stopped at a place called
Botero. Leslie's map said that it was fifty-nine kilometres from
Medellin; a sign over the platform confirmed 'KM 59'. We had
been travelling for two hours. I got out to stretch my legs.
Standing on the track, looking back at the train, I saw sudden
gouts of piss.

And then we were heading towards the tunnel of La Quiebra
once again, the mist still on the hills though it was mid-morning, and Leslie's map saying we had come sixty-eight kilometres
to Porcecito, where the letters ELN were written on the wall of
the general stores. In the carriage, a man selling green mangoes
was sharpening a knife and there was ash drifting in from the
sugar canes after a fire. The occasional *campesino*, or piebald
cow, peered from the cane. The *campesino* always wore a hat;
one favoured a homburg. The return of the tic-tac boy was her-
alded by his propositioning rattle and the man in the green shirt

was still reading his newspaper at the rear of the carriage, and
then everything went dark.

After the tunnel, and the sensation of threat in the blackened
carriage – a moment from the Hercule Poirot casebook – and
then the soldiers getting on at Limon to look for guerrillas, there
was an old boy moistening his lips, holding a leaf in his fingers.
He put the leaf to his lips, as though he was licking a Rizla. He
began humming through it. The effect was of a kind of castrato's
Jew's harp, if you can imagine such a thing.

It wasn't long before the train stopped and everyone got off at
the station of Cisneros, named after a pioneer of Colombian railways, a foreign engineer like my grandfather. I went to eat at a
cafeteria beside the track: *tinto* and eggs *revueltos* (scrambled,
with cheese) and *arapas*, cakes made out of maize which looked
like cloths for cleaning LP records and tasted of poverty. The
last letter Leslie had written in Colombia – the last one I could
find, anyway – was a fond note to his daughter in April 1957, a
month before he came home ('thank you very much indeed for
your interesting letters and for the excellent photographs. It was
nice to see your old phiz again even if only in print'). Leslie was
packing up the house in Mariquita. 'I have made a note about
the records but they will have to be of the long playing kind as
I am in a bad fix about baggage space and packing cases and
breakable articles such as records need plenty of padding. There
are no strong packing cases available as imports from abroad
have practically ceased and I have had to pay through the nose
for the few miserable cases available.' He was taking advantage
of a break in the timetable over Easter ('the only time in the year
when there are no trains on the National Railways'), another
pointer to me of how things had changed.

Leslie was disturbed by another mysterious military caller.
This time, it was a Colonel Prado, plus party ('the good lady,
five daughters and one son'). They had come by car from Bogota
to stay at Number One, according to a handwritten postscript,

but nothing was prepared so 'they stayed in No. 5 until the house was made ready and bang went my packing'.

Leslie wrote, 'Being Good Friday I was alone in the house but they brought a very excellent picnic meal, which I shared – this saved me preparing my own meal but drinks, chiefly minerals, were on me.' Where was Isabel when this was going on, I wondered. I hardly expected Leslie's correspondence to refer to her, but all that stuff about saving him from preparing his own meal – that was laying it on a bit thick, wasn't it? Unless Isabel – and Elvia the cook, come to that – were absent, with their families over Easter. Leslie's boy absent, too. Or had my grandfather already sent his Colombian family away for good, made other arrangements for them now that he was going back to his wife and daughter?

As usual, his letter talked about his work. He had been handing over to a Dr Gomez. 'He will not stay here permanently, as he is Chief Engineer of the Railways, but it has proved impossible to find anybody else for the job. He intends to visit only four stations on the Ropeway – Mariquita, Fresno, Esperanza and Manizales – and will take the rest for granted. Goodness only knows how he expects to run the show if he never visits the line and is scared of travelling on the carriers. He is lame and cannot ride a horse.' The image that the letter left with me was of Leslie the engineer. 'Yesterday I had to work all day out on the line . . .'

The train, the *Ferrocarril de Antioquia*, clanked past the *cafeteria*: an old lady setting her heirloom bangles jangling. I watched the carriages go by from my table. It was hard to credit that it was the same train that had rocketed through the tunnel at La Quiebra. *A runaway train.* Perhaps this usage wasn't confined to trains themselves, I thought – trains that skipped the rails, trains that were lost – but could also apply to people riding on trains, people who were running away as surely as stowaways. *A runaway train.* The last carriage went by, the one I'd travelled in. Gripping the handrail in a pair of stout gloves, and unmistakably fulfilling the role of guard for all that he was in mufti, was the man in the green shirt.

I finished my meal. Was the truth of it that my grandfather couldn't bear to be parted from the railways and *El Cable*, from this beautiful country; that he had been running away, apprehending as well as any of the consultants who would subsequently attend his bedside that the leaving of Colombia was the death of him?

9

The Last
Adventure

It was Ash Wednesday when I went to Mariquita to find my Colombian uncle. I got up before dawn at a hotel high in the coffee belt, and went out past the night porter who was asleep under a blanket in the lobby, and a man in a suit who was reading a newspaper in the doorway. There was a cathedral opposité the hotel, but no sign of devotion there or anywhere else. I caught a taxi with a broken windshield to the bus depot. There was no railway to Mariquita any longer, so it would have to be a *buseta*.

The bus followed a route through the mountains where men were tilling earth in fog. Mile after mile, these were some of the most broken-down *fincas* I'd seen. There were people living on top of their own refuse, their children playing in it – though the area seemed far from over-populated; quite the reverse, in fact – and a family with their cattle standing about outside their own back door. There was breakfast at a bend in the road called Albania, the food booths with their familiar fly-screens of offal, and I drank *tinto* thinking of my grandfather resting at this place on his treks by mule through the *Cordillera* to the stations of *El Cable*, the Manizales-to-Mariquita ropeway. He would be gone for days, the faithful Reina and a mule boy for company, Lucky Strikes and whisky, and a bed with the families of British engineers living on the route. There was a ropeway station at Papal, and a man called Rowe and his wife living in a bungalow with a corrugated roof and a view across the mountains; at another stop was a Mr Batchelor, a man who lived on strong tea and cigarettes and was as thin as a rake. Years separated my grandfather's last journey through Albania and my visit; a much shorter time elapsed between the latter and a guerrilla raid on the police station at Albania, in which five officers were shot dead.

The bus corkscrewed down the mountains and there were men breaking in a horse, one riding it round and round a paddock, the other, holding a rein, the fixed point of the circle. The sun was climbing as we descended, flooding light onto vertiginous slopes packed with rhododendron. They were darker than the varieties I was used to, and with a smaller leaf – they had been coffee bushes all along. We went through Padua and Fresno, and there people bore the mark of the cross on their foreheads for the beginning of Lent. A fat man had been sweating: the grey ash had run on his brow and he looked as though he was just coming round after a faint. In the days when my grandfather ran the mountain ropeway, the engineer who was based at Fresno used to collect specimens of spiders and poisonous snakes and send them home to Britain in jars of alcohol. Towards the end of the bus journey, a crocodile of children boarded, to go a mile or two to school, and a man with buckets full of pale cheeses.

The rooftops of Mariquita were glimpsed from a hilltop, and suddenly the town was upon us, shade-giving trees lining the streets and a profusion of bars and cafés. Men on bikes were pedalling tubs of drinks and there was a pleasant citrus smell – Mariquita was the *capital frutera*, the fruit capital of Colombia. It was only a few miles away from Honda. But this was the difference between being merely hot and wet all of the time, on the one hand, and in a roiling *bisque* of sweat, on the other; this,

and the absence of the Magdalena, which turned in its bed at
Honda like a man with a fever.

I looked at men on the street, election posters on lampposts,
thinking, 'Is that him? Could that be my uncle?' As I've said, I
had no success in finding my uncle's birth certificate. My friend
Dom had suggested calling at the mayor's office in Mariquita, in
case there was a register of foreigners: that would give me the
Frosts' old address, the place where I might find Number Two,
assuming that it was still standing. So I went through my story
at the mayor's office and spread my dog-eared photographs on
a desk. The name Frost didn't mean anything; an official
thought that Number Two – *all* that republican-style architec-
ture, he said – had been done away with. He looked at my
pictures. This, this one interested him: a postcard which my
mother had kept, showing the plaza in Mariquita, the church in
the background, an obelisk. But of course the obelisk wasn't
there any more, the official said. A stout woman appeared from
another office and went through my photos like a witness: she
said 'no' when confronted with pictures of Leslie, 'no' to
Number Two, 'no' to the domestic help. This, this was the
plaza, with the church, she said. Was I aware that the obelisk
had gone?

It emerged that a man who ran a hotel on the road out of
town knew a lot about the history of Mariquita, the old ropeway and the *ferrocarril*. I took a cab and went to see him. The
Hotel Marqueta was a would-be theme park, with the town
itself as the theme. There was a mural of *El Cable* on a wall, and
an old granite pile – a fragment of one of the foundations of a
ropeway tower – carefully placed beneath, in a rock garden
which was completed by other stones of historic interest. Carp
and catfish basked in a pool. Two pneumatic figures painted on
a wall represented Mr and Mrs Prehistoric Colombia.

When he appeared, the hotelier was like a character in a
play, a man who makes his bow at a turning point in the
action. It was difficult to say how old he was; he had a neat
moustache and a confident bearing, and he was the man behind

the commemoration of Mariquita achieved through his hotel. His name was Guillermo Giraldo. He produced a large, typed volume on *El Cable* and thumbed through it. The name Blackett appeared, but none of the others I knew, certainly not Frost.

The hotelier realised he knew a man I should be talking to: Don Rosendo Dias, a nonagenarian who had once been a mechanic on the ropeway. The hotelier telephoned him. Certain snatches of their conversation leapt out: the hotelier trying to get the deaf Don to hear him, for one – and then repeating what the Don was telling him. '*Supervisor, si,*' repeated the hotelier, and, '*Number Two, Number Two.*' He led the way to the Don's house on his scooter, a poised and enigmatic outrider guiding my taxi through the streets of Mariquita.

The Don was a lively old party in beaten-up boots. 'I am ninety!' he said with a note of surprise. He seemed pleased to see me, exercising English niceties perhaps learned from *los ingleses* many years before and not used very often since. 'Sit down, sit down,' he said to me, and, 'Mister Frost.' He was the first person I'd met in Colombia who remembered my grandfather. 'I was in and out of the ropeway offices all day long, so I saw everything,' he said. A member of the Don's family, who was removed from him by an almost impossible number of generations, was sent to prepare *tintos* while the Don and I sat in a passage by the door. I showed him my pictures. He said, 'My glasses are not here today,' and held the photographs up to his eyes in the style of an old professor of mine, whose weakness used to be punished by a bombardment of paper aircraft when he turned his back in the lecture theatre. The Don now scrutinised me. 'You look like him, the same height,' he considered. 'Though you are broader.' Mr Frost had been a good man, a respectable man. The Don remembered him leaving *El Cable* – in '45, was it? His memory was faulty, after all: Leslie was still working on the ropeway in the mid-1950s. The Don himself had gone to work for the Americans, in a fruit company, after the ropeway had shut down. He recalled the house at Number Two, he said. Did it still stand? He didn't know. The name

Quintero struck a chord, the name of the Frosts' cook, whose niece might perhaps have been Leslie's mistress, but it was only a name to the Don now.

However, the hotelier had thought of another ropeway veteran, a younger man, a stripling of seventy-eight: he was moving the plot along nicely. Oscar Pozada Perez also remembered my grandfather. 'Yes. He flew to London in a tin can, didn't he?' But Oscar was sick, ill with thrombosis, older-seeming than the Don. He sat in his kitchen with a newspaper in his lap, under a window which showed avocados swelling on a tree. There was a wooden rail in his kitchen, like a piece of gym equipment, to enable him to move a little. His wife looked at my pictures. She came to the photograph of the girl, her chin cupped in her hand; the girl who might have been Leslie's mistress. And she said, 'Quintero.'

So my mother was right – this was the girl! But hang on a minute: all Oscar's wife was doing was confirming her name, a connection with the cook. She wasn't saying anything about the girl's life. And then it seemed she wasn't saying anything much at all.

'Quintero? Quintero? I don't know a Quintero.'

'But you just said –'

But she couldn't remember what she'd just said. Perhaps it was just too long ago, I thought, my grandparents and the rest of *los ingleses* all dead, no one left alive who could recall any of it distinctly. Perhaps my uncle himself was also dead, although judging by the state of the birth certificates for Mariquita, confirming that would be easier said than done. What if I could find no proof that he had ever existed? There were the letters to my mother from her Colombian friends – though these had been too painful to keep – and of course Leslie's admission, but I was looking for something more tangible.

Jesus and the Virgin were behind glass in the stone church of *La Ermita*, as though the pilgrims who came to adore them

were window-shoppers, which I suppose they were. The dona-
tions box was secured with a combination lock of the sort you
might see on a safe, just in case you had forgotten that you
were in Colombia. *La Ermita* was the only reason visitors came
to Mariquita, although it also occupied a footnote in the
nation's history as the spot where the founder of Bogota,
Gonzalo Jimenez de Quesada, had died of leprosy in 1579. It
was half-past four in the afternoon, with one of the congrega-
tion climbing to his feet to ring the bells, and all around,
Spanish-looking faces, Indian faces, with streaks of ash on their
brows. Instead of lighting candles, petitioners were burning
children's dollies made out of wax. I had a sense of despair
about finding my uncle: I didn't think I'd find a record of his
baptism. It was a christening of someone whose name I didn't
know.

When I had arrived in Colombia, I had half-expected – even
half-hoped – that my uncle would be dead. Anything but a tan-
gled ball of a life, I thought, perhaps at an end, perhaps not,
involving a string of forwarding addresses, casual jobs, conflicting accounts, unconfirmed sightings. In *La Ermita*, the
memory made me squirm. Did I have an obligation to my uncle?
His birth had not been acknowledged by my grandfather – at
least, not formally. He had been left behind by Leslie and never
introduced into the catholic club of our family. Now, very possibly, it was too late. But having said that, what debt was owed
to an uncle, a *half*-uncle, maybe a late uncle, whom I'd never
met?

I had a drink, a sundowner, like Leslie used to, though mine
was a *leona cerveza*, a Colombian beer, rather than his preferred whisky or gin. It was tantalising to think that his son
might be no more than a few hundred yards from the bar, perhaps having a drink himself. In the end, being in Mariquita
had very little to do with any responsibilities incumbent upon
me because of the fact that my uncle and I were kin. I didn't
want to see him because I thought I should; I wanted to see him
because I wanted to see him, it was as simple as that. I was

curious to see what he looked like – *who* he looked like – the
same impulse that makes us pore over the dough-like features
of babies, no better informed than when we started. I wanted to
meet him: I wanted to see what he was like, to see if I liked
him, to see if I was like him. But these impulses were going to
be thwarted.

I had reckoned without the resourceful hotelier. That night
he introduced me to a man who had known Leslie's mistress, or
said he had. Her name was Isabel, said Carlos Hernandez, confirming what my mother had remembered at the hypnotist's.
She was *una morena*, a dark girl, an Indian. Carlos was a stocky
man in a white T-shirt embossed with the slogan 'National
Playday for Health'. His father had worked on the Mariquita
railway for forty-four years, and Carlos from time to time had
taken rum to the house where Isabel lived with *Señor* Frost. 'I
began helping *los ingleses* when I was about sixteen and she
wasn't much older than me but she was already tall and pretty,'
he said. Isabel was the daughter of a man called Antonio
Carrero, a mule driver.

I said, 'She definitely lived in the house?'

'*Claro, claro.* Number Five. She was much admired because
she had a big house,' said Carlos. 'She was a *coqueta*, flirta-
tious, but after she started living with *Señor* Frost, she became
very serious. She hardly ever left the house.' Carlos remembered seeing her when she was pregnant, but he had never seen
my grandfather and Isabel with a child. 'After the railways were
nationalised, I didn't see any of them again. I remember seeing
Isabel when she was carrying the child, she was eighteen, and
then about two years later the railways were nationalised. I
didn't see her again after that.' He had never known the child's
name, he said.

'Was the affair a scandal?'

'No, not in Mariquita. It wasn't a scandal because it was con-
cerning people who were "over there", as we used to say, *los
ingleses*. No one was surprised.'

'What was life like in the house?'

'*Bien, bien.* There were English people all around.' Carlos remembered *los ingleses* as well as my mother; he could even remember some of the Christian names she had forgotten. 'Mr Blackett lived at Number One; Alexander Kippen at Number Two; at Number Three was Louis Birchall, chief mechanic. There was also the accountant, Mr Cooper, who used to teach boxing. And your grandfather, who was the engineer of the *ferrocarril* and *jefe* of the cable. From Monday to Saturday, they worked. Maybe on Sundays or holidays, *fiestas*, they drank – that was when I would bring rum. The English often met on Sundays at the house of a man called Jimmy Hughes in Honda. He had an ironmonger's shop.'

'How have things changed since my grandfather was here?'

'My father used to be the paymaster for the railway, he had the money in his saddlebags and he went from station to station on the ropeway to pay the staff,' said Carlos. 'There wasn't any trouble at all. He could go anywhere with all this money.'

'*Ahora?*'

'Now? Oh! You can carry money now if you like but it will disappear.'

The next morning, I found Number Two, Mariquita, where Carlos had told me I would, near the overgrown tracks of the disused railway, and looking very much like the property in my grandfather's photographs. Beyond a pair of faded gates was a well-established drive which appeared to have had a pair of furrows ploughed into it, as though the owners had embarked in a limited way on market gardening. Where these ruts converged was a weathered-looking bungalow with a red roof of corrugated iron overhanging a verandah. In the shade of this roof, on this wide verandah, Leslie had liked to smoke his cigarettes and drink his drinks and make his plans. I thought again of the South American homestead of Graham Greene's *The Honorary Consul*: 'On the verandah of the rambling bungalow Charley Fortnum sat before a bottle of whisky, a syphon and . . . two

Number Two, Mariquita

clean glasses'. None of these bibulous artefacts was in sight: the place was now owned by a pleasant young man, not perhaps a drinker himself, who told me that he administered a *finca*. But the park benches on the verandah, the lanterns – they might have been here when this was the Frost place, also the insect-screens over the windows, the mesh here and there showing signs of having been patched. What about the fish pond? Hadn't Mum said something about a fish pond? It seemed it had been absorbed into a neighbour's garden.

The pleasant young man and an older woman – the maid, I decided – let me look over Number Two. There was a large, tiled hall, a large bedroom on either side of it; one of these had been the drawing room, according to a sketch my mother had made from memory. At the far end of the hall, a patio full of bright red flowers with a bright green parrot on a perch was partly enclosed by two wings in which the remainder of the

rooms were situated, including a dining room with a lustreless
chandelier and another bedroom, perhaps the maid's. This was
notable for a shrine to several saints: I couldn't have seen
Leslie, a Christmas-and-funerals churchgoer, giving it house-
room. He was C of E, and he didn't bother with church in
Catholic Colombia – it wasn't much of a hardship to him.
Neither he nor Peggie had objected to my mother going with
the maids.

To the rear of the bungalow had stood stable yards and the
lodgings of the mule boys. These had gone. The adjacent property was another bungalow of the republican school, perhaps
Number Three, occupied by Mr Birchall when Carlos
Hernandez had been a teenager delivering rum, but I didn't see
any other buildings of this style, and it appeared that Number
Five, where Leslie had lived with his mistress and she'd nursed
his son, had been torn down.

How had it happened, I wondered, my grandfather and
Isabel? She had been around the place, around Leslie, because
of Elvia the cook. Elvia had been her aunt. Isabel was a *coqueta*,
according to Carlos – perhaps she'd thought she was on to a
good thing. But she was eighteen, Leslie fifty-five. It was more
likely that he had seduced her, wasn't it?

It was the start of Lent and there was going to be a lunar eclipse.
It was against the backdrop of these portents that the stagey
character of the hotelier made his most dramatic entry yet. At
his hotel, beneath the painting that might have been entitled 'At
Home with the Pre-Colombians', he delivered the stunning
aside: 'I have found your uncle.'

My uncle! My Colombian uncle, my uncle in the jungle – so
he *was* alive! This carried the shock of revelation all over again,
after the setbacks with birth certificates, the imperfect recollec-
tions of old age. 'His name is Federico Forero,' said the hotelier.
It was a common name, he said; a *humble* name, was how he
put it. Perhaps it was as common as mine. 'Your grandfather

didn't give his name to his son,' he said – a little tartly, I thought.

No, not his surname – perhaps that had been withheld from the birth certificate, too – but my grandfather *had* given him a name nonetheless, a Christian name: Federico, as in Fred Leslie Frost. The hotelier was holding another one of his large volumes: I didn't know if it was a set of accounts or a volume of historical research. Perhaps it was a crib for his lines.

I congratulated him. 'You're a detective,' I said. A detective was a racier part to play than a hotelier.

'I'm not a detective but a historian.' If he had been a character in a play, you would have said that his dialogue was a little wooden. He only had something to say when it was time to move things along. 'Your uncle lives in Honda,' he continued. Would you believe it – sweaty old Honda! I'd passed right through the town and never even imagined . . . 'He would like to meet you. This afternoon, at two o'clock.'

I was dazed. I was excited: it was a journalistic excitement, a sense of getting the story (so often, the story eludes you). I had been approaching this moment, anticipating it, since my mother had first planted the idea of Leslie's son in my mind. But there was an excitement of another kind, too, one you felt in the bones: the incredible idea that a man who lived on the banks of the brown Magdalena, in the middle of Colombia, a country as remote in every way as you could imagine, was an intimate relative, was family. I was excited but I was also uneasy. It was all very well rushing off to bag your material. But this was my own flesh and blood – I was no closer to knowing what obligation I owed him. I wondered: would any irreversible corner be turned?

The action was moving fast. The hotelier had traced the Frosts' former cook, Elvia Quintero, who was the aunt of Leslie's mistress. He had also found a cousin of Federico's – Elvia and the cousin lived near each other in Mariquita. Under any circumstances other than an impending lunch-date with my long-lost uncle, these would have been enthralling discov-

eries. As it was, I went to morning coffee at Elvia's distracted
by what the hotelier had told me and in a state of agitation: I
was going to meet my uncle at last. What would he be like?
Come to that, how on earth had Sr Giraldo found him? I supposed it had helped that Mariquita was a small town – about
25,000 people – the sort of place where everyone knew everyone else. In the hotelier's line of business, and with his interest
in indexing and cross-referencing, perhaps he really *did* know
everyone else. Had the breakthrough come with something that
Carlos, the former rum boy, had said? Had there been a clue, a
clue I'd missed, in our meetings with Leslie's elderly ex-
employees, Don Rosendo and Oscar Pozada? Something in the
hotelier's manner discouraged close scrutiny – it would have
been like asking a master illusionist to explain his tricks, you
felt – and I never solved the mystery of how *he* had solved the
mystery of my missing uncle. He had, and that was all that
mattered at the time. The funny thing was, when he told me
that he'd found Federico, I realised I had never really expected
to.

Elvia was a woman with a happy face and a blue, polka-dot
dress. Her home was also a shop, like the shanty in Bellen
Saffra, Medellin, where the beguiling Constanza had taken me
to meet her family. Elvia's place was a sweetshop, but she also
had beer, and the last word in free-range poultry: chickens
enjoying the run of the entire house. My uncle's cousin, Luis,
was a bald man who didn't drink, smoke or eat meat, he told
me quite soon. He could recall Leslie teaching him to dance as
a little boy – this backfired, leaving Luis for many years with
no confidence on the dance floor (another Colombian my
grandfather had screwed up, I thought to myself).

Elvia, now seventy-five, remembered my family clearly.
'Your grandfather always had a bad chest,' she said.
'Rosemary – how she loved to ride!' Elvia brought out her old
photographs, and we found that they featured some of the
people who were in mine: it was like playing Snap, or Happy
Families. Elvia's collection included photographs of my mother

as a teenager, pictures of her I'd never seen before. They looked like publicity stills for *National Velvet*. Elvia said that I reminded her of Rosemary. 'You are tall like Federico, like Mr Frost.' Here was the familial impulse, comparing so-and-so with his father, his nephew. Federico was also dark, Elvia went on, dark like his mother. Her name wasn't Isabel at all, it emerged; it was Beatriz.

But this wasn't the most important thing I learnt about her. She had borne my grandfather not one hoped-for son, but two. The second child arrived two years after Federico – in 1957, after Leslie had come home. Beatriz was pregnant by him when he left. The child died in infancy, aged fourteen months. Did my grandfather know about him, I wondered. I assumed he did. I was sure my mother didn't.

A mangy kitten wound itself around the legs of my stool. Elvia said Beatriz herself had died at the age of twenty-five. I thought of the plot of *La Maria*, the first novel in the country's literature, the original Colombian love story: boy meets girl; boy goes to England; boy pines for girl and vice versa; girl dies. Leslie wouldn't have known about Beatriz's death, I supposed. I wondered whether he had thought about her much after he went home. My mother said that she had written to him – it was one of her letters that Peggie had discovered. Had Leslie written back?

Beatriz had died in hospital, in childbirth. It was a child by another man, and it had also failed to survive. Elvia said, 'Your grandfather left some kind of letter for Federico. I don't know what happened to it after Beatriz died, but he always knew about his father.'

Elvia wanted to show me her house. A big concrete sink was overflowing with pots and pans, and there was a parrot on a chair in a bedroom. In the garden grew lemons, mangoes and mandarins, and a cat was asleep on a tree stump. There was the sound of *chicharras*, cricket-like insects. In this shady place, Elvia broke off a leaf from the branch of a bush, folded it in half and gave it to me to taste. It was bitter and it made my mouth tingle. It was the same plant my mother had chewed as a girl; her Colombian friends had given it to her to relieve stomachache. This was the electric chewing gum of *coca*, the raw material of cocaine.

The women of Mariquita were pretty. I thought I saw what Leslie did in *colombianas*: the dark hair and dark eyes; the kind of make-up that men noticed (but British women thought too much); tight tops and trousers, or summer dresses. There was a fashion for revealing necklines and thin shoulder straps and push-up bras. I was going back to the hotel to dress for lunch with my uncle, my last change of clean clothes, the shirt and chinos I'd been saving for an embassy grandee in Bogota. A stout man on a moped went by in a T-shirt which read, 'My Next Husband Will Be Normal'.

In a taxi with the hotelier and Luis, I rolled my uncle's name around my tongue, trying it out, getting used to it, deciding how to address him: '*Tio Federico*; Uncle Frederick; Fred; Uncle Freddie.' I was nervous. how would Federico react to me? I would strike him as glaringly strange. Apart from our shared blood, the genealogical coincidence that Leslie was Federico's father and my grandfather, we had nothing in common, I guessed. It occurred to me that I had had more of Leslie than he had: my grandfather had left Colombia two years after Federico was born, so he had been around for only the first couple of years of his son's life; I was born in 1961 and Leslie died in 1966 (the firm of W.A. Truelove & Son Ltd had confirmed by letter that '2 car(s) will leave' at 1.25 p.m. on Friday 25 February 'joining the hearse at our Cheam office, High Street, Cheam. Service Randalls Park Crematorium, Leatherhead. Time Due 2.00 p.m.'). So I'd had five years with Leslie, though not much to show for them, other than memories of haircuts at home and the smell of bay rum.

Strictly speaking, my uncle was half-English, but to all intents and purposes he would be Colombian through and through, I predicted to myself in the back of the taxi. He had a humble name, the hotelier had said – was he trying to prepare

me for something? When my mother had first mentioned
Leslie's son to me, I had played a game of tinker, tailor, soldier,
sailor with him: the career options I had entertained for him
were peasant, football star, presidential hopeful, narco-baron.
Peasant looked the most likely role, now. This had been to my
advantage, I saw. A man with a humble name, living off the
land in an out-of-the-way place like Honda – this wasn't the
background to a life of frenetic mobility. Federico hadn't fallen
far from the tree. If Leslie had sired him in a big city, in Bogota
or Cali, say, tracking him down would have been hopeless.

We made a turning in Honda just where the touts operated,
where I had alighted from the Bogota bus, and pulled up outside a smart, one-storey house near the railway line, the spur
which the presidential carriage of STF had taken before the
excursion from La Dorada. A cluster of people of mixed ages,
whom I now know to have been a fraction of the family Forero,
came to the door and showed us in. I was conscious of several
well-padded, well-turned-out aunt figures, and some formal,
uncomfortable-looking Spanish furniture. But principally I was
having my eye drawn to a framed portrait which occupied
pride of place on the wall: my grandfather looked down
genially upon this strange living room, like the patriarch of the
family, in a misty-edged blow-up which showed him wearing a
grey suit jacket and a good, grey, spotted tie. It was astonishing
to think that his image had been presiding over this hearth at
the same time as it surveyed ours. Beside Leslie was a striking
if solemn-looking woman, the suggestion of Indian in her features, a long, clear face and red, red lips: this was Beatriz. Her
photograph had perhaps been enlarged slightly out of proportion with his in the process of making the montage. My change
of clothes paid off because one of the aunts remarked on how
clean I was. 'The English all look like film stars,' she added,
which I suppose was true in the sense that the English tend to
be white and so do film stars, although perhaps the aunt was
thinking of my grandfather, a ringer for one of Hollywood's
greats.

Leslie Frost and Beatriz Forero

Down a set of steps was a courtyard and a table surrounded by even more Foreros. Today, the day of an eclipse, was also by chance a birthday in the Forero family – though these presumably came thick and fast – and there was a good showing for lunch. I nerved myself to meet my uncle. There were three or four candidates among the lunch party. I made my way around them all – affably dumpy guys with, surely, no trace of the Clark Gable features, the lean Frost genes – before asking, as politely as I could, if the real *Tío Federico* would please stand up. But he wasn't there, not yet. In fact, it wasn't even his house, it was the home of an aunt, an aunt who had raised him after Beatriz died. Federico was expected to the birthday party. He had no idea that I would be there, poor man: all he had been told was to expect a cousin, but cousins were like flies in Colombia.

We ate turkey risotto. The hotelier told my story to the wordless Foreros, not leaving out, but neither overstating, his

own crucial role. It was his big speech. '*Finalidad!*' he concluded, making the word sound like '*Voilà!*', and spreading his
arms. I passed around my travelworn pictures and in return I
was shown a family album: Leslie was on the first page, cast in
the role of dynast, of founder, in the pose seen in the sitting
room. A page or two later, there he was again, in Oxford bags
and a sleeveless sweater in a perhaps cooler spot than the
Magdalena Medio. This wasn't a photograph I had seen before.
Leslie wasn't alone in it. There were other figures:
Colombians, Foreros, joining my grandfather on a day in the
country. This harmless snap had caught him red-handed in
his other life.

There was a hubbub among the non-dining Foreros in the sitting room and into sight at last came the imposingly tall and
brown and rangy man who was my Uncle Federico. Everyone
rushed to put him in the picture, to introduce uncle and
nephew. Federico was at a loss for words. He was a big, confident man without a thing to say for himself, a gameshow
contestant who thought he'd have more bottle until the time
came. We shook hands. He clasped my arm. I thought – I actually *thought* – about hugging him, but then thought better of it:
I had less bottle than I thought I had. This was my *uncle*!

I said, 'Is this a shock?'

'Yes, of course.'

'Good or bad?'

He laughed, my uncle laughed. He had a head of slightly
wavy black hair, coloured grey here and there, and a Zapata
moustache. His eyes were like Leslie's, and his nose was longer
and narrower than the classic Forero feature on view. He was
wearing a check shirt, open in the Honda heat, and a pair of
Levi's which hung slack over his backside. He sat down and this
was the cue for the hotelier to reprise his set piece. My uncle
began to drink beer straight from the bottle. I started asking him
questions. Lunch was set before him but it went untasted as I
asked away, the whole contingent of Foreros looking on.

I said, 'I should let you eat. I'm just so excited to meet you.' I decided to tell Federico about myself and my family in Britain. 'After Leslie left Colombia in 1957 he came back to England and he opened a post office. But he wasn't very well and he died in 1966.' *Had Federico known*, it occurred to me too late. I said, 'I don't know if you know that.'

'1966?'

'Yes.'

His expression was as opaque as his father's could be.

I said, 'Well, anyway, my mother – your half-sister – got married to my father and they had three children. I'm the eldest. My mother's still alive. Dad died last year.' I told Federico what I did for a living, that I was single. In practice I was telling the Forrero clan, and there was giggling at the latter disclosure.

Federico said that he'd like to show me his farm. That way I'd meet his wife and children. His *other* children, that was to say. Somewhere among the crowd was his eldest boy, good-looking and thoroughly Colombian, though perhaps he would grow as tall as his father in time. The *finca* was only half an hour away. It was decided. We would go in my uncle's antique Land Rover.

'British,' I said.

'Yes, the Land Rover is very good. But you have to be brave to ride with me,' he said, smiling. His voice was deep, but soft, quiet.

Federico's height made him eye-catching. I was talking to someone else, an aunt, not looking at Federico, who was going around the Land Rover to open the driver's door – and I saw in the corner of my eye a strikingly unusual figure, a fellow *gringo*, perhaps. I actually looked around to see who it was, to see my new uncle. Among our party were the aunt who had brought Federico up after Beatriz's death, Federico's son, Cousin Luis, me, and an unmarried aunt who was coming along, it was claimed, in order to give me the once-over as a prospective mate. It was a family outing, the sort of thing Leslie had been up to when he was compromisingly photographed in Oxford bags and sleeveless sweater.

The road went north and alongside it were railway lines. It was the road I had once taken from Honda to La Dorada, with a church rising from the jungle like a chess piece overlooked on a lawn. We stopped at a village where Federico bought *cervezas* and *gaseosas*, and then we turned onto an unmade road and went for a mile or perhaps two, at which point we broke down. After a time, during which an embarrassed Federico tried unsuccessfully to start the Land Rover again, we abandoned it and set off on foot in two different directions, Federico and his son going back the way we'd come, to beg a set of wheels from a neighbour, and the rest of us hiking through the hot and ululating river basin towards the still-distant farm, Cousin Luis talking unstoppably about humanism, and the spinster picking fruit off trees in an embittered way, and something in the undergrowth making a noise like a fax machine. I thought of Federico's remark, 'You have to be brave to ride with me.' No sooner had he ceased to be lost in Colombia than I was. Our ramble took us to a stream. Boys were bathing. A woman was washing clothes. We crossed a dry river bed. Finally, *Tio Federico* was clattering up behind us in a borrowed pick-up.

We came upon the *finca*. It was as isolated as Number Two, Mariquita had been in the days of the Frosts. Federico had called it *La Esperanza*, meaning hope. It was the home of a *campesino*, wooden walls with almost every trace of pink paint washed out, a tin roof and a concrete floor, a yard where a pair of old boys were sawing timber. There was a screened-off *baño*. There was no electricity, no telephone, there was no post. A car came out specially, Federico told me. At first sight, his circumstances were rudimentary; but the house was a good size, and Federico's children wore shoes and well-kept clothes: there was a pretty daughter and a boy of eleven, Federico Junior, Leslie's name passed on to another generation.

My uncle's wife, Miriam, was a year younger than him but looked older, filled out where he was spare; and you thought, how was a woman supposed to keep her looks in the middle of the jungle? 'They mature early there' – that was my mother's remark about the girl who had been Federico's mother, but the other side of it was that women were also quicker to mature in the more euphemistic sense of the word, half-dead at forty. Federico had met Miriam at the little place where we had collected refreshments. They weren't man and wife, in fact. Though no one quite said as much, I formed the impression that the experiences of Federico's childhood – not only Leslie's disappearance but also Beatriz's involvement with another man – had left him unprepared for married life, or perhaps I should say, prepared for a more informal arrangement.

I said to him, 'All I know about you is that you were born in 1955. What happened to you after that? Did you go to school, for instance?'

'No, I never went to school properly.'

'Why not?'

'I couldn't afford to. After my mother died, I started work.'

'I thought Leslie left you and your mother some money –'

'– *Nada, nada, nada. Nada!*' cut in the aunt who had raised Federico. Federico himself, *tranquilo*, said he didn't know about that. He was only seven when Beatriz died. 'My mother was very good, very nice, but she never spoke to me about my father,' he said. Like Elvia the cook, he was unaware of what had become of the letter my grandfather had left for him.

'Did you and your mother stay on at the house, Number Five?'

'I can't remember – I think so but I can't remember. I know we lived at Mariquita.'

In his own home, a dog slumbering under the table, Federico little by little became more expansive. He told me he had 800 hectares of land. He grew maize and raised gamine white cattle. He was involved in a scheme to coordinate local farmers and press for better infrastructure. While we were talking on the stoop, one of his neighbours came through on his way to town, bumping down the track from his own *finca* some miles further up the Magdalena, and it was clear by the way this man talked to my uncle – particularly by the way he listened to him – that

Federico was respected, he was seen as a man with get-up-and-go, with unforced authority.

I said, 'Do you like your life here? I suppose you must do, but a lot of people would think it was a very tough life for you all.'

'*Siempre duro*' – things were always hard. But it wasn't a bad life, Federico added. He had once dreamt of doing other things, but without a good education, the dreams had been impossible.

'When I was trying to imagine you, I thought you might be a footballer, you know, like Asprilla –'

'– *como Asprilla!*' Federico laughed.

'– or a guerrilla or a *narco*.'

'A guerrilla? No, definitely not that.'

The aunt who had been like a mother to Federico butted in, 'He is very intelligent. He has taught himself. He can fix any machine.'

'Can he fix a Land Rover?'

Federico laughed. He was remarkable, I thought – *not* a narco-baron or footballer or politician, but everything you could want in a long-lost uncle, all the same: handsome, assured, a figure of integrity. I stole long looks at his hands: it was the baby-watching impulse again. My mother was disappointed with her hands, my dad's long fingers one of the things she'd liked about him. Federico's hands were not large, his fingers not long – but broad, brown and knotty as wood, the hands of a workman, a farmer, the hands of my mother's brother. My hands were alien-pale in comparison; in the humidity, the fingertips had puckered as if they had been in the bath too long. Around my uncle's wrist was an old, metal watch.

I asked if he was angry with Leslie. 'Sometimes,' he agreed with great reluctance. 'A little bit, but he wasn't here. What could I do? I was here by myself.' His taciturnity, his can-do self-reliance: his father had left him something, after all.

'Leslie – he had two daughters?' he asked me.

'One.'

Federico Forero (right) and his family.
The author is second from right.

'And two sons.'

'That's right.' I told Federico that Leslie had always wanted a son. He must have been proud of him, despite everything. Federico told me a story about trying to find his father when he was a boy. He knew that Leslie had been a foreigner, a *gringo*. There was a *gringo* pilot at the little airstrip in Mariquita. One day the young Federico went out to the airstrip and asked the pilot, 'Can you take me to my Daddy?'

I had to call my mother – but they couldn't place international calls from the hotel in Mariquita, so I went to the *Telecom* office across the street. A handwritten sign, lashed to the double doors, made it clear that the office was closed. It was something to do with a *petition*, a claim – industrial action, by another name. Men were lounging flat out on the counter. When I pressed a quizzical face to the glass, one of them wagged a finger at me with a look of infinite judiciousness. Nobody seemed to mind this inconvenience – other *Telecom* offices in Mariquita remained open.

My mother had been so excited, or disturbed, that she hadn't been sleeping, she said. I told her all about Federico, how he resembled Leslie. I took a deep breath and I told her about the other boy, Federico's brother, Leslie's second son. I waited for my mother's reaction and she said, 'It's not a very good line, is it?' I didn't have the nerve to tell her again until much later.

'When you come back, you must stay at the *finca*,' Federico was saying. 'We can go for a swim and fish in the water hole.' We were in Mariquita, outside my hotel, hugging each other – unapologetically, now. And then he was getting back into a Dodge or a Chevvy, an American car from the 1950s. We had been out driving with various Foreros. If I had been looking for a large family circle, it was here. Federico said, 'I'll be waiting at the *finca* for you. *Muy lindo.*' My last sight of my uncle was of him waving, waving from the rear window of the 1950s car. The old-fashioned metal watch. My grandfather's hand.

10

Cathedral
of Salt

My blind date with a kidnap specialist began with an afternoon at Ivan's, and Ivan sitting in an armchair wearing a woollen hat. 'I know I look ridiculous – I don't care,' he said. He was complaining of a cold. We had caught a flight from Medellin to Bogota that afternoon and he had travelled with his eyes shut, ostensibly because he was feeling poorly, but also, I suspect, because he'd had to come and razzle me out of the airport bar, where I was drinking with the improbably encountered Dr Manuel Lopez of the rail operators, STF. Lopez, taking the same flight as us, had been sublimely unperturbed by the looming departure time. I was watching my watch: we were due to take off at 2.37. It was 2.22; then it was 2.25. At 2.26, Lopez had ordered another round. I thought: Lopez ought to know what he's doing, he probably travels like this all the time – seldom by train, I imagined – and, more importantly, he's Colombian, he understands that timetables and schedules are merely advisory. Then Ivan had appeared, all flustered, towing a little wheeled valise: 'Steve! That's the last call! Didn't you hear it? We have to go right away!' Lopez extinguished his cigarette lugubriously. 'Well, I was waiting for *him*,' he said. I felt like the American journalist in *The Killing Fields* – Sidney Schanberg, was it? – aloofly trying the patience of his interpreter.

It wasn't Ivan's place, strictly speaking, but his parents'. He had moved back in with them some years ago on his return from studying and translating in the United States. When I had first come to visit, I couldn't believe what I saw: a bungalow ringed by a metal fence and dwarfed by its sturdy girders. You would have thought it was a tantalisingly well-stocked field hospital in the middle of a combat zone. The young woman in a starched white pinafore who had admitted me into the compound had enhanced this image, although she had turned out to be a maid rather than a nurse.

Inside the bungalow, the decor and most of the possessions gave the impression of a time-capsule sealed in the 1970s or early 1980s. The day room in which Ivan now tended his cold was really a roofed-in patio, or should I say rockery: a trail of granite slabs led like stepping stones to the part of the bungalow where Ivan's parents had their quarters. There were paperbacks of things like *Kramer vs. Kramer* and a wall of Betamax cassettes. We had the television on – an American sitcom dubbed into Spanish – and Ivan was liverishly taking and making calls on his cellular phone. The maid brought us trays of late lunch – pea soup, *frijoles*, potato salad, rice, chicken – every item in its own dish, like a small, informal banquet. Ivan's parents were not at home, the distinguished orthodontist and his wife. I gathered that Ivan's mother could be suffocating; I considered the trail of stepping stones, the trenches between them. I wondered whether they weren't as conducive to domestic peace of mind as the stakes around the property.

In Medellin, Ivan and I had been for a pizza. He had sent his back – twice. Teenagers were queuing outside a cinema, the girls in trendy army pants, all unconscious of the fact that men were wearing such clothes in deadly earnest elsewhere in the city – unconscious of it, or just indifferent: you might as well have expected youngsters in Belfast not to go out or wear fashion during the Troubles. From the street stalls, Ivan had picked out a new watchstrap. The vendors of religious bric-a-brac were selling ephemera associated with St Gregorio, the saint in the three-piece suit, including statuettes like the one I'd bought in Manizales. Ivan said, 'My aunt was a great believer in St Gregorio. She was rather an unhappy person.' Her parents hadn't bothered to get the aunt an education – 'I shouldn't judge,' said Ivan – and she had ended up looking after them when they became elderly. At length the aunt married, but her husband was an alcoholic. The couple adopted a child, 'but there was something wrong with it.' Ivan shrugged. 'Well, there would be,' he said.

Our hotel in Medellin was beside a fruit market, in a red light district, one of the girls on the corner a transvestite with such a prominent Adam's apple, it made me think of a snake swallowing a pygmy. I lay in bed listening to the noise of the streets: cars changing gear, taxi horns, the barely audible bass rumble of the metro. I was going home. My mother had told me there was news of Federico: a first letter from the lonely *finca*. This in turn was proof that the postman had got through with *her* letter. Federico wrote, 'I had the pleasure of reading the mail that you sent . . . in which you say that everyone is in good health, working, the small histories of our family. Truly we take great pleasure in hearing about the past.' He said he had been surprised to discover his English family. 'We will investigate further.' Federico included 'news of us here on the farm': the children were busy at their studies, looking forward to a school holiday. 'They are anxious to know you all.' Miriam was well, Federico said, collaborating with him in his work, looking after the children and animals. 'Of myself I tell you that I am well, working on the farm and enduring life with patience'. I anticipated going back to the *finca* one day, getting to know the Forreros, taking my uncle up on the offer of some fishing, a little swimming in the water hole. Perhaps I would even introduce Federico to my mother, his half-sister.

At the maximum security bungalow in Bogota, one of Ivan's friends rang to say that he'd fixed Ivan up with a blind date. The blind date was cover for the friend, Tom, who was married but taking out a woman he fancied, with Ivan and his companion making up the innocent-seeming foursome. Ivan sat in his arm-chair with his tray of lunch in his lap and fussed. 'I bet she'll be cheesy.' He tried to persuade me to go instead of him – Tom sold kidnap and ransom insurance, he said. Well, *I* was on. But this arrangement wasn't ideal, I felt; how would Ivan's date feel, meeting me instead of the *bogotano* she had been expecting? 'She'll love you. Women adore foreigners,' said Ivan. The sitcom had ended and now there was one of the new episodes of *Mission Impossible*. Ivan said that he had enjoyed *Star Trek – the Next Generation*, though not the original show.

I demanded a receipt for some money I had given him: more Sidney Schanberg on my part, I'm afraid. I didn't have any use for the receipt – it had been Ivan's idea, originally – but he was making such a song and dance about his cold that I cruelly insisted that he take the opportunity of being near his computer to print me what I was owed. He kept his computer in his bed-room, like a teenager. While we waited for the receipt to print off, Ivan took down a black-and-white photograph from a book-shelf, a portrait behind Cellophane. 'Tell me what you think of that face,' he said. I was looking at a kindly, Asian woman of early middle age. She had long dark hair.

Ivan surprised me by saying, 'Doesn't he have the warmest eyes you've ever seen?' This was Ivan's guru, it seemed. He had another picture of the same man, by now distinctly aged. 'That was taken minutes before he died. Look at his eyes!' Ivan had a paperback of the guru's teachings. 'When I heard about him, I had to find out more.' From my experience of him, Ivan was good-humoured, kind to children and animals. But there was another side to him; he had a dry sense of humour, a finicky side, a mean streak.

He was coming round to the idea of the blind date, despite his cold, and having to go to Cartagena early the next day, to provide simultaneous translation at a conference. He had per-suaded me to try a hotel in the prosperous north of the city,

which happened to be near the restaurant where the date had
been fixed. It was modern, sleek, with every facility, and it was
absolutely identical to every other businessman's hotel: there
were glass-sided lifts rising from the lobby floor, but in my sev-
enth-storey eyrie, I missed the draughty hotel in Candelaria,
and wondered why I hadn't noticed at once that the new place
had carpeted floors – not the polished boards and terracotta of
my old haunt.

I hadn't been in my room long when Ivan called. There was
a problem with the date. Ivan's friend, Tom, had gone to the
appointed eaterie and found that the girls, apparently not caring
for the menu or the prices, had left. It didn't sound promising,
but Ivan picked me up anyway: no woollen cap now, but a scarf
around a tweedy sports coat in the manner of a don.

In the chic north of the city, designers kept their boutiques
ablaze late, with no screens or shutters to spoil the window
dressing. The roads were wide, the pavements deserted. There
were no vagrants. There were new, trendy diners and a palpable
absence of Bogota unease. I studied the over-priced menu in the
window of an Italian restaurant, clearly popular with well-to-do
bogotanos. The wine waiter was delivering heavy, costly-looking liquor to a party of four near the door. There were no wine
glasses on their table but chunky laboratory vessels which were
full of ice and colours at the margins of the vintner's spectrum.

Ivan had been given the coordinates of the rearranged date in
a call from Tom, the kidnap specialist. The location was a
restaurant in a converted house, with a carved wooden staircase
as a talking-point, and lots of candles. There was already a party
of five by the time we arrived: Tom, putting on a little weight,
losing a little hair, in a windcheater; his would-be squeeze,
Anjela; and Ivan's date, a pouch-cheeked woman with a grating
voice. The other two were a woman who didn't speak English,
or so I was told – later, and suddenly, she broke into it without
a hitch, and no wonder: she had been living in Florida for
years – and a man whose son was driving racing cars in Britain.
Apart from Ivan and myself, everyone at the table appeared to

have children aged eighteen or more, though this seemed improbable in the case of everyone except Tom.

   Tom spoke English, or American, very well; his mistress-in-prospect, less so, though she and I managed to get through why I was there, the names of old British rock bands (Bread, the Electric Light Orchestra) and some jokes about Ivan – Anjela decided he looked more like a priest than a don. There was mulled wine. When we'd arrived, the others had just lost interest in a plate of sweetmeats – the last we were to see of dinner. Tom was reticent about his business, but did say, 'We've got someone kidnapped at this time. They've had him one or two months – no, wait – he was taken in January!' This seemed to make the point, conceded by Tom, that Colombians had become inured to kidnapping. 'They don't even mention it on TV,' he said. Some people overreacted, took out so much security, invested in so many devices and services, that they only served to draw attention to themselves as worthwhile targets; to emphasise their kidnappability, as Ivan might have put it. Other people just didn't take out enough security, said Tom. 'Go figure!' He didn't discuss specifics – perhaps he didn't care to: that's certainly what his manner suggested – making out it wasn't actually his area. 'We have people who advise on the technical stuff.' The main thing was to avoid routine. 'A client said to me, "But this means we'll never be able to lead a normal life." I nearly said to him, "Hey, this is Colombia" – you know?'

Poor old Tom, versed in the arts of risk-avoidance, kidnap management, had no means of handling his date, who was as unsteady and exciting as gelignite. There would be no eating, we must dance, Anjela more or less decreed. The women present had been given advice on where to go dancing by their teenage children. We walked across a pleasant green, where sales of paintings were held on Sundays, to a bar done out in a kitsch, Christian-y way. There were more candles and a folk trio and *bogotanos* singing along at tables laden with *aguardi-ente* bottles, tables too densely packed to leave room for a dance floor. We arrived in ones and twos, took stock, waiting for Anjela. The general view was that the bar was fine. But no: Anjela had to dance. I wondered where we were going next.

Anjela consulted Ivan – Ivan the amenable, Ivan the priestly conciliator. I can't imagine that he can have voiced anything more than the most elliptical endorsement of the bar, or the most ambiguous reservations about moving on elsewhere. But at all events, Anjela's objections evaporated: we went ahead and found a cramped table and ordered red wine and *aguardiente*. We joined in the singing. There was a Beatles medley. Tom leant across the table to me: 'They knew you were coming!' he said. Anjela couldn't sit still, getting up every few moments to get a better view of the trio, dancing on the spot. The folk singer came round to meet his public – moustache, bald spot, leather waistcoat – and I wondered if I could possibly have mistaken him for anything else.

As the band struck up with one particular number, everyone in the place got up, and I was tapped on the shoulder by a brown-skinned *bogotana* who had been sitting at the next table. '*Queres bailar?*' she said. We embarked on a salsa, my left hand in hers, the other on her very trim waist. Her name was Marcella, she was twenty-four and she worked in Switzerland for IBM. She had come home to see her family. But where was *I* from? For want of anywhere better known, I said *Londres*. After a moment, Marcella said, 'That's all right,' making me think that she was contemplating jetting in from Geneva for assigna-tions under the clock at Waterloo Station. She had an odd, high voice, and a mole in the middle of her forehead. She was attrac-tive. The transparency of her motives was almost blush-making: I wondered whether Beatriz had ever entertained notions of becoming Sra Frost, with the security of a ring and a British passport. I told Marcella how soon I was going back to Britain. It was tomorrow. But at what *hour*, Marcella enquired. In the evening, I said. After a moment, she repeated, 'That's all right.'

But later she must have decided that it wasn't all right after all, because she looked at me and said, 'I'm going to my friends now,' and returned to her table.

We had some food, finally, some *tapas*: small, fried new potatoes, *chorizos* and yucca. 'You like yucca?' asked Tom. He was getting on about as well with the flighty Anjela as Marcella had with me. Anjela had a way of looking at you, talking to you for a moment, making you want the moment to be longer – and then going, and not getting back to you until she had been round everyone else, and you knew you had her figured – until she was back talking to you again. She was thirty-eight, divorced with one child. 'I'm looking for a prince,' she told me over the music, the tipsy singing.

'Well, perhaps he's here, right now,' I heard myself say, going in to bat for the out-thought Tom, but Anjela didn't think so, and nor did I: Tom the kidnap specialist, whose job was all about risk, whose job was to *take* risks, was just too risk-averse for Anjela. Tom's face betrayed all his worries about his family. 'I suppose I'd better get home. My wife will be wondering where I am!' was his wretched way of laughing things off as we went back to our cars.

Ivan drove me to my hotel. He hadn't chipped in any money on our night out – I had the impression that friends like Tom knew about this side of him. I told Ivan that his blind date had nice legs. 'I like her,' he said. She had survived two divorces, marrying 'way too young' the first time, and latterly to an alcoholic. For a time, she'd lived away from the city, on a farm, and had received death threats from local gunmen – it wasn't clear of which stripe, perhaps not even to her. I was saying to Ivan that he should think about whether he fancied her. If he didn't, what was the point? He said, 'Oh do you think so?' and I wondered whether I heard sarcasm in his voice. But then I considered: perhaps he really does welcome my advice, as he said he did, for what it might be worth. Perhaps he was merely humouring me. I'd been thinking that Ivan was a terrible warning; a vision of the future, if I wasn't careful. Living with mum (not *that*, surely); living for himself if not entirely by himself; pernickety; a tray on the lap and freelance work and a Cellophaned picture of a guru on a bookshelf.

I woke next day with an impulse to see *La Catedral de Sal*. The salt cathedral was said to be the most impressive man-made sight in Colombia. It was about an hour's journey by car, on *Carretera del Norte*. Prehistorical deposits and encrustations of sodium chloride had made a gargantuan salt cellar of a mountainside at a place called Zapiquira. It had been exploited since well before the Spanish conquest, and after the muscular Christianity of the colonists had taken hold, miners had hewn a Catholic shrine out of one of the crystalline faces. During the 1950s, my grandfather's final years in Colombia, a subterranean cathedral had been excavated at Zapiquira – three cavernous naves with crudely sculpted columns and a towering, illuminated cross. I had read that this inside-out – or, rather, outside-in – basilica was so huge that it had been possible to make a tour by car: there had been a tunnel of brotherly love. *Nuestra Señora del Rosario,* the Virgin of the Rosary, the patron of colliers, had lent her name to the salty see upon consecration in 1954. But cracks appeared in the salt cap and the cathedral was declared unsafe and closed in 1990. Work began on a sturdier church which was eventually opened five years later.

A *mestizo* in a homburg with a beaten-up Japanese saloon agreed to take me to the cathedral. We left Bogota in rain; the clouds surrounding the tops were more than ever like cigarette smoke, like cigarette smoke glimpsed across a room, moving slowly, light slanting onto it. The road to *La Catedral de Sal* was known as the road of death, according to a sign warning of traffic accidents. There was a long stretch of corrugated roof at the roadside, like the cover of a cattle market, and beneath it Indian women cooking sides of meat in fiercely hot metal teepees, the roof blackened by the smoke. Another place sold eggs – the kiosk itself had a facade white and ovoid as an egg. In a well-mowed municipal park, boys were playing soccer on pitch after pitch: the little league all seemed to be wearing blue shirts — hundreds of them.

The cathedral was at the end of the railway line out of Bogota, the Nemocon line, the route of the *Aguardiente Express*, as sluggish as the Colombian football team. I had come tantalisingly close to seeing the cathedral on the day I had taken the *Aguardiente Express*, but in the end the best I had managed was the Museum of Salt at Nemocon. I'm afraid the *Museo de Sal* had been as dry as its subject, a series of glass cases in which miniature figurines posed tableaux from local history; this was meted out in absurd salami slices — ten years at a time since the discovery of fire, or so it had seemed. The guide had been a bossy young woman with a large mouth and a dying fall to her pronouncements.

From the car, I could see the fishbone of the railway line. There was supposed to be money on the way at last for the abandoned railways of Colombia. Forty years after the routes that Leslie had mapped had been handed over to the government and allowed to fall into decline, there were moves to pump-prime the railroads with foreign investment. The entire network, such as it was, had been put out to tender, according to José D. Lievano, who was the closest thing I could find to a minister of railways, though some measure of the still-lowly status of his office could be gleaned by the fact that his car park in downtown Bogota was protected by a man with a duck rifle. Colombia was about to discard the old system, in which the state-owned *Ferrovias* maintained the track and the private sector STF was responsible for operations. 'This was a marriage,' said Sr Lievano, smartly turned out for our interview in a tie with a motif of horsey tack, and unable to suppress a wince of disbelief that his English caller had not thought better of road-worn jeans. 'But the marriage didn't work out. *Ferrovias* had the job of fixing the line, but it wasn't close enough to STF to commission repairs when and where they were most needed;

it usually fixed the line where the train *didn't* go, because of political reasons. That's why I call it a bad marriage.' Sr Lievano, guarded behind spectacles and tombstone teeth, didn't elaborate about the political reasons, but I thought I could hazard a guess. Senators and regional politicos would see votes in keeping the line up to scratch for members of the electorate who were in the habit of catching one of Colombia's few trains, or making their own transportation with *brujitas*. The guerrillas, too, liked to see the railway . . . To make matters worse in the 'bad marriage', a senior manager at *Ferrovias* had been accused of embezzling $18 million. Despite the loss of this untrifling sum, it was Sr Lievano's view that the troubles of the railways had nothing to do with a shortage of investment.

'What about the guerrillas, drug-running?'

'The line is very rarely attacked by the guerrillas – blown up, I mean.' The minister of railways believed there had been explosive sabotage perhaps two or three times in the past five years, on stretches of the Atlantic route favoured by coal exporters: an underestimate, judging by what I had discovered, but all the same it was true that Colombia's almost hysterically destructive factions gave the railways a comparatively easy ride. 'It's curious, I guess. Maybe the guerrillas don't see money there, in railways. In the oil industry, in other foreign interests, they see money. As for drugs, no.' Sr Lievano paused. 'The traffickers prefer something a little faster, I think. And there aren't enough trains.'

But things were changing. There was a new philosophy. The government had come round to the idea that railways were complementary to roads and rivers. There was a new plan. Operation and infrastructure would be under the same roof, and in private hands. The first route on offer was the Atlantic service itself, the greatest railway in Colombia, the longest uninterrupted man-made link in the country, the stretch which included Leslie's old La Dorada line. The successful bidder would be given the opportunity to redevelop this railway, plus a sweetener from the government of $140

million, and the right to levy tolls on the freight moved along
the most northerly section of the line, from La Loma to Santa
Marta, which were estimated to be worth $40 million a year. Sr
Lievano said, 'We want somebody to fix the line and to give
the answer to the problems of transportation.' Companies from
South America and Europe had expressed interest, he said.
The line out of Cali, the route followed by the Cocaine Train,
was also in the window: one Iberian–Colombian consortium
had expressed interest. It was looking for $120 million from
the state in development money. It had been decided to restore
the old railway stations – about 200 of them, half of the original total – with luck as successfully as the vaulting temple on
the Manizales line. Some would be returned to their original
use; others would be turned over to the mayors in the towns
where they stood, with a view to them being used as municipal offices or cultural centres. The Colombians were beginning
to appreciate the inheritance of their railways, as they were the
aerial ropeway which had once been suspended across the
Andes.

The *mestizo* and I stopped to buy coffee – though there was
none – at a shack where chickens turned on a spit. There was a
seedy-looking European in a well-used tracksuit and a toupee.
He was Swiss, he said. Was I North American? He wanted to
know about immigration to the United States. But what was he
doing here in the first place? 'A *chica*,' he said, with a roué-ish
expression. He had bulging blue eyes. I thought of Nicholas,
the émigré Swiss of Cali with the teased coxcomb and
Colombian spouse and the jokes about the many children he
had sired. Who would have thought the Swiss were so fond of
sex? The chickens completed another baleful revolution. I told
the man with the toupee that I didn't think he'd have many
problems settling in the United States, at least not compared to
a Colombian. 'I've been working on a farm,' said the Swiss,
gazing out at the *altiplano*: this appeared to be a complication,
his job. 'And there's so much paperwork . . .' He had done nothing about naturalisation, and he never would, a move to the

States just a dream in his *aguardiente* cups – unless by chance I had been an attaché who could have written the visa out for him there and then.

Carretera del Norte didn't look very much like 'the road of death'. But the Colombia you encountered every day, the Colombia of mountains and rivers, pack mules and soot-trailing *busetas*, of maudlin *vallenato* music and maize cakes, was an incongruously beautiful backdrop for guerrillas and death squads and drug gangsters. I recalled the old joke about God designing Colombia, giving it the best of everything, every blessing, until the angels demanded an explanation – and the Almighty said, 'Relax, you haven't seen the Colombians yet.'

We passed a paddock of lush-looking grass, glossy with sunshine, a *vaquero* straddling his mount on a hemp saddle. A tin roof on two poles shaded half an old lorry tyre: a homemade water-trough. There was a breezeblock house, a lean-to under a polythene tarpaulin, a TV aerial on a long bamboo mast.

Was Colombia still on the road of death? There were conflicting indicators. The new president, Pastrana, was enjoying a honeymoon period, though a politician from anywhere else but Colombia might already have been dreaming of a quickie annulment: political atrocity raged, with a spectacularly grisly conflagration after an oil pipeline was dynamited; a marathon public sector strike shut down many key services. No honeymoon at all, on the face of it; but importantly, a dialogue between the state and Colombia's clandestine factions, tentatively embarked upon before Pastrana was elected, continued to be patched through over the interference of violence. A month before he assumed power, Pastrana had visited the leaders of FARC in the southern province of Caqueta. As president, he passed a decree recognising the political status of FARC: a European observer was bound to recall steps taken to include hard-liners in Ireland and Spain in mainstream politics. The new leader also made the considerably more exotic gesture of offering to withdraw the army from an area the size of Switzerland.

In October 1998, Pastrana went on a state visit to Washington, the first Colombian president to do so in more than twenty years. Harvard-educated, fluent in English and with many friends in the United States, he was as fêted as his predecessor, the disgraced Samper, had been humbled. That said, the trip didn't go off entirely smoothly. Apart from the embarrassment of the Colombian air force Hercules impounded at Fort Lauderdale with a ton of coke in the hold – a darkly comic throwback to the Samper incumbency – Pastrana stirred things up himself by challenging the fundamental assumptions of the West's 'drug war' against his country. It was an expensive waste of time and effort, he said. It was an obstacle to a peace settlement in Colombia, which was the prerequisite for any satisfactory outcome to the drugs problem. Pastrana argued that tactics like spraying *coca* bushes and opium poppies with herbicide were so clumsy that they were counter-productive, the almost inevitable side effect of ruining perfectly harmless crops a sure way of turning ordinary Colombians against the campaign. The guerrillas had told the new president that they were willing to join forces with him to curb drugs. But first it was necessary to staunch the bloodshed of Latin America's longest-running conflict.

Congress decided to give Pastrana the benefit of the doubt, not to mention $2.6 million, some of it in the form of top-of-the-range Blackhawk helicopters for the Colombian police. His homeland was now the greatest beneficiary of United States tax dollars after Israel and Egypt, receiving $280 million in fiscal 1999. The Clinton administration made the right noises about the peace initiative – 'There is enormous respect for President Pastrana, for his plan and where he is going,' said the Treasury Secretary – but the main interest was in what the new Colombian leader could do to keep his country's notorious export off Main Street, USA. Republicans attached a condition to the aid. As though they hadn't been listening to their visitor, they stipulated that it would be cut off if Pastrana's peace efforts interfered with established anti-drugs programmes. Speculation grew that his gamble in demilitarising 15,000 square miles could give hawks in Washington a pretext for intervention: they would no longer be meddling in sovereign Colombia, the argument went, but in a Marxist banana republic which was only notionally connected to the internationally recognised nation. Officials in Washington expressed the view that FARC could take power within five years unless checked, but they denied that the United States would take part in Colombia's internal conflict.

At home, Pastrana's project didn't impress the right-wing paramilitaries. They killed ten people and abducted fifteen in the town of San Carlos in Antioquia; they murdered eleven in Altos del Rosario in Bolivar: the gunmen worked from lists, as usual, and as usual they dragged people from their homes and shot them while their families and neighbours looked on helplessly and in horror. What was different about these attacks was what the death squads had to say in the graffiti they left behind: 'Pastrana is twisted' was the message. A group calling itself R-20 used chainsaws to torture and beheed peasants near Vegachi, in Antioquia. Eleven died and thirteen were kidnapped. The monitoring group Human Rights Watch was now attributing 60 per cent of the most flagrant abuses in Colombia to the paramilitaries. They, or their friends in the army, were suspects in the murders of four prominent trades unionists as a national strike closed schools and left hospitals providing only emergency care. The dispute began after Pastrana introduced austerity measures intended to reduce the country's budget deficit, and the privatisation of inefficient state concerns; he ended up authorising pay rises worth 15 per cent just to get Colombians back to work after a month-long shutdown. By the winter of 1998–99, Pastrana had declared a limited state of emergency, just like his predecessor had done, assuming absolutist powers to make laws as high interest rates and overdue debts threatened to set off a banking crisis.

In spite of the president's overtures to the leftists, the guerrillas hadn't laid down their arms. In skirmishes with the security forces, they continued to take and make casualties, and the Marxist ELN group was accused of bombing an oil pipeline near Segovia, sending a fireball of crude through two hamlets, incinerating at least seventy people. The rebels claimed it had been a mistake. A woman called Nury Velasquez, whose son and three grandchildren were among the dead, told reporters, 'Hell is here on Earth. After this, there can be no other hell for these poor people.' It was the same Segovia which had been visited by appalling paramilitary violence ten years earlier.

A Japanese businessman with interests in coffee and emeralds was abducted from his farm in central Colombia. The government's anti-kidnapping office said the disappearance of Shimura Shoro, who was sixty-nine, brought to 954 the number of people taken in 1998; an independent organisation which counselled kidnap victims and their families, *Pais Libre*, published their own only slightly more shattering calculation of 1,577; though that was for the first eight months of the year alone.

It was a different country from the one my mother remembered; she hardly recognised my descriptions of Colombia. Clearly, it had changed in the forty-odd years since she had last visited. It had always been strangely violent, but it had grown more violent – and as a result, more strange, more remote. Hopes rested with the Pastrana government, but they weren't high hopes. Colombia had been the country of my mother's childhood, a magical place of sun and mountains and animals. She had grown up talking and reading in Spanish, and thinking like a Colombian, she said.

On the road to Zapiquira, I remembered an incident which had highlighted my mother's Colombian attitudes (though it had happened in England). There had been a rat in the cellar. Perhaps it had been disturbed by the removal men. Although it might have sensed that the house was emptying, it wasn't behaving in the classical rat manner, getting out first. It was sickly looking, according to an eyewitness, and didn't look as though it was going anywhere. The cat couldn't be persuaded to behave in the classical cat manner, either, so my mother went to find the wooden mallet – formerly used, I seemed to remember, for knocking home tent pegs – and bludgeoned the rat to death. As I knew she would, she invoked her Colombian upbringing: the matter-of-fact chicken-throttling; the day when the dog produced thirteen puppies and the cat seven kittens and 'my father very determinedly got seven assorted whelps and went off and drowned them'. I picked up the rat between two pieces of plywood and, at my mother's suggestion, left it in the middle of the garden, for the crows. Within minutes, it had gone. Mum said that her neighbours had been complaining about a rat, they might have poisoned it. I pointed out the food-chain implications. 'Well, there are too many crows anyway,' said the girl from Mariquita.

It was a year since my dad had died and the house had been sold, the house where my brother and sister and I had grown up, completion pencilled in by an odd coincidence for the anniversary of his death. A cocktail shaker belonging to Leslie had turned up in all the clearing out and Mum had put it on one side for me in case I wanted it. He had loved a party, she said. He was the life and soul on the cruise ships, once he had a few drinks inside him: I thought of the photographs of him in the costume of a Scottish drunk. Mum was talking quite a lot about him. In a story I didn't fully grasp, she said that Leslie would gather cobwebs in the morning in Colombia and use them to test his homemade instruments – an unforgettable picture was conjured of this immensely practical man double-checking his calibrations with the filigree of spiders' webs.

They found the emphysema when he was already in hospital, Mum said. He was undergoing tests for cancer. It was around then that Gran discovered the letters from Beatriz, discovered what had happened in Mariquita. She had gone round to her sister's, to my Aunty Joan's, and come right out with it as soon as Joan had answered the bell, on her doorstep. 'She was terribly hurt,' my mother said.

Leslie began by passing it off to Gran as a fling. Then he'd asked her, 'Does Rosemary know?'

'She's never mentioned it but I think she does.'

Mum told me, 'I knew, but I kept it to myself. It shocked me – I suppose because my father had always been so strict. My reaction was, "How *could* he?" It seemed so hypocritical. But then, as you grow up, you get to know about men and what they do.'

Later, during a downpour, as Mum and I were getting drenched, she said, 'It could come on to rain.' One of Dad's trusty jokes. We were in the churchyard, with my sister. Because of the move, there wouldn't be time to come up on the anniversary itself. The churchyard was well-kept but not prissily so: the stalks of wild flowers seeming to pick up the static, the atmospherics, between the summer storms; the sky black; chalky gargoyles over the church door – the one we had filed in and out of at the funeral – a tree with leaves the colour of red cabbage. Dad would have known the name of it; or if not him, then his dad, Uncle Stephen, my other, reluctant grandfather. Mum was kneeling, clipping grass with a pair of kitchen scissors, grass from around the flat tablet with Dad's name on it. There were fresh flowers: gold carnations for him, and pink for Gran ('She liked pink'), who had her name on another plaque close by. My mum began trimming the grass around that, too, and I saw, or perhaps I simply noticed for the first time, that Leslie's name was on it beside Gran's. But his remains had been laid to rest miles away, in a cemetery by a dual carriageway, the one I'd been taken to as a boy.

Yes, said Mum, she'd asked to have Leslie's name added to Gran's, and she had often thought of moving him, but what was the point, really? The man who had led a double life was even buried in two places.

On the way to the Cathedral of Salt, I thought: I came to Colombia in my mid-thirties, the age Leslie was when he had moved his family to Manizales in order to take up a position with the La Dorada company. My mind had been full of death, the death that seemed synonymous with Colombia in the 1990s, the long-ago death of my grandfather, the death of my father. I had found the Colombia I had been expecting, the Colombia I deserved, perhaps – though not even I could have overlooked the life I found in everybody. I wouldn't forget the Stag's Head, or the *mariachi* men of Caracas Avenue; *La Cigarra* in Manizales; the man in a café outside Cali who 'ate from the same plate' as the *narcos*; Constanza, the beauty of the Medellin *barrios*. I wouldn't forget Uncle Freddie and the Foreros of Honda. My family.

I had met my uncle on the day of an eclipse, and this had turned out to be rather apt. For a time, meeting him had obscured everything, but then the moment had passed, and presently it had taken its place among what Federico called 'the small histories of our family'. I had finally plucked up the courage to tell Mum about Federico's brother, the second son Beatriz had borne Leslie. '*Really?*' said my mother. '*Two* children?' I was afraid that the second son would be a double blow, twice as bad as one, but it was all so long ago that in the event it wasn't half as bad, nowhere near half as bad.

Zipiquira was the last place in Colombia; the final entry in the gazeteers and guidebooks. It had grown up around a refinery for processing salt. This stood at the foot of the mountain where the cathedral itself had been hollowed out. Because of the cathedral, the town had developed a tourist industry of sorts, shops selling bright blankets and toy *busetas*. I bought a cheap pamphlet, climbed a steep road, and came upon a portal like the entrance to a mine shaft: I went down the cathedral.

'Neither the most thrilling account of adventure nor the best novel of action, perhaps only the ancient epic poems, can describe the expedition of several men that under Jimenez de Quesada came from the Atlantic Coast to the centre of the continent,' the cheap pamphlet began understatedly. It was an account of how the Spanish under de Quesada discovered the

Indians' salt racket, and brusquely assumed the franchise. The author, Oswaldo Diaz, went on in the same shrinking style as he described the experiences of the conquistadors: 'They suffered all sorts of penalties, faced great dangers, had to fight with wild Indians, unexpected animals, a vegetation that tried to imprison them within its tentacles, unknown illnesses, poisoned arrows and also had to fight hunger. They came through forest and swamps and had to climb mountains that seemed to touch the sky with its snow-capped peaks. What led them and gave them incentive to persevere in this extraordinary and wild undertaking? Salt.' Over centuries, the local Muisca tribe had found a way of drying out the raw material of the mountain over their fires, reducing it to glittering loaves. The beauty of this was that the salt was portable; it was the original takeaway. The Spaniards persuaded the Muisca to let them have the recipe. It was the beginning of a complex relationship between the Christians and the Indians and, though Diaz didn't say so, a dubious one, too: 'In this way the Indians exchanged the salt of the land for the salt of religion . . . they redeemed with salt their souls for heaven.'

Mining began in 1808, under an expatriate engineer, a German named Jacobo Wiesner. The enterprise was as precarious and foolhardy-seeming as the aerial ropeway of *El Cable* a century later. Hitting his rhetorical stride at last, Diaz wrote, 'What is interesting to note is how the miners with poor tools, risking their lives second by second among landslides, outbursts of power and dynamite, in the middle of lethal gases, in the darkness of almost a hundred years barely broken with the dim light of tallow candles, breathing an impure air and under the threat of imminent dangers, continued excavating the land in galleries, tunnels and caves – in summary, a frightening labyrinth – to extract the raw salt.' This was processed: dried in moulds made out of mud.

It was little wonder that the miners murmured their prayers to the Virgin of the Rosary, made a rough little altar, an oil lamp burning on it. They wanted to erect a more enduring shrine, but the vapours in the mine would have tarnished a metal cross, corrupted a ceramic image. So they adapted the technology they were using to withdraw the salt: they baked a statue of mud, and erected it in a salty grotto. The same unvarnished piety guided the development of the subterranean cathedral, established on top of the mine shafts. The architect was a man called José Maria Gonzalez Concha. According to the rococo prose of Oswaldo Diaz, 'his fine art rejected all decoration that could tarnish the primitive cyclopean character' of the mountain void. Dr Gonzalez himself said he hoped that 'in this church of salt . . . in its absolute purity, is a reflection of the soul of the believer . . . a prayer, a meditation raised on the mysteries of Christ.'

A file of people was coming and going out of the mountain, like termites, and there was a curious odour of sulphur. By a blueish light – the rays of neon strip bulbs, diffused through the cured gloom – it was possible to make out representations of the stations of the cross ('Jesus falls to the ground of second time') in the tunnel descending to the nave. The rebuilt cathedral had been inaugurated by former President Samper. It was capable of holding 10,000 – like a nuclear bunker, or a dance venue – but what it put you in mind of, with its crannies and recesses, was a series of burial chambers, the pickled air perhaps encouraging this.

I thought of Leslie, buried in two places. What did I know about my grandfather that I couldn't have told you before I visited Colombia? Without a prompt, I could now recount his biography: the birth in 1900, the first year of the century, the final century of the millennium; the military father and florist mother; the apprenticeship; the courageous war service; the marriage to my gran; the arrival of my mum; the years as an engineer in Sudan and Colombia. I had been through Leslie's papers, and his file at the railway archives in Bogota. I had seen the ruins of *El Cable* and travelled across Colombia with my grandfather's map on what was left of the railways that he had known, now set to receive a despaired-of reprieve. I had found his old house at Mariquita. I had found his son – yes, I'd had the feeling I was closer to my grandfather when I was with Federico: the Frost features, the almost period quality of can-do masculinity; not forgetting the familiar photograph in the sitting room in Honda, as iconic in its way as the bust of Valderrama I had sheltered behind on Medellin's *La Setenta* when England played Colombia.

Of the two of them, father and son, Federico should have been the more exotic, the harder to make out: a Colombian, a *campesino*. Leslie ought to have been easier to read. His deeds were all done, immutable. But the principal witness to them was beyond recall, and they were open to interpretation, to revision. History was mendacious. There was the fact of my grandfather's service in the Royal Flying Corps, but then there were the lies about his age, the undisclosed career as a teenage fighter ace over France. There was the marriage, the family: the wife and the daughter. And then there was the house in Mariquita, the young, dark mistress, the sons. I thought about the statuette of St Gregorio which I'd bought in Manizales, the saint who manifested himself in the garment of an accountant, and then of Leslie, wearing his pullover and opaque expression in the old black-and-white portrait, changing for his undercover role among the Foreros into Oxford bags and sleeveless sweater. There was Leslie the Victorian paterfamilias, and then there was the earthier man who had lived in Mariquita with Beatriz. My grandfather was like a cathedral of salt himself.

At the heart of the diocesan bunker was a domed ceiling. By the undersea light, I saw that it was marbled with salt, and growing stalactites of salt – they looked like drying icicles of builders' grout. Tour guides passed beneath this ceiling, trailing their crocodiles of visitors. I could taste salt on my lips, the savoury faith of Zapiquira ('they redeemed with salt their souls for heaven'). It was time to confess to guilt. I couldn't doubt that Leslie, a private man and, as it turned out, a secretive one, would have disapproved of what I had been doing. I considered

his case. He had been separated from his loved ones, from
Peggie, and a long way from home – though I increasingly felt
that his real home had been Colombia all along. Apparently, he
had believed that the woman he had married was no longer
able to provide him with all the comforts of a wife. The relationship with Beatriz had been a sexual one, and it had clearly
put a spring in the old boy's step – I thought of him taking the
air in the Mariquita *paseo*, Beatriz at his side and their son in
his pram. Though this involvement had harmed people I loved,
I didn't begrudge it, for what that was worth. I could certainly
understand it.

I didn't think it had been love. Perhaps it was just the done
thing on the La Dorada. Louis Birchall, chief mechanic, who
lived at Number Three, Mariquita – Leslie's colleague and
neighbour – he had set up home with *his* Colombian mistress,
the woman who kept her hand in a pocket of her skirt because
of a missing finger, though there was no record of any children
at Number Three.

Leslie had written, 'Apart from family reasons, it has never
been my idea or wish to become a permanent resident of
Colombia.' His Colombian family hadn't been sufficient reason,
apparently. Perhaps he had declared himself as Federico's father
on his birth certificate and it had simply gone astray; certainly,
he had given his son his name. Perhaps he had left the boy and
his mother provided for, in spite of what Federico's aunt had
said. Perhaps he hadn't known – even Beatriz herself hadn't
known – that she was pregnant with a second child when he
left. But he had never gone back; never written, to my knowledge. And the name Fred: the truth was that he had never liked
it (because it had been *his* father's, the Major's?). That's why he
was always Leslie.

I didn't think it had been love but I didn't know: the delays
over his return to England might have been filled with indeci-
sion, Leslie missing his wife and daughter but desperate at the
thought of being parted from his beautiful, young mistress and
the longed-for son who had come along after he had given up

hope of this ever happening. Did he know that this was his 'last adventure in life'?

My guilt lifted when I realised that the secrets of my grand-father's heart were safe, though I suppose I ought to have viewed this as failure. The moment I had felt that I truly knew him was in the presidential carriage, on the old La Dorada line, the Railway of Little Fish; a moment he would surely have been happy to share with me if he could. He was there in the person of the shrewd engineer with a pocketful of pens, a boyish enthu-siasm for trains undimmed, with the heat and green of the Magdalena basin passing by the window of the carriage and the prospect of a glass of whisky.

In the dugout cathedral, there was a repent-making moment when the lights went out . . . then once more the crystals of salt glimmered in the uneven floor. There was a copy of a detail from the ceiling of the Assisi chapel, Man touching God, and a great marble cross, and large, looming shadows. You thought of the goodness of Christ, submerged in this blessed, unholy coun-try, going on in the darkness.

Acknowledgements

With grateful thanks to: Rosemary Smith; Dom Young; Ivan Zagarra Cayon; *Sociedad de Transporte Ferroviario*; Guillermo Giraldo; and to Zaiba Malik; Bill Dunlop; Cat Ledger; Richard Beswick; Antonia Hodgson; Helen Pisano; Jim Gray; Peter Barron; Tim Dee; Stephen Rankin; Julian Hadden. Brief portions of the text originally appeared in the *London Review of Books* and the *New Statesman*. Photographs by Leslie Frost and Stephen Smith.

SS, March 1999, Leeds

THE LAND OF MIRACLES
A Journey Through Modern Cuba

Stephen Smith

Christopher Columbus described Cuba as 'the most beautiful land that human eyes have ever seen'. Tourist brochures describe it as a Caribbean paradise of shimmering beaches, salsa and cigars. *Cubans* describe it as 'The Land of Miracles' in ironic tribute to the privations of life in a communist country long after the rest of the world has junked Marx.

It is through this land of cutbacks and economic instability that Stephen Smith travelled. Searching for both the real Cuba and Fidel Castro, the man who has shaped the island's history for nearly forty years, Smith dines on giant rat, checks into a Love Hotel, poses as a second-hand arms dealer and gets his head down on Castro's bed. With disarming wit and considerable insight, he discovers a country ruled by Marxist tenets yet dependent on tourism, a country where communism and voodoo co-exist, and where Castro's influence continues to throw a long shadow.

'Fascinating . . . genuinely brilliant' Jon Snow, *Observer*

'He is the best sort of reporter; detached, ironic, yet well-versed on the terrain he's exploring . . . a compelling portrait of a society on the verge of an ideological breakdown'
Douglas Kennedy, *Independent*

'The best guide to this beautiful, bedevilled island. Unfailingly well-written' *Sunday Times*

'Essential reading' Norman Lewis

Abacus
0 349 10813 7

TIME AMONG THE MAYA

Travels in Belize, Guatemala and Mexico

Ronald Wright

'A superb travel writer' *Observer*

Often called the Greeks of the Americas, the Maya created one of the world's most brilliant civilisations. Despite a mysterious collapse in the ninth century and Spanish invasion in the sixteenth, seven million people in Guatemala, Belize and southeastern Mexico still speak Maya languages and preserve the Maya identity today.

Ronald Wright set out to discover their ancient roots and the extent of their survival. At once a riveting journey and the study of a civilisation, *Time Among the Maya* embraces history, politics, anthropology and literature. Written with wit and wisdom, this is travel writing at its broadest and best.

'*Time Among the Maya* shows Ronald Wright to be far more than a mere storyteller or descriptive writer. He is an historical philosopher with a profound understanding of other cultures' Jan Morris, *Independent*

'There is a short litany of first-class travel writers – Bruce Chatwin, Jan Morris, Paul Theroux – to which you may add Ronald Wright' Patricia Rolfe, *Bulletin* (Australia)

'Outstanding . . . Wright draws on his experience to make the old Maya as real as the new Guatemala and it is all delivered with great style' *Sunday Times*

Abacus
0 349 10892 7

TRAVELS IN A THIN COUNTRY
A Journey Through Chile
Sara Wheeler

Squeezed in between a vast ocean and the longest mountain range on earth, Chile is 2,600 miles long and never more than 110 miles wide – not a country which lends itself to maps, as Sara Wheeler found out when she travelled alone with two carpetbags from the top to the bottom, from the driest desert in the world to the sepulchral wastes of Antarctica.

This is Sara Wheeler's account of a six-month odyssey which included Christmas Day at 13,000 feet with a Llama sandwich, a sex hotel in Santiago and a trip round Cape Horn delivering a coffin. As eloquent, astute and amusing as her first book, *An Island Apart*, *Travels in a Thin Country* confirms her place in the front rank of today's travel writers.

'Notably well-written, perceptive, lively and sympathetic. Very well-worth reading' *Daily Telegraph*

'Always lively and informative . . . a perceptive and entertaining account' *New Statesmen*

'Confident and witty . . . not only informative geographically, historically and politically, but also light-hearted and amusing' *The Traveller*

Abacus
0 349 10584 7

ALMOST HEAVEN

Travels through the Backwoods
of America

Martin Fletcher

'An enthralling, addictive book to compare with John
Steinbeck's *Travels with Charley* or Bill Bryson's *Lost
Continent*' *Daily Express*

After seven years as Washington correspondent of *The
Times*, Martin Fletcher set off to explore the great
American 'boondocks' – the raw and untamed land that
exists far from the famous cities and national parks. His
extraordinary journey takes him to amazing communities
outsiders have never heard of, to the quintessential
America. He encounters snake-handlers, moonshiners,
and communities preparing for Armageddon; goes bear-
hunting and gold-prospecting; meets truckstop preachers
and Death Row inmates. From the eccentric but friendly
to the frankly unhinged, the inhabitants of backwater
America and their preoccupations, prejudices and
traditions are brought vividly to life.

'Sharply detailed and warmly insightful . . . fascinating
and consistently enlightening, wonderfully funny and
unbelievably true' *Time Out*

'Surprising, entertaining and original . . . a pleasure to
read' Nigel Williams, *Sunday Times*

'Very appealing . . . I highly recommend this book'
Independent on Sunday

'A triumph of a book' *Economist*, Books of the Year

Abacus
0 349 10935 4

BEYOND THE PYRAMIDS

Travels in Egypt

Douglas Kennedy

'Seems to me to have the satisfying insights of a Paul Theroux' Maeve Binchy

Beyond the Pyramids is a delightfully wry chronicle of travels through a country of incongruity – an Egypt encompassing a diversity of cultural influences which often belies its image of 'archaeological theme park'.

With an acute eye for the unusual, the interesting, or the plain absurd, Douglas Kennedy takes us on a continually surprising tour beyond the pyramids, to a place where Bedouin in an oasis watch American television; where monks in the desert are computer literate; and where an entire community of Cairo's poor have set up home in a cemetery.

'Kennedy writes with clarity and isn't scared of sticking the knife in, yet his criticisms are underlined with concern, not contempt' *Time Out*

'Douglas Kennedy takes on modern Egypt with a vigour uncommon in travel writing' *The Times*

'He has a gift for sliding in and out of diverse communities and recording his impressions entertainingly . . . this is the first book of a born traveller' *Guardian*

'One of our best travel writers' Philip Kerr

Abacus
0 349 10607 X

SHADOWS AND WIND

A View of Modern Vietnam

Robert Templer

'The best introduction to Vietnam I have read. It is the story of a proud and tragic country, that lost two million people from famine at the end of World War II, turned for its salvation to communism, only to lose millions more in its war against capitalism . . . Templer tells of a government that clings tenaciously to power and a people who aspire for more than their rules can offer. He charts the growth of prostitution, drug addiction and the inevitable spread of HIV. His tales of official corruption include the Interior Ministry, which runs not just the police, but the VIP club in Hanoi "where a bevy of women with sprayed-on tight dresses shuffle unenthusiastically around the floor each night as they wait for foreign men" . . . both a good read and a more complex view of Vietnam' *Times Educational Supplement*

'A portrait of a country where, contrary to most Westerners' preconceptions, the Vietnam war is already history and the most pressing concern is how to afford a new Honda Dream scooter' Edward Marriott, *The Times*

'In a convincing blend of colourful reportage and trenchant analysis, Robert Templer blows away the myths that have misinformed the world about this deeply troubled country for too long' *Financial Times*

'Important, thought-provoking and will probably be banned in Vietnam, although much read by expatriate Vietnamese' *TLS*

Abacus
0 349 10819 6

A SIMPLE BRAZILIAN SONG
Journeys Through the Rio Sound

James Woodall

'A journey right to Brazil's musical heart . . . passionate
. . . enjoyably offbeat' *The Times*

In *A Simple Brazilian Song* James Woodall shows us a
complex and vividly colourful country through the
medium its inhabitants understand best: their music.

Brazil lives for its music. James Woodall discovered this
when, in 1992, he first interviewed one of Brazil's greatest
singing stars: Chico Buarque. The writer began an affair
with Brazilian music which initially took him to Rio de
Janeiro, Chico Buarque's – and samba's – home city. There,
he discovered the city's immodest beach culture, got
horribly sunburnt and took part in Carnival. Picking up
Portuguese on the hop, Woodall then moved north to
Bahia, where he talked to Chico Buarque's great musical
contemporary, Caetano Veloso.

Back in Rio, he spent more time with Chico: what he
learnt about this charismatic artist and the strange,
dangerous city where he lives has produced a book
which is as much a hymn to Rio as it is to the
intoxicating music that beats at its heart.

'Woodall captures the exhilaration as well as the grime
and sweat of Rio and its music . . . a book that is filled
with lyrical references and which has an hypnotic
rhythm of its own' *Mail on Sunday*

'Woodall seems consistently to ask the right questions
. . . always engaging' *TLS*

'His writings on the music have lasting value' *Q*

Abacus
0 349 10849 8

Now you can order superb titles directly from Abacus

☐ The Land of Miracles	Stephen Smith	£7.99
☐ Time Among the Maya	Ronald Wright	£7.99
☐ Travels in a Thin Country	Sara Wheeler	£7.99
☐ Almost Heaven	Martin Fletcher	£6.99
☐ Beyond the Pyramids	Douglas Kennedy	£7.99
☐ Shadows and Wind	Robert Templer	£8.99
☐ A Simple Brazilian Song	James Woodall	£7.99

——————————————— ⟨ABACUS⟩ ———————————————

Please allow for postage and packing: **Free UK delivery.**
Europe: add 25% of retail price; Rest of World: 45% of retail price.

To order any of the above or any other Abacus titles, please call our
credit card orderline or fill in this coupon and send/fax it to:

Abacus, 250 Western Avenue, London, W3 6XZ, UK.
Fax 020 8324 5678   Telephone 020 8324 5517

☐ I enclose a UK bank cheque made payable to Abacus for £ . . . . . .
☐ Please charge £ . . . . . to my Access, Visa, Delta, Switch Card No.

Expiry Date ☐☐☐☐   Switch Issue No. ☐☐

NAME (Block letters please) . . . .

ADDRESS . . . .

Postcode . . . . Telephone . . . .

Signature . . . .

Please allow 28 days for delivery within the UK. Offer subject to price and availability.
Please do not send any further mailings from companies carefully selected by Abacus ☐